Mountain Biking
Northern California

Help Us Keep This Guide Up to Date

Every effort has been made by the author and editors to make this guide as accurate and useful as possible. However, many things can change after a guide is published—trails are rerouted, establishments close, phone numbers change, facilities come under new management, and so on.

We would love to hear from you concerning your experiences with this guide and how you feel it could be improved and kept up to date. While we may not be able to respond to all comments and suggestions, we'll take them to heart and we'll also make certain to share them with the author. Please send your comments and suggestions to the following address:

The Globe Pequot Press
Reader Response/Editorial Department
P.O. Box 480
Guilford, CT 06437

Or you may e-mail us at:

editorial@globe-pequot.com

Thanks for your input, and happy travels!

A FALCON GUIDE ®

Mountain Biking
Northern California

Roger McGehee

FALCON®

GUILFORD, CONNECTICUT
AN IMPRINT OF THE GLOBE PEQUOT PRESS

AFALCONGUIDE ®

Cover photo © Cheyenne Rouse Photography
All interior photos by Roger McGehee

Library of Congress Cataloging-in-Publication Data
McGehee, Roger.
    Mountain biking Northern California / Roger McGehee.
        p. cm. — (A Falconguide)
    ISBN 1-56044-747-8
    1. All terrain cycling—California, Northern—Guidebooks. 2. Bicycle trails—California, Northern—Guidebooks. 3. California, Northern—Guidebooks. I. Title. II. Falcon guide.

GV1045.5.C22 C256 2001
796.6'3'09794—dc21

                                        2001031564

Manufactured in the United States of America
First Edition/First Printing

Contents

Dedication

I dedicate this book to my biking buddy and friend Don (Vivican) Flint, who has shared many spiritual mountain biking moments with me. Not only will I continue to carry his spirit with me as I ride, but everyone that buys this book will, too.

Special thanks!

No one writes a book by himself—many thanks to all those who shared their information with me. Thanks also to the many land managers who checked my ride descriptions for accuracy and added valuable comments. I realize that many of the land managers fear added impact and conflict on their trails because of the publication of this book, but I have faith that you, the reader and rider, will use this book to reduce your impact on the trail and that you will contribute to a lessening of trail conflicts.

Don (Vivican) Flint

Introduction

In *Mountain Biking Northern California,* I try to teach the concept of low impact. Hopefully the trails will be better off because of this book. I have faith in people and in education, and believe most trail damage occurs because people don't realize they're harming the trail and don't know how to avoid doing so. (I apologize if I repeat myself often throughout the book, but I want to make sure that the message about low-impact riding reaches everyone, even if you do only one ride in this book.) I'm also donating all of my proceeds from the book to the International Mountain Biking Association (IMBA). I encourage you to join IMBA, a group that works hard to assure our access to singletrack and to maintain and build new singletracks. Visit IMBA's Web site at www.imba.com for more information on becoming a member.

I've divided northern California into four sections. Part 1 of this book covers the southern coast ranges from Monterey to San Francisco. Part 2 covers the northern coast ranges from San Francisco to the Oregon border. The southern Cascades and northern Sierra Nevada from Mount Shasta to Yosemite National Park are described in part 3; part 4 encompasses the southern Sierra Nevada from Yosemite National Park to Sequoia National Park. Some of the trails are "classics"; some are newly built. All pass through natural areas and possess scenic attributes.

THE WEATHER

Northern California weather is fairly simple: Pacific storms begin to roll in during October and November, intensify during December, January, and February, and decrease during March and April. Altitudes above 3,000 to 4,000 feet will receive some snow; those above 6,000 to 7,000 feet may have snow lingering into the summer months. Pacific storms seldom occur in summer. Thunderstorms sometimes occur in the southern Cascades and Sierra Nevada in summer—especially during August. Summer fog is a frequent phenomenon in the coast ranges near the ocean. The coast ranges and lower altitudes in the Sierra Nevada can become quite hot in summer; whereas the higher altitudes in the Sierra can fall below freezing at night during the summer.

THE LAND

From west to east, northern California consists of the coast ranges, the Central Valley, the Sierra Nevada, and the western edge of the Great Basin desert, with the Cascades extending down into northern California from Oregon. Several of the rides described in this book are in the Sierra Nevada surrounding Lake Tahoe—the largest high-altitude freshwater lake in California and perhaps the most beautiful mountain lake in the world.

One ride traverses the bottom of a cliff beside a waterfall and leads through a grove of California redwoods in a temperate rain forest in the northern coast ranges. Another passes by alpine lakes in the high Sierra. Still another leads along a rushing stream in the high desert. California is famous for its diversity!

HEALTH AND SAFETY

Poison oak grows in the coast ranges and below 4,000 feet in the southern Cascades and Sierra Nevada. It's sometimes impossible to avoid hitting poison oak on narrow singletrack. I've found that washing any exposed body parts immediately after a ride usually removes the oils and prevents a reaction. Placing your bike and shoes in the sun will allow the oils to evaporate.

Ticks are common at lower altitudes throughout northern California, mostly in late winter, spring, and early summer. Check your body frequently to catch them before they burrow in deeply. Ticks love out-of-the-way and/or hairy places, although they've been known to burrow in anywhere. If you locate one, grasp it near the head with a sharp pair of tweezers and pull gently for a couple of minutes; it should let go. The area might be discolored for a few days. Watch for the appearance of a ring around the bite and flu-like symptoms. If these develop, please see your doctor, because it might indicate the presence of Lyme disease.

Rattlesnakes are also common at lower altitudes throughout northern California. Fortunately, they're quite secretive and shy, but I have seen people surprise them on bikes, once resulting in a rider nearly being bitten. (Fortunately, the snake hit the bike frame rather than his leg.) This is just another reason to ride slowly and watch the trail in front of you.

Mountain lion encounters are not common, but these cats may be anywhere. They're extremely secretive; you probably won't see one. But if you do encounter one on the trail, stop, stand tall, hold your bike between you and the lion, and slowly back away while looking at the animal. In the unlikely event that a mountain lion attacks, fight back aggressively, using your bike as a shield.

Wild pigs are common in some regions within the coast ranges. They're actually a cross between feral pigs (escaped and naturalized) and wild boars (also introduced). Although they can become quite large and are very strong and fast, they won't bother you unless you try to approach them. Keep your distance!

Heat exhaustion is sometimes a problem in hot weather. It seldom occurs when you're drinking enough water. But limiting your pace and resting regularly will help prevent it.

Hypothermia is a real danger when you get wet in cool or cold weather. If there's any chance that it might rain or become foggy on your ride, take rain gear. Simple plastic rain gear might save your life. Wearing noncotton clothing is also helpful.

Adjust your seat properly. If the front of your seat is too high, or if the seat is set so far back so that you're forced to sit on its front, you may injure delicate organs in your crotch area. This affects both men and women.

Besides adequate water, high-calorie snacks, and rain gear, you should carry the following with you on every ride: extra tube or tube repair kit, pump, tire irons, Allen wrenches, and a chain tool. I also carry some water purification tablets, a quarter, a $5.00 bill, a small knife, and an extra car key. If you head off in late afternoon, be prepared to spend the night: Take some extra food, extra water, and extra clothes. If you're forced to spend the night on the trail, use pine needles, twigs, leaves, or bark to insulate yourself. You can sleep quite warmly and comfortably this way. It's not a good idea to walk or ride out in the dark.

While riding, keep track of your directions. The sun rises in the east and sets in the west. At noon the sun is to the south of you. Stay found and you'll never become lost.

Let someone know where you're going in case you become injured or lost. If you do get lost, don't wander around looking for the trail or another way back. Try to follow your tracks back to the trail. If this isn't possible, then stay put until someone finds you.

REGULATIONS

Many public lands require that helmets be worn. Personally, I can't understand why anyone would want to ride without a helmet. I've cracked several of mine, either by landing on my head or by hitting my head on low limbs.

Many public lands also have a speed limit for mountain bikes—usually 15 miles per hour. In addition, you're often required to slow to a walking pace when visibility is limited (usually less than 50 feet).

Many public lands are open only between sunrise and sunset.

Not all singletracks within public land are open to mountain biking. It's your responsibility to make sure you're riding on legal trails. All the trails described in this book were legal when I rode them. But trail designations change. If you're following a ride in this book and come across a trail that has been closed to biking, please don't ride it. Check with a land manager to make sure that all the described trails are still legal.

Be sure to check the local regulations when you arrive at the trailhead.

MINIMIZING YOUR IMPACT ON TRAILS

A rolling tire on a hard surface doesn't cause significant impact. But if the surface isn't hard, or if the tire isn't rolling—or it runs off the trail—then damage can occur.

I see five main problems:

- Allowing your bike to run off the trail. This causes erosion of the trail edge and therefore narrowing of the trail. If you find that you're repeatedly running off the trail, perhaps you should practice on wider trails or ride at slower speeds until you have better control over your bike. Everyone runs off the trail every once in a while, but please don't make a habit of it.

- Allowing your back tire to lock up when going downhill, causing the tire to dig into the trail. A sliding back tire is fairly useless in slowing you down and causes heavy trail erosion. Keep the back wheel turning! I find that it helps to pump my rear brake lightly and quickly and to keep my weight far back—even behind the seat on steep downhills. If something is too steep for you to ride without sliding the tire, please get off and walk the bike down.

- Allowing your bike to slide around corners, causing lateral erosion of the trail. Sliding around corners has become an acquired skill for many riders, but it does cause a great deal of trail erosion. Riding a corner cleanly—without sliding—is harder to do, but preserves the trail and demonstrates superior bike-handling skills. I have also noticed "chatter marks" just before a corner, indicating that riders were going too fast and had to slow down too quickly prior to the turn. Keep your speed low, and slow down gradually.

- Riding through deep mud, causing deep ruts, which act as erosion trenches. The wonderful thing about modern mountain bikes is that they're light—which means they can be picked up and carried through deep mud. (The bad thing about clipless pedals is that people hate to click out and get their cleats muddy. Don't let this inconvenience keep you from walking your bike through deep mud.)

- Riding around natural barriers and water bars, which widens the trail and contributes to erosion. Half the fun of riding singletrack is to succeed technically—to ride over roots and rocks and water bars. If you meet up with an obstacle that you cannot ride, please get off your bike and carry it over the obstacle rather than riding around it. If you want to ride on narrow singletracks, ride in such a way as to keep them narrow. If you're not willing to keep singletrack narrow, you can ride on dirt roads.

Low-impact riding not only prevents erosion of trails but also preserves our right to use singletrack trails—and might even lead to the opening of more trails for our use.

IMPROVING YOUR RIDING TECHNIQUE

Singletrack mountain biking differs from dirt-road mountain biking in that singletrack trails tend to be narrower, steeper, with sharper turns, and with unavoidable obstacles such as rocks, ruts, roots, and water bars. Sometimes they're built along the sides of steep slopes with varying amounts of exposure.

Riding on narrow trails means you may not have any choice in where your bike needs to go—your line has been determined by the trail builder. If your wheels go off the trail, both you and the trail can be injured. Before heading down a singletrack for the first time, practice riding on narrow sidewalks or between obstacles. If the trail is narrow and deep, you'll also need to avoid hitting its sides with a pedal. Generally, go slower on narrow singletracks than you'd ordinarily ride.

Steep downhills can be quite challenging. What you don't want to do is let your weight get too far forward. If your front wheel hits something and your bike suddenly slows, your body could be thrown forward, the bike could flip forward, and you could go sailing over the handlebars. You need to have a strong upper body (push-ups!), and to keep your weight back. In general, the steeper the descent, the farther back your weight should be. It's not unusual to keep your body in back of the seat on very steep descents. Use enough front brake to help keep your speed under control, but not so much that your bike might hit an obstacle and come to a stop or that your front tire might begin to slide. Use as much rear brake as you like up to the point where it begins to slide. (The farther back your weight is, the more effective your rear brake will be.) A sliding tire is fairly useless in helping you maintain your speed. In general, if you start to lose it, let go of the brakes; the bike will usually recover. Loose rocks can pose special problems, making it difficult to brake without sliding. Sometimes the bike will jackknife as the rear slides around. (This usually means your weight isn't far enough back.) You may need to let the bike move a little faster than you'd like until you reach firmer ground. If your front wheel needs to ride up to get out of a dip or over a rock or over a log or water bar—get off the rear brake! (The rear brake tends to hold the front wheel down, preventing it from riding up. In fact, getting off both brakes when the front wheel needs to move up is best.) And most important, if you can't ride a section without sliding your rear tire, please get off the bike and walk it through.

I'm still working on sharp turns. Many of you will find that you can turn sharply in one direction but not the other. This is probably the same side you use to get on and off your bike. Practice getting on and off on the "wrong" side until you feel comfortable doing it. You may find that your bike just doesn't want to turn. Make sure you're not applying too much front brake—it will prevent the bike from turning and increase the probability that the front wheel will slide out from under you. Practice leaning your bike into the inside of the turn while moving your body toward the outside. Your body may resist this movement, especially if there's a cliff. But your bike won't turn if you can't get your weight toward the outside of the turn, so force yourself to do so. If you're turning left, push your handlebar to the left and away from you. Keep your weight directly over the inside edges of the tires, just as you would keep your weight over the edges of skis as you turn—the sharper the turn, the greater the lean. Placing all your weight on the outside foot will help you lean the bike toward the inside and will help you keep your weight toward the outside—over the inside edges of the tires. The steeper the descent of the trail as it goes around the turn, the farther back you'll need to keep your weight to prevent the rear tire from sliding. On steep uphill turns you'll need to pull your body up hard with your arm toward the outside of the turn. (Pull-ups help.) The bike won't turn until your weight is moved to the outside of the bike.

Obstacles pose a special problem. To get over a root, water bar, or rock, approach it at a right angle, compress the front of the bike just before hitting it, and pull up with your arms as you reach it. The front wheel will then hop over it. Next, shift your weight forward and let your rear wheel hop over it. (Practice riding up higher and higher curbs.) If you have enough speed and wish to jump over the obstacle with both wheels—compress the entire bike just before hitting it and pull up and forward with your arms. If your timing is correct, you'll sail right over. If you're riding uphill, you'll need to throw your weight more forward as you go over an obstacle. Riding downhill, shift your weight less forward as you go over. Releasing both brakes helps greatly, but apply them gently after the jump if you need to, so as to avoid skidding. If you must cross an obstacle at an angle, exaggerate your movements to jump over it without touching it or to minimize the force with which your bike hits it. And if you can't jump over an obstacle, please get off and carry your bike over it rather than riding around it. Riding down a drop-off requires that your weight be shifted way back and that you stay off the front brake. (Practice riding off higher and higher curbs.) Riding over a sharp, deep dip requires that you at least hop the front wheel over it (compress and pull). Better yet is to hop the front wheel over it, then the rear wheel over it; or you can hop the entire bike over it at once.

Don't look down at what your front wheel is about to experience. Instead, be looking ahead. Your brain requires time to respond and has a good memory of what you saw moments before. By looking ahead, you give your brain enough time to process what it has seen and to respond appropriately and accurately. Look at where you want to ride instead of what you don't want to hit. You automatically ride toward whatever you look at. Look for a good line through the rocks and ruts, and you'll follow this line. But if you look at a rock or rut that you don't want to hit, you'll hit it for sure! With practice you'll be able to quickly spot a good line, then relax and ride down it accurately. If you spot a section that you know you can't ride, stop the bike before you get to it and walk through. When you find yourself in a difficult section, don't hit the brakes, but relax and ride through it—especially on steep downhill sections. Trying to stop in the middle of a difficult section is a sure way to fall. Riding through is usually successful.

If you're riding across a steep slope and feel your bike beginning to slide down and off the trail, force yourself to move your weight toward the direction in which the bike is sliding (the downhill side). This will cause the bike to stop sliding and turn uphill. If out of fear you move your weight away from the direction of the slide, your bike will slide out from under you for sure.

The front brake can be your best friend or your worst enemy. It's the more effective brake and can be safely used when traveling straight on a stable surface. But when turning or riding on a loose surface, ease off on the front brake, get your weight back, and rely more on the rear brake.

MINIMIZING TRAIL CONFLICTS

It takes more than one person to cause a conflict, so here are some ideas for all trail users to help decrease the severity and number of conflicts.

First, check your attitudes. Don't judge others who use the trail. Regardless of the manner in which they use the trail, they're basically out there to enjoy nature and enjoy their sport, whether it be hiking, backpacking, horse riding, or mountain biking. These forms of trail use have been shown to be similar in impact, and all are valid ways to enjoy natural areas.

All trail users are responsible for being alert and for watching and listening for others. But the faster you're moving on a trail, the more alert you need to be. Headphones, loud conversations, and daydreaming contribute to a loss of alertness.

All trail users should stay to the right of the trail. This allows people to approach and pass each other easily, and removes any indecision about the proper side on which to pass.

Faster users should slow down when approaching blind curves so as to not surprise anyone on the other side. Sometimes this requires a much slower speed than the customary 5 miles per hour. In general, you're riding too fast if:

- You must slide your tires to stop or slow down when you're surprised by the presence of other trail users.
- Other trail users seem nervous as you approach.
- You cannot look up and smile at other trail users as you pass.
- You feel out of control.

Faster users should take care not to throw dust or mud onto others.

Uphill mountain bikers usually have right-of-way over downhill riders. (It's hard to get going again after stopping on an uphill climb.) The rider on the cliff side of a trail usually has right-of-way over the rider on the bank side. (The rider on the bank side can simply lean on the bank, allowing the cliff-side rider to safely pass.)

Hikers and equestrians have right-of-way over mountain bikers. This means you should stop and move your bike to the side of or off the trail, if necessary, before hikers and equestrians feel compelled to do so. Horses feel more comfortable when you're below them rather than above them.

Talk to the horses as they approach. It doesn't have to be anything intelligent; just use a soothing voice. If you approach hikers and equestrians from behind, let them know you're approaching before you get close enough to frighten them. You may have to wait until equestrians have found a wide place, moved their horses off the trail, and turned the horses around so that they can see you. Please be patient! Horses vary a lot in their responses to mountain bikers. More experienced horses may pay no attention to you. Less experienced horses may panic easily. Follow the instructions of the rider.

Trail users need to get used to each other. This will decrease fear. It's interesting to note that bicyclists are not afraid of other bicyclists, hikers are not afraid of other hikers, and equestrians are not afraid of other equestrians. The more we know about each other, the less we fear each other. Concentrate on similarities—not differences. We're all out there for the same reasons: to enjoy nature, and to enjoy what we're doing.

IMBA Rules of the Trail

Thousands of miles of dirt trails have been closed to mountain bicyclists. The irresponsible riding habits of a few riders have been a factor. Do your part to maintain trail access by observing the following rules of the trail, formulated by the International Mountain Bicycling Association (IMBA). IMBA's mission is to promote environmentally sound and socially responsible mountain biking.

1. Ride on open trails only. Respect trail and road closures (ask if not sure), avoid possible trespass on private land, obtain permits and authorization as may be required. Federal wilderness areas are closed to bicycles and all other mechanized and motorized equipment. The way you ride will influence trail management decisions and policies.

2. Leave no trace. Be sensitive to the dirt beneath you. Even on open (legal) trails, you should not ride under conditions where you'll leave evidence of your passing, such as on certain soils after a rain. Recognize different types of soils and trail construction; practice low-impact cycling. This also means staying on existing trails and not creating new ones. Be sure to pack out at least as much as you pack in. Some of the rides feature optional side hikes into wilderness areas. Be a low-impact hiker, too.

3. Control your bicycle! Inattention for even a second can cause problems. Obey all bicycle speed regulations and recommendations.

4. Always yield trail. Make known your approach well in advance. A friendly greeting (or bell) is considerate and works well; don't startle others. Show your respect when passing by, slowing to a walking pace or even stopping. Anticipate other trail users at corners and blind spots.

5. Never spook animals. All animals are startled by an unannounced approach, a sudden movement, or a loud noise. This can be dangerous for you, others, and the animals. Give animals extra room and time to adjust to you. When passing horses use special care and follow directions from the horseback riders (dismount and ask if uncertain). Chasing cattle and disturbing wildlife is a serious offense. Leave gates as you found them, or as marked.

6. Plan ahead. Know your equipment, your ability, and the area in which you're riding—and prepare accordingly. Be self-sufficient at all times, keep your equipment in good repair, and carry necessary supplies for changes in weather or other conditions. A well-executed trip is a satisfaction to you and not a burden or offense to others. Always wear a helmet.

Keep trails open by setting a good example of environmentally sound and socially responsible off-road cycling.

How to Use This Book

Each ride description in *Mountain Biking Northern California* follows the same format:

Location: This is the general location of the ride, in reference to a city or other major landmark.

Distance: This is the total distance that you travel, either in a loop (loop), or out to a point and back again (out-and-back), or from one point to another point (point-to-point). I measured all distances with my trip cyclometer. Yours will probably be adjusted differently, but most are within 5 percent of the signed mileage.

Time: This is how long it should take intermediate riders—such as myself—to do the ride, allowing time to stop and look at the scenery and check this book and maps. It does not include time for lunch, swimming, napping, and so on. Please include extra time for these important activities.

Elevation gain: This is the total elevation gain. My cyclometer keeps track of every climb on the ride and adds all the climbs together for a cumulative elevation gain. The total elevation gain, more than any other parameter, will help you judge the effort and energy that you'll need for the ride.

Tread: This describes the surface of the trail: singletrack, doubletrack, dirt road, paved road, wide or narrow, hard-packed, sandy, rocky, loose, rutted, and the like.

Aerobic level: This is determined by the length of the ride, the amount of time the ride requires, and the amount of climbing involved. A ride that extends for 5 to 10 miles, lasts 1 or 2 hours, and climbs 1,000 feet or less will probably be listed as easy. A ride that extends 10 to 15 miles, lasts 2 to 3 hours, and climbs between 1,000 and 3,000 feet will probably be listed as moderate. Strenuous means you'll be exercising hard for a long time. A ride that covers 15 to 30 miles, lasts between 3 and 6 hours, and climbs between 3,000 and 5,000 feet will probably be listed as strenuous. Please don't attempt a strenuous ride unless you're in excellent physical condition. Take extra food and water. And note that a ride rated easy or moderate may have strenuous sections.

Technical difficulty: I've rated each ride on a scale of 1 to 5. A rating of 1 is smooth asphalt or smooth dirt: technical skills aren't needed. A rating of 2 means minimal technical skills are needed, such as being able to ride on a narrow trail, being able to ride on gravel or other loose surfaces, and being able to ride over small water bars, bumps, ruts, roots, and rocks through gentle terrain with little exposure. A 3 rating tells you that intermediate technical skills are needed to ride the majority of the trail—you should be able to ride over larger water bars, bumps, ruts, roots, and rocks through steeper and looser and more exposed terrain. A ride rated 4 calls for advanced technical skills, such as being able to ride steeply downhill on a loose and rocky surface. A section of trail rated 5 is not ridable—push or carry your bike through this section. Basically, I consider myself an intermediate rider. If I find myself walking a large portion of a trail because it's too demanding technically, then I assign it a rating of 4. If I can ride all or most of the trail but it takes my full concentration and some-times takes me to my limit, then I rate it a 3. If I can ride all or most of the trail without concentrating much and am not challenged by its techni-cal nature, I rate it a 2. And of course, a 1 is assigned when no technical skills whatsoever are required—trails I could ride without my hands if I wanted. Most rides involve several technical designations. Be sure that you can ride the maximum technical designation, or that you'll be able to carry your bike through the more technical sections.

Highlights: These are the things I really appreciated about the ride. I hope you do too.

Land status: Here I list the land administrator.

Maps: I always list the U.S. Geological Survey (USGS) maps that cover the area of each ride, but many of these singletrack trails have been built since the USGS maps were last updated, and therefore aren't shown on the USGS maps. Many private topographic or shaded relief maps are being printed these days; I recommend these when appropriate. Sometimes the only map of a trail is a hand-drawn, photocopied map provided by the public agency involved. Sometimes the only map is the one in this book.

Access: Here I explain how to get to the trailhead and describe the serv-ices available at the trailhead.

Notes on the trail: General information you might want to know about the ride: the trails, the scenery, the natural history, the history, and so on.

The ride: Here I list mileage landmarks: trail junctions, creek crossings, vista points, points of interest, general landmarks, and anything else that might help you find your way or add to your education, enjoyment, and safety.

MAPS

The maps in this book are not meant to be substitutes for detailed USGS or local trail maps, but should prove to be helpful in combination with other maps. Each map should be used in conjunction with the ride descrip-tion.

ELEVATION GRAPHS

The elevation graphs show changes in elevation for each ride. In general, the steeper the graph, the steeper the climb or descent. The technical difficulty of each ride segment is also shown. Use each graph in conjunction with the ride description.

FINAL WORDS

I promised land managers that their trails will be no worse for wear, and might even be better off because of this book. I trust you'll use the following ride descriptions respectfully, trying to minimize your impact on the trails and on other trail users. I also ask that you try to educate others to the need for low-impact and considerate riding.

Spread your hard-earned money around: Pay for parking at the trailheads, buy things from local stores, stay in local motels. Singletracks will stay open to mountain bikers if the local people want them to stay open. Give them a reason to keep these trails open to you!

I hope you enjoy these rides as much as I have. See you on the trail.

Legend

Interstate		Campground	
U.S. Highway		Picnic Area	
State Highway/ County Road		Buildings	
Forest Road		Peak/Elevation	X / 4,507 ft.
Interstate Highway		Bridge/Pass	
Paved Road		Gate	
Gravel Road		Parking Area	
Unimproved Road		Boardwalk/Pier	
Trail (singletrack)		Railroad Track	
Trailhead		Cliffs/Bluff	
Route Marker		Power Line	
Waterway		Forest Boundary	
Intermittent Waterway		Radio Tower	
Lake/Reservoir		Map Orientation	N
Meadow/Swamp		Scale	0 0.5 1 MILES
Mining Site			
Bridge			

Ride Locations

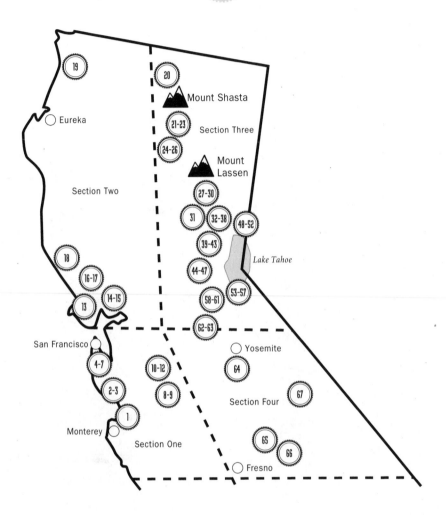

19

20

Mount Shasta

Eureka

21-23

Section Three

24-26

Mount
Lassen

Section Two

27-30

31 32-38 48-52

39-43 Lake Tahoe

18

16-17

44-47

14-15

13

53-57

58-61

San Francisco

62-63

4-7

Yosemite

10-12

64

2-3

8-9

67

1

Section Four

Monterey

Section One

65

66

Fresno

Northern California
Sections and Chapters

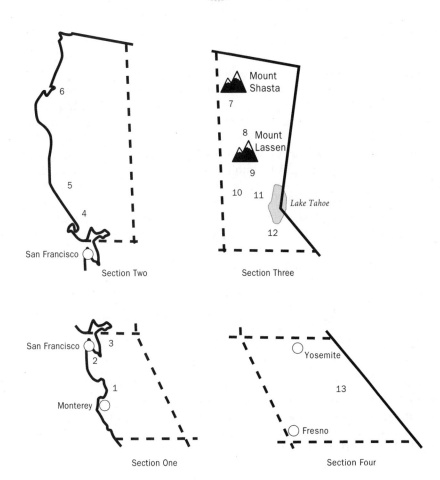

Southern Coast Ranges

This section includes rides from Monterey to San Francisco.

In many places valleys separate inland coast ranges from their coastal counterparts. These inland coast ranges seldom experience summer fog; they usually receive less winter precipitation and get significantly hotter in summer than do their coastal counterparts. Conversely, the outer coast ranges see frequent summer fog and associated cool temperatures during the summer, along with significantly higher precipitation during the winter. The summer fog contributes to the growth of redwoods in the outer coast ranges.

In general, the wildflower season begins early in the coast ranges, with the first flowers appearing in January in the warmer areas, and the last flowers fading in August where it's moister. Grasses turn green as early as December and remain green until May in drier areas—until July in moister areas. California's coast ranges are known for their bright green color in winter and spring, and for their golden color during the summer and fall.

Poison oak is heavy in all regions. Ticks are also common throughout the coast ranges from early spring through summer

Monterey Bay Area

Monterey Bay marks the southernmost extent of significant redwood forests. Beautiful examples of redwood forests exist in Wilder State Park and in Soquel Demonstration State Forest. Fort Ord Public Lands are composed of live oak forests, chaparral, and grasslands.

Most trail surfaces here are composed of compacted sand that has been uplifted. As a result, these trails are easily eroded; take extra care to prevent your rear tire from sliding. Concentrate on keeping your weight back and use the front brake more when descending, unless you're in the process of turning. These sandy trails are especially vulnerable to damage when wet.

Campgrounds and motels are abundant throughout the area, but usually require reservations during the summer months. If all the campgrounds are full along the beaches, try Mount Madonna County Park on California Highway 152 between Watsonville and Gilroy. Forget about finding a place to camp on a summer weekend without reservations! Bike shops can be found in Monterey and Santa Cruz.

Fort Ord Public Lands

Location:	6 miles west of Salinas and about 7 miles east of Monterey on California Highway 68.
Distance:	10.6-mile loop.
Time:	1.5 hours.
Elevation gain:	About 1,800 feet. Lowest elevation is 250 feet; highest elevation is 600 feet.
Tread:	Mostly singletrack, some dirt road.
Aerobic level:	Moderate, with some strenuous climbs.
Technical difficulty:	2–3 (mostly 3).
Highlights:	Views of Salinas Valley and Monterey Bay, wildflowers and green hills in spring (March through June), and abundant wildlife. (Bobcat sightings are common; I've even seen a road-runner!) No motorized vehicles may use the dirt roads and trails.
Land status:	Bureau of Land Management.
Maps:	USGS Salinas; a free well-drawn topographic map is also available at the trailhead.
Access:	Coming from the south of Salinas on U.S. Highway 101, take the Monterey Peninsula exit. Coming from the north of Salinas on U.S. Highway 101, take the second Monterey Peninsula exit just south of town. This road eventually becomes California Highway 68. Continue west as California Highway 68 becomes a freeway. The trailhead is located at the end of a long grassy strip 0.8 mile after the freeway becomes a two-lane road. If you find yourself at the turnoff to Laguna Seca, you've gone too far. Turn back and again look for the long grassy strip beside the Toro Creek Estates.

Notes on the trail: Be sure to pick up the free map available at the trailhead, but note that what the map calls a "Trail" is often just about impossible to ride, whereas a "Single Track Mountain Bike Trail" is likely ideal. You'll start out on Toro Creek Road, climb up through grassy hills on Trail 45 to Oil Well Road, climb Trail 10 to the top of the ridge, and descend on

Fort Ord Public Lands

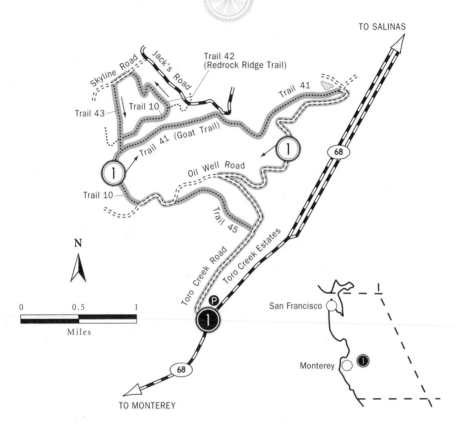

TO SALINAS

Trail 42
(Redrock Ridge Trail)

Skyline Road

Jack's Road

Trail 41

Trail 43

Trail 10

Trail 41 (Goat Trail)

Oil Well Road

Trail 10

Trail 45

68

N

0   0.5   1

Miles

Toro Creek Road

Toro Creek Estates

P

San Francisco

Monterey

68

TO MONTEREY

the technically challenging Redrock Ridge Trail (Trail 42) through chaparral and oaks and poison oak. You'll then ride a short distance on Skyline Road before heading up Trail 43, only to descend for a long way on Goat Trail—the longest "Single Track" here—which roller-coasters down to a small lake at its terminus. Then return to your car via Oil Well Road and Toro Creek Road.

The quality of the singletrack and the scenery here make this a worthwhile trip. Most of the trails are sandy and become ridable within a few days of a major winter storm. Please don't ride them when they are wet. The temperatures are moderate during spring and fall. In summer it may be either uncomfortably hot, or cool and windy if the fog is in. These trails are easily eroded; please prevent your rear wheel from sliding or walk your bike down sections that you cannot ride without sliding. Many

Andrew enjoying singletrack on Fort Ord Public Lands.

people use these trails, so slow down when your visibility becomes limited to avoid surprising them. Remember to yield them the right-of-way.

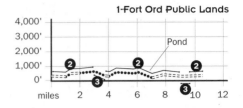

The Ride

0.0 Begin riding on an unnamed dirt road.

0.1 Turn right at the T onto Toro Creek Road.

0.8 Dive down into a sandy creek bed (keep your weight back!).

0.9 Turn left onto Trail 45.

1.0 Ignore Trail 46 and continue to climb steeply on the singletrack/recovering dirt road.

1.3 Turn left onto Oil Well Road (dirt).

1.9 Turn right onto Trail 10. This is another dirt road recovering to singletrack.

2.5 Ignore the Goat Trail for now and bear left to continue for a short distance on Trail 10.

2.6 Major intersection. Turn right and head up the old dirt road (Trail 10). After the initial steep climb, this road turns into a gentle roller coaster.

3.1 Top of the Redrock Ridge Trail. You might want to put your seat down a bit, because this next trail involves some fairly technical downhill. Keep your weight back to avoid sliding your rear tire. Walk your bike if you cannot ride without sliding. Use the front brake more, except when turning.

3.4 Look out for the steep, rocky drop-off, followed by sandy sections and a very steep downhill.

3.8 Bottom of Trail 42. Turn left and ride a short distance on Skyline Road (dirt).

4.0 Turn left onto Trail 43. This is a nice singletrack on which to ascend. Watch for poison oak.

4.5 You're back at the major intersection. Bear left onto Trail 41 (the Goat Trail). This wonderful, hard-packed, and mostly smooth singletrack is basically downhill, but it roller-coasters a lot, especially toward the lower end.

6.8 There's a picnic table next to a small lake.

7.3 End of Trail 41. Turn right onto Oil Well Road (dirt).

9.1 Turn left onto Toro Creek Road (dirt).

9.7 Back at the junction with Trail 45, head down into the wash.

10.5 Turn left onto the unmarked trail leading a short distance back to your car.

10.6 Back at your car.

Wilder Ranch State Park

Location:	5.1 miles northwest of the intersection of California Highway 17 and California Highway 1 in Santa Cruz, on California Highway 1.
Distance:	13.2-mile loop.
Time:	2.5 hours.
Elevation gain:	About 2,000 feet. Lowest elevation is 200 feet; highest elevation is 750 feet.
Tread:	Mostly singletrack, mostly hard-packed.
Aerobic level:	Moderate.
Technical difficulty:	2–3 (mostly 3).
Highlights:	Shady redwood groves, flower-filled meadows, views of Monterey Bay, small streams. No motorized vehicles are allowed on the trails.
Land status:	Wilder Ranch State Park.
Maps:	USGS Santa Cruz. A free, good topographic map is also available at the bookstore in the working ranch.
Access:	At 5.1 miles northwest of the intersection of California Highways 17 and 1 in Santa Cruz, turn left off California Highway 1 at the sign for Wilder Ranch State Park. There's a spacious parking lot. The trailhead begins at the northeast corner of the lot. Bathrooms and water are available.

Notes on the trail: This is a very busy place—especially on weekends—with other mountain bikers, equestrians, and hikers. Please ride responsibly and courteously. This is also the habitat of a rare species of red-legged frog whose existence is being threatened by people stirring up sediment as they cross the creeks. Please carry your bikes across all creeks that don't have bridges, and walk carefully on the exposed rocks when crossing.

The singletracks here pass through beautiful redwood forests with a bright green ground cover

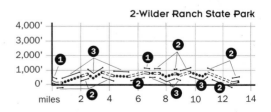

2-Wilder Ranch State Park

Wilder Ranch State Park

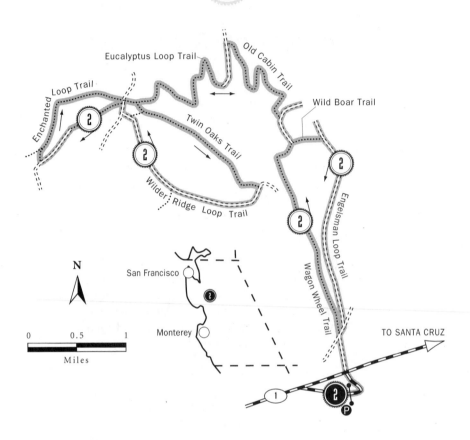

of redwood sorrel. Although poison oak is abundant, the trails are wide enough so that you usually won't come in contact with it. But to be safe, wash up after your ride—and also check for ticks. Because of the easily eroded soils, riding at Wilder within a couple of weeks of a major Pacific storm isn't appropriate. In fact, portions of the park don't dry out (and are closed) until early or midsummer, depending on the year. It's wise to call ahead to ask about the conditions of the trails. I'd hate to see you arrive and not be able to ride some of the lovely trails!

The Ride

0.0 Leave the parking lot at its northeast corner and follow the paved service road down to the working ranch.

0.2 Turn into Wilder Ranch at the sign. A sign will instruct you to dismount and walk your bike through the ranch. Stop off at the bookstore to pick up a free topographic map of the state park. Ride through the tunnel. The paved road turns to dirt.

0.4 Ride over the cattle guard. There's place for donations at the large map. If you can't afford to donate to trail maintenance and you live nearby, the state park staff will gladly accept your help in maintaining these trails. You might also want to check out the poison oak display on the bulletin board.

0.5 Go right at the dirt-road junction.

0.6 Several dirt roads take off from this point. Take the one to the far left. You'll see a sign for the Wagon Wheel Trail. It will soon turn into a singletrack and is designated one-way uphill so as to minimize trail conflicts and trail erosion.

Note: The Wagon Wheel Trail has been closed to all users until a way to protect the habitat of the red-legged frog along this trail can be found and implemented. Hopefully by the time you read this, the trail will be reopened. If not, please turn onto the Engelsman Loop Trail at this point, turn left onto the Wild Boar Trail at mile 1.8, and arrive at the top of the Wagon Wheel Trail at mile 2.0. Then skip ahead in this description to mile 2.2.

0.9 The trail travels alongside a creek through a cool and shady area. The trees growing in the creek with grayish bark are alders.

1.1 Everything looks very lush. The bright green ground cover is composed of redwood sorrel. Redwood trees are appearing—and giant chain ferns. Don't forget to carry your bike across the stream whenever the trail crosses it and to walk lightly across the rocks.

1.6 Until now the trail has been climbing unnoticeably. At this point, it begins to climb more steeply. Sticky monkey flowers and wild morning glories appear among the rocks.

2.2 You're at the end of the Wagon Wheel Trail. Hang a left onto the dirt road and pedal up.

2.5 Trail junction. Turn left onto the Old Cabin Trail (singletrack). Remember to adjust your speed to the degree of visibility as you head down to the creek.

2.8 Dismount and carefully cross the creek in order to protect the red-legged frogs.

3.4 You're now crossing over an area that stays wet and muddy late in the season. Please prevent any more resource destruction by carrying your bike through any mud here.

3.4+ Trail junction. Turn left onto the Eucalyptus Loop Trail. At this point, it's a dirt road.

3.7 The dirt road narrows to a wide singletrack as it enters a live oak forest.

3.9   The trail heads steeply down to the creek. Only advanced riders will be able to ride down without creating resource damage, and even they should carry their bikes across the water to prevent siltation and damage to the organisms that live downstream.

4.0   The wide singletrack narrows and passes through a redwood forest carpeted with redwood sorrel.

4.1   Dodge the poison oak.

4.3   Another chance to carry your bike across a creek.

4.4   Trail junction. Bear left onto the Twin Oaks Trail and pass through an oak forest, followed by a redwood forest, followed by a bay forest, followed by a meadow of wildflowers.

4.6   Ignore the old trail coming down from the right.

5.3   The Twin Oaks Trail ends as you're dumped out onto the Wilder Ridge Loop Trail (dirt road). Turn right and climb steeply.

5.5   Take the left fork for 100 feet to a view of the entire Monterey Bay area. Then return and continue the way you were going.

6.0   Pass by Zane Gray Cutoff and continue climbing on the Wilder Ridge Loop Trail.

6.5 +   Ignore the connector trail to the Twin Oaks Trail and follow the dirt road as it makes a sharp turn around a fence.

6.7   Turn right onto the paved road.

6.8   Ignore the singletrack taking off to your right.

6.8 +   The pavement turns into dirt. Three singletracks await you on your left. Take the one that requires making the sharpest turn, almost 180 degrees from the direction that you were going. This is the beginning of the Enchanted Loop Trail.

7.0   After traveling through a dense forest, you suddenly find yourself on another dirt road. Turn right.

7.5   Leave the dirt road and bear right onto the singletrack to continue on the Enchanted Loop Trail.

7.5 +   When the singletrack forks, take the right fork. At the junction 100 feet beyond, again take the right fork. This is a continuation of the Enchanted Loop Trail. It's a steep, downhill, technical singletrack, passing through a forest of redwood trees, sword ferns, and redwood sorrel. If you choose to ride it, keep your weight back behind the seat and use your front brake heavily except when your front wheel is turned. If you begin to lose it in a technical section, let go of both brakes and roll through it. Let off the brakes when riding over water bars or roots.

7.7   Get your weight way back and release the brakes as you go over the drop-off. Glide gracefully down into the forest.

8.2   You have a choice: You can proceed straight ahead, or turn right. Both ways will get you to the top. I prefer the right fork.

8.7   You're back where you started riding on the Enchanted Loop Trail. Turn left onto the dirt road, ride for 100 feet through a sandy section, and turn right onto the singletrack. You're back on the Eucalyptus Loop Trail.

8.9 This is where your turned down the Twin Oaks Trail. Bear left to continue on the Eucalyptus Loop Trail—the same trail that you rode up earlier. The trail is very tricky as you enter the forest, with a steep drop-off followed by an angular water bar. Unless you're an expert, best walk your bike.

9.7 Turn right onto the Old Cabin Trail. (You also rode this earlier.)

10.5 Cross the creek. Listen for the nervous song of the canyon wren as you pump or push uphill.

10.8 Turn right onto the dirt road and head down.

11.1 You're back at the top of the Wagon Wheel Trail. This time bear left onto the Wild Boar Trail. (You can't go down the Wagon Wheel Trail, because it's one-way.)

11.3 Turn right onto the dirt road (Engelsman Loop Trail) and stop for a moment for one last look at Monterey Bay. *Warning:* It's easy to gain too much speed on this dirt road. Erosion trenches and sand pits sometimes await you. What's the hurry, anyway? If you hit a sand pit, force your weight far back, let go of the brakes, keep your front wheel pointing straight ahead, and float through it.

12.3 Steep descent.

12.5 Steep descent. You're at the bottom of the Wagon Wheel Trail. Proceed down the dirt road for another 100 feet and take the left fork. Head for the corral, ride along the fence, go over the cattle guard, ride through the tunnel, and get off and walk your bike through the working ranch.

13.0 Hop back on your bike, turn right onto the paved road, and pump up to the parking lot.

13.2 Back at your car. I advise you to wash your body as soon as possible to remove poison oak oils and to check for ticks. And take that silly grin off your face!

Soquel Demonstration State Forest

Location:	9.7 miles east of California Highway 17 on Highland Way, about half an hour south of San Jose.
Distance:	14.3-mile loop.
Time:	3 hours.
Elevation gain:	About 2,600 feet. Lowest elevation is 600 feet; highest elevation is 2,500 feet.
Tread:	Paved road, dirt road, and hard-packed single-track with short rocky sections.
Aerobic level:	Moderate, with one long strenuous climb.
Technical difficulty:	1–4 (mostly 3).
Highlights:	This region really feels remote, and it is. No motorized vehicles are allowed on the single-tracks. The singletracks themselves are challenging and fun, and pass through dense forests of madrone and redwood, with occasional views of Monterey Bay.
Land status:	Soquel Demonstration State Forest is managed by the California Department of Forestry and Fire Protection for forestry education and research.
Maps:	USGS Laurel, Loma Prieta (the trails are not shown). A free map of the trails is also available at the trailhead.
Access:	From San Jose, take California Highway 17 south toward Santa Cruz. Take the Summit Road exit as you approach the summit of the Santa Cruz Mountains, and follow it southeast as it becomes Highland Way at 5.0 miles. (The Summit Center Store at 3.7 miles is your last chance to get bottled water, cold drinks, and food.) Continue on Highland Way until you spot a dirt road passing over a bridge to your right at mile 9.7, and park. A small green sign beside the bridge reads: SOQUEL DEMONSTRATION

Soquel Demonstration State Forest

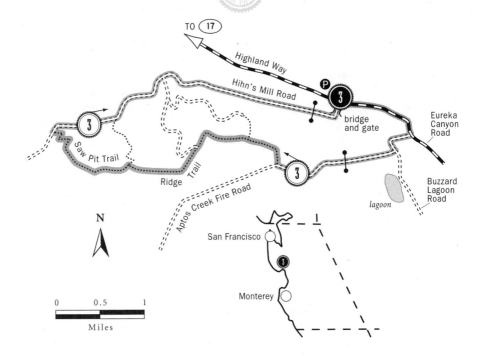

STATE FOREST. (This bridge and parking area are located at a low point in a redwood forest. If you find yourself driving back uphill, you've gone too far.) Grab your bike and get ready to ride south on Highland Way. (You'll be returning to this spot via the dirt road passing over the bridge.) No water is available at the trailhead.

Notes on the trail: Although this ride requires you to climb 350 feet on a paved road, another 700 feet on dirt roads (to reach the upper part of the singletrack), and then another 1,000 feet on a dirt road (to return from the bottom of the singletrack), it's well worth the workout. Although it's tempting to ride fast on these trails, you need to be prepared for other users, including other mountain bikers, and slow down considerably when visibility becomes limited. When you meet other trail users, yield the right-of-way to them by stopping and moving off the trail. The land manager is especially concerned that equestrians and hikers feel safe and welcome. Please be extra considerate of them. The manager is also concerned that you stay on the trails, don't trespass on private property, and stay away from areas that are closed due to logging.

The singletrack varies from lightly technical to highly technical. The more technical sections are short, making it easy to carry your bike over them if you cannot ride down them without sliding your rear tire. The singletrack traverses a north-facing slope on the boundary between madrone and redwood forests along the top of the ridge, and through redwood forests on the way down from the ridge to the bottom of the canyon. The last leg of the ride passes along a shaded creek for several miles.

These trails shed water amazingly well, but there are times after large winter storms when it would be best to let them dry out for a week or so before using them. Summer temperatures are often moderate because of the close proximity to the ocean. At times it can be cold and foggy even in summer.

The Ride

0.0 Climb on paved Highland Way along Soquel Creek under shady and cool redwoods.

1.9 Turn right onto Buzzard Lagoon Road (dirt) and continue climbing.

2.9 The road forks at this point. Bear right onto Aptos Creek Fire Road (no sign) toward the sign for Forest of Nisene Marks State Park. This is a good place for a break: It's cool and shady, and you'll soon be climbing on a hot, exposed, south-facing slope.

4.0 Go under the closed state park gate and continue to climb on Aptos Creek Fire Road beside manzanita, ceanothus, and live oak shrubs.

5.1 When the dirt road widens a bit and a view of Monterey Bay appears on your left, look for a (currently) unsigned singletrack taking off to the right. This is the entrance to the upper part of Soquel Demonstration State Forest. It's also the high point on this ride. (If you find yourself going downhill on the dirt road, you've gone too far.) Once you're inside the state forest, there's a display with maps. Get ready for a bumpy ride with dips, trenches, and stumps on which to catch a pedal.

5.8 Trail junction. You've been riding on the Ridge Trail. Bear left and continue riding on the Ridge Trail. (The right fork would take you down the Corral Trail.) Before the next junction you'll be faced with two extremely steep, but short, hills to climb. Keep watching

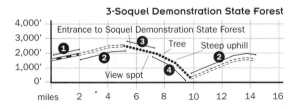

3-Soquel Demonstration State Forest

for stumps that can grab your pedal. Also watch for a rocky downhill section that tends to funnel you right into a tree.

6.6 Trail junction. You've just passed by an unsurfaced heliport surrounded by bright blue bush lupines, and providing a nice view toward the northwest. Bear left to continue on the Ridge Trail.

7.3 View spot. After winding through a forest of madrone trees, the trail passes by a picnic table with a view of Monterey Bay. This is a perfect place for a rest, snack, or lunch break. The trail becomes very smooth and playful until the next intersection. Watch your speed on this section. I saw a large tree claim the bike of a rider who was going too fast. He had a long walk back to the car.

7.7 Trail junction. Bear left to continue on the Ridge Trail. After a short, playful section, the trail becomes steep and rutted. For the sake of the trail, walk your bike if you cannot ride without sliding your rear wheel.

8.4 This short section is very steep and loose. Rocks and roots will try to divert or stop your front wheel. Only experts should ride it. Shortly thereafter is an impossible-to-ride uphill section. Ride up as far as you can, then get off and push.

8.6 This looks like it should be a trail junction, but it isn't. The sign marks the end of the Ridge Trail and the beginning of the Saw Pit Trail. It also marks the last—and best—section of singletrack. *Warning:* This section will throw everything at you, including steep downhills, sharp drop-offs, sharp turns, water bars, trenches, pits, and strategically placed trees in a dense grove of redwoods. While concentrating on the trail, please remember to be alert to other trail users.

9.8 Junction with Hihn's Mill Road (dirt). Well, it's all uphill from here! Fortunately, the dirt road follows a stream through cool redwood forests, and it's a middle-chain-ring climb.

10.5 The Tractor Trail meets Hihn's Mill Road at this intersection. Continue on Hihn's Mill Road.

11.8 The Sulfur Springs Trail meets Hihn's Mill Road at this intersection. Continue on Hihn's Mill Road. If you smell noxious gases, it's likely a result of the numerous sulfur springs in the area. If you don't want to go back to your car just yet, ride up the Sulfur Springs Trail to its junction with the Corral Trail, then up the Corral Trail to its junction with the Ridge Trail, and do the ride again.

12.5 This is a great creek for cooling off on a hot day—or for washing off any poison oak oils that you may have accumulated on your legs and arms.

14.1 Locked gate. Bike around the gate, past the sign for Soquel Demonstration State Forest, and continue on Hihn's Mill Road.

14.3 Bridge and parking area at the junction of Hihn's Mill Road and Highland Way.

Western South San Francisco Bay Area

This western, outer, coast range receives an impressive amount of rainfall and frequently experiences summer fog. As a result, temperatures are moderate and lush forests tend to grow there. Where fog tends to linger, redwood forests thrive. This area is very close to major metropolitan areas and therefore receives a lot of use—especially on weekends. Extra care must be taken so that you don't surprise other trail users. Always yield to them by stopping and moving off the trail before they feel compelled to do so. Motels and bike shops are abundant in the nearby cities. Campgrounds exist at Portola State Park and at Big Basin State Park. Reservations are suggested in summer—especially on weekends.

Like most of the trails in the coast ranges, the surfaces are easily eroded and require that you prevent your rear tire from sliding by keeping your weight back. They should not be ridden in wet weather.

Saratoga Gap Loop

Location:	At the junction of California Highway 35 (Skyline Boulevard) and California Highway 9, about 1 hour south of San Francisco.
Distance:	13.2-mile loop.
Time:	3 hours.
Elevation gain:	About 2,700 feet. Lowest elevation is 1,400 feet; highest elevation is 2,750 feet.
Tread:	Hard-packed singletrack and dirt roads.
Aerobic level:	Strenuous.
Technical difficulty:	2–3 (mostly 3).
Highlights:	Dense forests of live oaks, Douglas firs, madrones, and bays, views of the Pacific Ocean, wildflowers in spring and summer, and a lot of very nice singletrack. Motorized vehicles are not allowed on these trails.

Saratoga Gap Loop

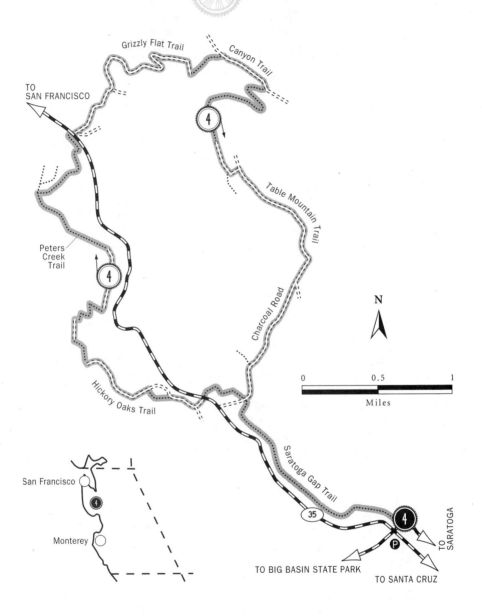

Land status:	Saratoga Gap Open Space Preserve, Long Ridge Open Space Preserve, and Upper Stevens Creek County Park.
Maps:	USGS Mindego Hill; a well-drawn topographic map is also available at the trailhead.
Access:	The trailhead is at the junction of California Highway 35 (Skyline Boulevard) and California Highway 9. You can reach this junction by driving south from San Francisco or west from Saratoga. Park in the large parking area on California Highway 35. No bathrooms or water are available. Carefully ride across California Highway 9 to reach the trailhead.

Notes on the trail: This loop is composed of several nice singletrack trails tied together with narrow to wide dirt roads. The first part of the ride is gentle; the second half dives deeply into a canyon and then climbs steeply out. Avoid doing this ride in the middle of a hot day, as the long climb out of the canyon in the heat can be brutal. A beautiful creek runs through the bottom of the canyon—a perfect place for a picnic! These trails become quite muddy in winter, and are usually closed to horses and bikes. Even if they're open, please don't ride them when they're wet. Most of the trails meander through forests of live oaks, madrones, bay, and Douglas fir. Poison oak is abundant, and so are ticks.

Please be gentle with these trails by preventing your rear tire from sliding as you descend and turn. Walk your bike through technical sections that you cannot ride without sliding. Many people use these trails, especially on weekends. Please slow down considerably when visibility becomes limited, and yield right-of-way to other trail users. The land manager asked me to remind you that helmets are required, there's a 15-mile-per-hour speed limit, and the preserve is open between sunrise and half an hour after sunset.

The Ride

0.0   Begin this ride on a 1.7-mile singletrack. This section is class 3 in difficulty because there are quite a few rocks, roots, steep downhills, and sharp turns to negotiate. Keep your weight back to avoid sliding the rear tire!

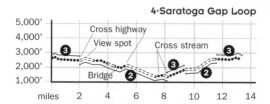

32

0.2 The large, beautiful orange-barked tree on your left is a madrone. Meander down now through a shady forest.

0.7 Ignore the singletrack descending from California Highway 35.

1.7 Cross over the dirt road and head for the singletrack on the other side. The forest becomes quite lush at this point.

2.1 The trail spits you out onto California Highway 35. Cross carefully, because vehicles travel very fast on this section of road. Head for the singletrack on the other side.

2.1 + The short singletrack joins a narrow dirt road.

2.2 Dirt-road junction: Swing to the right.

2.3 The dirt road heads to the right. A singletrack heads to the left. Take the singletrack, of course.

2.4 Take the short trail up to a view rock, if you wish. Enjoy the views of the surrounding hillsides covered with forests and the distant Pacific Ocean.

2.6 Turn left onto the dirt road.

2.7 Leave the forest and climb a steep, grassy knoll.

3.1 Bear right onto the singletrack and head for Grizzly Flat Parking.

3.4 Intersect a dirt road (Ward Road). Bear left onto the dirt road marked: TO GRIZZLY FLAT PARKING.

3.4 + Junction of Ward Road and Long Ridge Road. Turn right onto the Peters Creek Trail (singletrack). This is a beautiful singletrack that switchbacks down the hillside; many of the turns are quite tight.

3.9 Cross a bridge over a small creek and ride through a lush forest.

3.9 + Cross over the dam of a small lake to your right. (The lake is on private property.) The singletrack ends at a dirt road. Turn left onto the dirt road.

4.1 Notice the scarlet larkspur in bloom in late June. Pass through an older forest. The trail is lined with stinging nettles—don't touch them, especially with bare legs! It's hard to tell if this is a narrow dirt road or a wide singletrack.

4.5 Turn right to continue on Peters Creek Trail toward Grizzly Flat Parking. The narrow dirt road has now narrowed to a singletrack.

4.9 Turn right to Grizzly Flat Parking.

5.0 Cross over a wooden bridge and turn right to continue toward Grizzly Flat Parking. Get ready to climb!

5.4 You're spit out onto California Highway 35 again. Carefully cross the highway and head straight down the Grizzly Flat dirt road. (Ignore the dirt road that heads off to the right.) Get ready for a long descent.

6.6 Ignore the wide singletrack coming up from the right.

7.4 Trail junction: To your left is a sign that reads: CANYON TRAIL, .5 MILE. To your right is a fence with a sign that explains that this is a wintering site for ladybugs. In late June I saw thousands of them flying around. You might as well travel straight and down to Stevens Creek to wash off, have a rest, and enjoy the coolness of the place. It looks like the trail should cross the creek at this point, but it doesn't. When you're ready to ride on, go back to the sign and take the singletrack toward the Canyon Trail.

7.6 Cross the stream where a large Douglas fir has fallen over. The singletrack switchbacks sharply and climbs steeply through a shady forest. There's a lot of poison oak along this section.

7.9 Turn right to Stevens Canyon Road on a narrow dirt road.

8.2 Turn right to Saratoga Gap, 4.8 miles onto a singletrack. A sign alerts you to the fact that bicycles must ride one way. Fortunately, it's the way you're going. Cross over Stevens Creek again. Now the singletrack becomes class 3 and climbs steeply. Fortunately, you're climbing through a shady forest.

9.5 Turn right onto the dirt road.

9.6 Ignore the narrow singletrack on your right. (It's closed to bikes.)

9.7 Bear right onto a larger dirt road.

9.8 Notice the little grove of young giant sequoias. They're remnants of an old Christmas tree farm.

10.0 Follow the sign that requests bikers to travel one-way to the right. Continue to climb through a live oak and madrone forest.

10.6 Take the dirt road to the right at the T (uphill, of course).

11.0 The term *unrelenting* comes to mind.

11.3 You're at the top of the climb!

11.5 After a short downhill, you'll arrive at an intersection that you've seen before. Bear left onto the singletrack for the last 1.7 miles back to your car.

12.0 Notice the large, mature Douglas firs that line the trail.

12.5 Ignore the singletrack coming down from the right.

13.0 You're back at the large madrone. It's all downhill from here.

13.2 You made it! Suggestion: Wash off the poison oak oils and look for ticks as soon as you can.

Russian Ridge
Open Space Preserve

Location:	About 1 hour south of San Francisco near the northwest corner of Alpine Road's intersection with California Highway 35 (Skyline Boulevard).
Distance:	4.4-mile loop.
Time:	0.75 hour.
Elevation gain:	About 900 feet. Lowest elevation is 2,300 feet; highest elevation is 2,600 feet.
Tread:	Narrow to wide singletracks with some dirt road; hard-packed sand.
Aerobic level:	Easy, with some moderate climbs.
Technical difficulty:	2.
Highlights:	Just some nice singletracks passing through grasslands and oak forests with views of the Pacific Ocean in the distance and wildflowers in spring. No motorized vehicles are allowed on the trails. This is a good ride for beginning singletrackers.
Land status:	Russian Ridge Open Space Preserve.
Maps:	USGS Mindego. A well-drawn topographic map is also available at the trailhead.
Access:	From Interstate 280 in Los Altos Hills, take the Page Mill Road exit and head west for 8.5 miles. Cross Skyline Boulevard (California Highway 35) onto Alpine Road and immediately turn right into the parking area for Russian Ridge Open Space Preserve. An outhouse is available at the trailhead, but no water.

Notes on the trail: I was at first disappointed when the wide singletrack turned into a dirt road, then thrilled to find that the Ancient Oaks Trail was a high-quality singletrack. I was again disappointed when it suddenly came to an end on another dirt road, but couldn't believe the great singletrack that took off again along the top of the ridge and then back into the oak forest. For a short ride, this has some pretty wonderful singletrack.

Russian Ridge Open Space Preserve

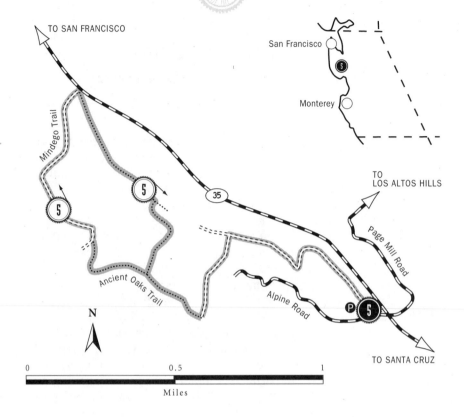

The land manager asked me to remind you that helmets are required, there is a 15-mile-per-hour speed limit, and the preserve is open between sunrise and half an hour after sunset. Lots of people use these trails, so please be extra careful not to catch them by surprise. To prevent erosion, please don't ride these trails when they are wet, and prevent your rear tire from sliding by keeping your weight back or by walking your bike down steep sections.

The Ride

0.0   Ride uphill on a wide singletrack.
0.3   The wide singletrack turns into a dirt road.
0.5   Trail junction. Go left to Ancient Oaks Trail onto another dirt road.
0.9   Take the singletrack to the right. This is the beginning of the Ancient Oaks Trail.

1.1 Don't forget to take your eyes off the trail and look at the Pacific Ocean on the horizon.

1.2 Turn left to Mindego Trail to continue on the Ancient Oaks Trail.

1.5 Very lush!

1.6 You're rudely dumped onto a dirt road (Mindego Trail). Turn right. Gear up for a granny-gear climb. I hope it's not the middle of a hot afternoon because there's no shade whatsoever along this dirt road.

2.3 You're at the Vista Point entrance to the preserve. Turn right onto the narrow singletrack and enjoy a middle-chain-ring climb to the top.

2.9 Turn right toward the Ancient Oaks Trail and head downhill on a sweet and narrow singletrack into the oak grove again.

3.2 You're back on the Ancient Oaks Trail where you were at mile 1.2. Turn left to retrace your "steps" back to your car.

3.5 Turn left onto the dirt road marked: TO RIDGE TRAIL.

3.8 Turn right onto the dirt road marked: TO ALPINE ROAD PARKING.

4.1 The dirt road turns back into a wide singletrack.

4.4 Back at the car. Do you have time to do it again?

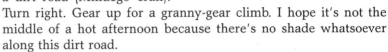

5-Russian Ridge Open Space Preserve

El Corte de Madera Creek Open Space Preserve

Location:	In the Santa Cruz Mountains, about 30 minutes south of San Francisco and about forty-five minutes north of San Jose, on California Highway 35 (Skyline Boulevard).
Distance:	14.8-mile loop.
Time:	3 hours.
Elevation gain:	About 3,100 feet. Lowest elevation is 1,430 feet; highest elevation is 2,465 feet.

Tread:	A mixture of singletracks and dirt roads, mostly smooth and hard-packed.
Aerobic level:	Strenuous.
Technical difficulty:	2–3 (mostly 3).
Highlights:	The largest system of singletrack available on the peninsula, many newly built. Lovely redwood groves and, if you're lucky, a giant salamander. No motorized vehicles are allowed on the trails.
Land status:	El Corte de Madera Creek Open Space Preserve, Midpeninsula Regional Open Space District.
Maps:	USGS Woodside. A free and well-drawn topographic map is also available at the Skeggs Point parking area.
Access:	From Interstate 280, take the California Highway 92 exit west, toward Half Moon Bay. At the top of the ridge, turn left onto California Highway 35 (Skyline Boulevard) and drive 8.8 miles to Skeggs Point parking area. An outhouse is available, but no water.

Notes on the trail: Please don't attempt this ride without strong intermediate technical skills. Doing so not only places you at risk but also endangers other trail users and adds significant erosion to the trails. This is a very popular area for mountain bikers, hikers, and equestrians. Please approach other trail users slowly and yield the right-of-way to hikers and equestrians by stopping and moving off the trail. Help preserve these sandy and easily eroded trails by keeping your weight far enough back that you don't slide on descents and turns. Dismount on sections that you cannot ride without sliding.

I first rode here several years ago and encountered mostly dirt roads, along with some sketchy, badly eroded singletracks. Since then the open space district has closed some of the inappropriate singletracks; with the help of volunteers, it has repaired others and built several new singletracks. The result is several miles of high-quality singletracks extending through beautiful redwood forests composed of California redwoods, tanbark oaks, and Douglas firs. Many thanks to the open space district, to the juvenile work crews, and to members of ROMP (Responsible Organized Mountain Pedalers).

I've tried to create a ride that includes the most and the best sections of singletrack. After experiencing what's available, you'll probably want to come back and ride some of them in the opposite direction. Basically, this ride includes the El Corte de Madera Creek Trail, Resolution Trail, Fir Trail, Sierra Morena Trail, Methuselah Trail, Manzanita Trail, Timberview Trail, Giant Salamander Trail, Leaf Trail, El Corte de Madera Creek Trail, and Tafoni Trail—in that order. You'll encounter many hikers from the

El Corte de Madera Peak
Open Space Preserve

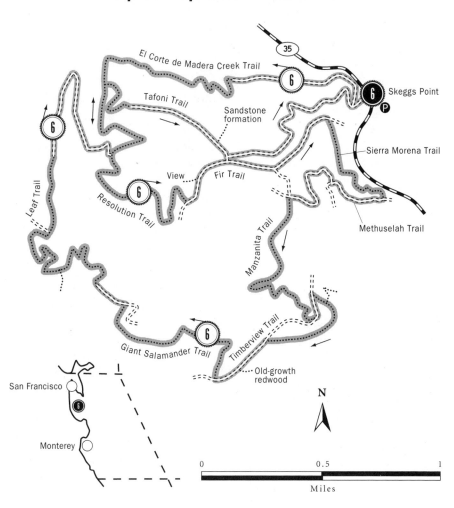

El Corte de Madera Creek Trail

35

Skeggs Point

Tafoni Trail

Sandstone formation

Sierra Morena Trail

Leaf Trail

View   Fir Trail

Resolution Trail

Methuselah Trail

Manzanita Trail

Timberview Trail

Giant Salamander Trail

Old-growth redwood

San Francisco

Monterey

N

0   0.5   1

Miles

6-El Corte de Madera Creek
Open Space Preserve

Creek

5,000'
4,000'
3,000'
2,000'
1,000'

miles   2   4   6   8   10   12   14   16

Sandstone Formation to Skeggs Point. Extra caution and consideration will be required in this section, especially on weekends. Please avoid riding when the trails are wet. Give them a few days to dry out after a major winter storm.

The Ride

0.0 Begin by riding north on the highway for 100 yards. Carefully cross the highway to the gated dirt road on its west side. At the gate a sign will lead you in the direction of the El Corte de Madera Creek Trail.

0.2 Turn right onto the El Corte de Madera Creek Trail (dirt road). You'll be riding steeply downhill. Keep your weight back, control your speed, and watch for other trail users. Be prepared for ruts, humps, and dips!

0.9 Turn left and cross the wooden bridge to continue on the El Corte de Madera Creek Trail (singletrack). Ascend gradually on the class 2, medium-width singletrack.

1.8 Junction with the Tafoni Trail. Continue straight on the El Corte de Madera Creek Trail as it becomes narrower, more exposed, and more technical.

2.4 Bear left to begin climbing on the Resolution Trail (singletrack). This narrow, class 3 singletrack starts off gradual and smooth, and ends up quite steep and rocky.

3.6 Turn left onto the Fir Trail (dirt road).

3.7 If you wish, travel a short distance up to Vista Point. This would be a great place for a picnic. On a hot day it's a good place to enjoy the ocean breeze, if there is one.

3.9 Intersection with the Tafoni Trail. Bear right to remain on the Fir Trail.

4.1 Intersection with the Methuselah Trail. Bear left to remain on the Fir Trail.

4.6 Turn right and head down the Sierra Morena Trail (singletrack). It's tempting to ride fast on this smooth, downhill singletrack, but you're very close to both the road and another access to the preserve; you might meet another trail user at any time.

5.1 The singletrack has dumped you out onto the Methuselah Trail (dirt road). Turn right.

5.4 At the junction with the Timberview Trail, bear right to remain on the Methuselah Trail. Prepare mentally for a steep climb.

5.9 Turn left onto the Manzanita Trail (singletrack). The Manzanita Trail passes through very sandy and easily eroded terrain. To preserve this singletrack, please don't allow your rear tire to slide;

keep your weight way back. If you can't ride it, walk it. If you can't ride over something, don't ride around it.

7.0 Turn left onto the Timberview Trail (dirt road).

7.2 A currently unsigned, but mapped (and therefore legal) single-track takes off to the right. It's not currently named on the map. This fun little singletrack passes through a cool redwood forest.

7.3 Bear right to continue on the little singletrack.

7.8 Bear left to rejoin the Timberview Trail (dirt road). This section is a lot of fun to ride, but keep an eye out for other trail users who might be heading down to the old-growth redwood.

8.1 Turn right onto the Giant Salamander Trail (singletrack). Giant salamanders occur along streams in redwood forests. I've seen only one in my lifetime—a huge individual, over a foot long! They're very rare. Please watch carefully for them, both to enjoy them, and to avoid hitting them. Review my speech at mile 5.9, then get your belly behind the seat, or get off and walk your bike down this initially steep, loose, and fragile section. This trail is going to throw a little bit of everything at you—sharp corners, trees, dips, humps, steep uphills, and steep downhills.

9.0 Turn left onto the Methuselah Trail (dirt road).

9.3 The dirt road becomes a singletrack that meanders gently down through a moist, cool redwood forest to El Corte de Madera Creek.

9.5 This year-round creek provides a cool and shady place to rest. If it's a hot day, I suggest wetting your hair before you begin the climb out of here. (You're at the lowest altitude on this ride; it's mostly up hill from here.) Cross the creek on the rocks or on the planks provided so you don't stir up sediments and cause siltation downstream. (Siltation kills aquatic organisms, including the endangered red-legged frog larvae.) Climb out of the canyon on a well-built singletrack.

10.3 Turn right onto the Leaf Trail (singletrack). The abundant leaves are from the tanbark oaks above. This trail roller-coasters high above the creek.

11.0 Bear right onto the El Corte de Madera Creek Trail (dirt road) and descend to the creek. On a hot day it really feels good gliding down this smooth dirt road!

11.3 Turn right at the pump house to continue on the El Corte de Madera Creek Trail (dirt road).

12.0 You're back at the lower end of the Resolution Trail. Turn left to continue climbing on the El Corte de Madera Creek Trail (single-track).

12.6 Turn right onto the Tafoni Trail (a sweet little singletrack) and continue to climb.

12.8 The singletrack turns into a dirt road that begins to roller-coaster steeply up and down. This section may not be very enjoyable if you're tired.

13.5 If you feel like exploring on foot and have the energy to do so, hide your bike and hike up to the Sandstone Formation. You'll find a variety of cavelike structures in the eroded slab of sandstone.

13.6 Bear left to remain on the Tafoni Trail (dirt road). This is the beginning of a long, smooth downhill. Many trail users will be encountered on this section, going and coming from the Sandstone Formation—including people pushing baby strollers, complete with babies.

14.7 After a short uphill grind, arrive at the paved road. Carefully cross the road and head along the shoulder for the parking area.

14.8 Arrive back at your car. If you're like me, you're tired but very happy! Stores with soft drinks and deli sandwiches are located about 3 miles north and about 4 miles south of here.

Whittemore Gulch Trail

Location:	On California Highway 35 (Skyline Boulevard), about half an hour south of San Francisco.
Distance:	7 miles, out-and-back.
Time:	1.5 hours.
Elevation gain:	About 1,700 feet. Lowest elevation is 550 feet; highest elevation is 2,100 feet.
Tread:	Mostly smooth, hard-packed singletrack; some dirt road with one steep, rocky, rutted, and loose downhill section.
Aerobic level:	Moderate, with one long, strenuous climb.
Technical difficulty:	2–3 (mostly 3).
Highlights:	Superb singletrack, both descending and ascending; views of forest-covered hills and the Pacific Ocean; wildflowers blooming late into summer; moist redwood groves. No motorized vehicles are allowed on any of the trails.
Land status:	Purisima Creek Redwoods Open Space Preserve.

Whittemore Gulch Trail

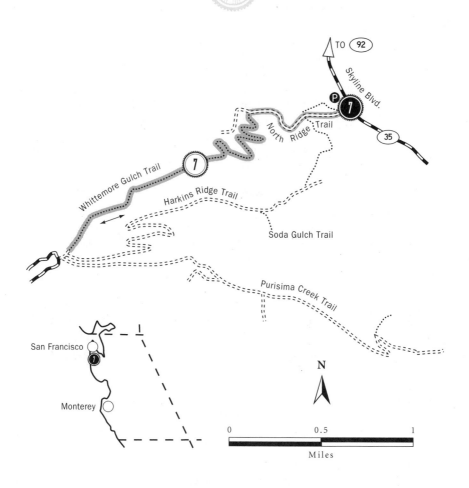

TO 92

Skyline Blvd.

P 7

35

North Ridge Trail

Whittemore Gulch Trail 7

Harkins Ridge Trail

Soda Gulch Trail

Purisima Creek Trail

San Francisco 7

Monterey

N

| 0 | 0.5 | 1 |

Miles

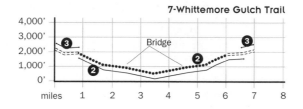

7-Whittemore Gulch Trail

4,000'
3,000'
2,000'
1,000'
0'

Bridge

3   2   2   3

miles 1   2   3   4   5   6   7   8

Maps: USGS Half Moon Bay, Woodside; a well-drawn topographic map of the trails is also available at the trailhead.

Access: When you're taking Interstate 280 from the north or from the south, take California Highway 92 exit west toward Half Moon Bay. When you reach the top of the ridge, turn left (south) onto California Highway 35 (Skyline Boulevard). Drive for 4.5 miles, and turn right into the parking lot. It's not well signed, so watch carefully. The lot is adjacent to Kings Mountain Country Store. An outhouse is available, but no water. Bottled water and other cold drinks are available at the store.

Notes on the trail: The North Ridge Trail is actually a dirt road. The first 0.3 mile is a steep descent with loose rocks and ruts. Past that point, you can concentrate on how green the surroundings are—even in late summer. Fog frequently bathes this hillside in moisture during the summer. The Whittemore Gulch Trail is a wonderful switchback descent into the redwoods below. Wildflowers adorn the hillside from March to September.

Winter rains make the trail quite muddy, necessitating a closure to bikes and horses, usually in November. The trail generally reopens in April or May, but may not become totally free of mud until midsummer.

This trail is highly vulnerable to erosion. Please don't ride this trail when it is wet. If you cannot ride a section without sliding your rear tire, please walk your bike through. Don't slide around turns. Ride or walk your bike over water bars, not around them. You'll encounter many other trail users, especially on weekends. Please ride in such a manner that you don't surprise them, and yield them the right-of-way by pulling off the trail.

Summer weather varies from warm when the fog isn't in, to cold, wet, and windy when it is. Although you can extend this ride by incorporating dirt roads, try to return to the trailhead via the Whittemore Gulch Trail—it's a great ride. As with any out-and-back ride, look back at each trail junction to make sure you'll be able to get back to the trailhead.

The Ride

0.0 Begin at the North Ridge Trail (dirt road). This section can be quite technical because of its steepness, loose rocks, and ruts.

0.3 Junction with the Harkins Ridge Trail. Continue straight on the dirt road. The road flattens out and becomes smoother past this point. Begin to notice how green everything is, even in late summer.

0.8 Turn left onto the Whittemore Gulch Trail (singletrack). Enjoy the great views of the surrounding forested hills and the ocean. Sunsets are particularly nice from here. (Planning to arrive at this point on the return trip at sunset is ideal.) Ride first through a Douglas fir forest and then down through chaparral with lots of yellow sticky monkey flowers and yellow bush lupines.

1.3 Trail junction: Take the steep switchback to the left to continue on the Whittemore Gulch Trail.

1.8 A series of wonderful turns drops you down into a redwood forest. Thistles, stinging nettles, and poison oak are abundant alongside the narrow trail.

2.5 Pass over a bridge over a small stream in a redwood and alder forest. It's always cool and moist here, even in the driest of years. The character of the trail changes now, from a narrow singletrack with a gradual descent to a wider, steeper, rockier, and often muddier trail without switchbacks. It's easy to pick up speed, but please ride slowly enough not to startle anyone or their horses.

3.5 End of the Whittemore Gulch Trail. You can turn around now and enjoy the trail in the other direction, or you might spend some time exploring the redwood groves around the lower trailhead before heading back. On the way back up the Whittemore Gulch Trail, you may find sections from here to the bridge too steep to ride. While pushing your bike, enjoy the views of the creek rushing below and the trees towering above you.

7.0 Back at your car.

Options:

1. If you have energy to burn, you can ride up the Purisima Creek Trail (dirt road) as far as you wish, then ride back, before heading back up the Whittemore Gulch Trail.

2. It's also possible to return to your car on the Harkins Ridge Trail (mostly dirt road), but it's incredibly steep, rocky, and loose in places.

Eastern South
San Francisco Bay Area

This area is dominated by Henry W. Coe State Park, which is about 1.5 hours south of San Francisco. The park contains a wealth of wildlife, including turkeys and the introduced wild pigs, which can sometimes be seen rooting under the oak trees. The best times to see wildlife are early morning and evening. Wildflowers are abundant from March through May, and the hills are green from January through May.

It can become quite hot here during the summer, making mountain biking less than enjoyable and even dangerous. If you do decide to ride in summer, I suggest you finish your ride by noon, or begin it in late afternoon. (If you choose late afternoon, be prepared to spend the night on the trail in case you or your bike has a serious problem. Take extra food, extra water, and something warm to wear.) Summer is also the season for small, annoying, sticky seeds that cling to your shoes, socks, and leg hair. I advise wearing long socks if you have leg hair—old ones, so that you can throw them away at the end of the ride. Ticks and poison oak are also abundant. Wash your body thoroughly and look for ticks after every ride. Spring and fall are the best times to mountain bike in Henry W. Coe State Park, although summer days when the fog is in can be quite pleasant, as can warm winter days between storms. To reduce erosion, trails are closed for 48 hours following storms in which more than half an inch of rain falls. Crossing streams can become dangerous in winter or early spring. If you're biking at these times, ask about current conditions at the headquarters.

The rides described in this chapter are not appropriate for beginners, because the singletracks tend to be narrow and technical. If you're not in good shape, please don't attempt any ride other than the Frog Lake out-and-back.

The first two rides begin at the southern entrances to the park. No facilities of any kind exist at these entrances—except for outhouses. The singletrack tends to be highly technical, and the climbs tend to be long. Signs may or may not be present. These trails are not heavily used, especially not on weekdays; you'll probably be on your own. If you're biking alone and become injured, and no one knows where you are, you may have to wait days for someone to come along. If you must ride alone, ride extra carefully and let someone know where you are. There's a campground at nearby Coyote Lake Park.

The last three rides begin at headquarters, at the main entrance. Rangers are on duty at the visitor center to give you advice. Maps and books are for sale. Bathrooms, water, and a campground are available. The newer trails, such as Flat Frog Trail and China Hole Trail, are very well built. Grades are less than 10 percent, which discourages water from running down the trail and often eliminates the need for water bars; it also eliminates the tendency for some mountain bikers to lock up their rear wheels and gouge out the trail on descents. They're also narrow, which prevents water from forming puddles, prevents mountain bikers from traveling much faster than other trail users, and makes mountain biking much more pleasurable.

Lyman Willson Ridge Road/ Grizzly Gulch Trail

Location:	Hunting Hollow Access to Henry W. Coe State Park, about 1.5 hours south of San Francisco and 9 miles northeast of Gilroy.
Distance:	11.7-mile loop.
Time:	2.5 hours.
Elevation gain:	About 2,250 feet. Lowest elevation is 900 feet; highest elevation is 2,300 feet.
Tread:	Paved road, dirt road, wide singletracks, narrow singletracks, mostly hard-packed with some rocks.
Aerobic level:	Moderate, with one long, strenuous climb.
Technical difficulty:	1–3 (mostly 3).
Highlights:	Isolation, wildflowers in spring, abundant wildlife, open vistas, oak forests and grasslands, and a nice descent on a narrow singletrack. No motorized vehicles are allowed on the trails.
Land status:	Henry W. Coe State Park.
Maps:	USGS Gilroy Hot Springs. A free topographic map is also available at the trailhead.
Access:	From Interstate 101 in Gilroy, take the Leavesley Road/California Highway 152 West exit. But instead of heading west on California Highway 152, head east on Leavesley Road. After 1.7 miles, turn left (north) onto New Road. After

Lyman Willson Ridge Road/ Grizzly Ridge Trail, Kelly Lake Loop

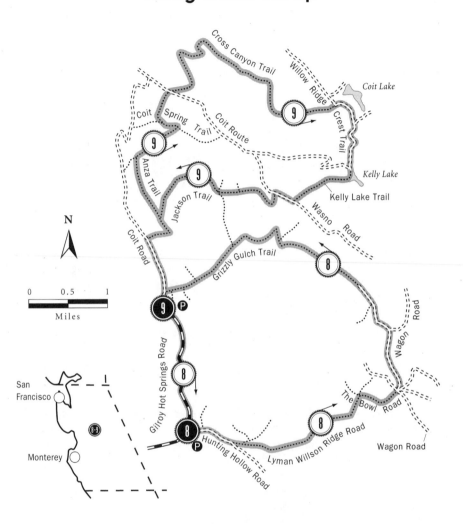

Cross Canyon Trail

Willow Ridge

Coit Lake

Coit Spring Trail

Coit Route

Crest Trail

Coit

9

9

Anza Trail

9

Jackson Trail

Kelly Lake

Kelly Lake Trail

Wasno Road

Coit Road

Grizzly Gulch Trail

8

9 P

Wagon Road

N

0   0.5   1
Miles

Gilroy Hot Springs Road

8

San Francisco

Monterey

8-9

8 P

Hunting Hollow Road

Lyman Willson Ridge Road

The Bowl Road

8

Wagon Road

8-Lyman Willson Ridge Road/ Grizzly Gulch Trail

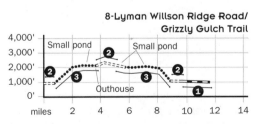

4,000'							
3,000'	Small pond		❷	Small pond			
2,000'	❷				❷		
1,000'		❸			❸		
0'			Outhouse			❶	
miles	2	4	6	8	10	12	14

0.6 mile, turn right (east) onto Roop Road. Follow Roop Road for 3.3 miles until it turns into Gilroy Hot Springs Road at the turnoff to Coyote Lake County Park. Continue on Gilroy Hot Springs Road for 3.4 miles until you reach the Hunting Hollow Access. Turn right and park. Outhouses are available, but no water. A nominal fee is charged for parking and day use.

Notes on the trail: You start off riding on a dirt road (Hunting Hollow Road), but quickly turn onto Lyman Willson Ridge Road, which is really a singletrack—sometimes quite narrow. Then you climb forever along the top of a ridge to the intersection with Wagon Road. This dirt road leads you down gently to the intersection with the Grizzly Gulch Trail, which starts off as a dirt road, becomes a wide singletrack, then becomes a narrow, downhill, frolicking singletrack that brings you down to the paved Gilroy Hot Springs Road and back to your car. Don't expect to meet anyone on the ride during the week. You may be the only human being for miles! Signs of other animals are abundant, though: coyote tracks and scat, deer tracks, fox tracks and scat, bobcat tracks, jackrabbit tracks, and evidence that feral pigs (wild boars) have been rooting under the trees. You'll be riding through oak forests and grasslands. Wildflowers are abundant in spring (March through May).

Do not attempt this ride on a hot afternoon. Most of the climb is without shade on a south-facing slope. If you do the ride in the evening, be prepared to spend the night in case anything happens to you or to your bike. (Take extra food, extra water, and something warm to wear.) Ride with someone, if you can. You're on your own out here—no one may come along for days.

These trails are easily eroded. Please don't ride them when they are wet. Please don't allow your rear tire to slide when descending or turning. Walk your bike through sections that you cannot ride without sliding. Ride or walk your bike over water bars, not around them.

The Ride

0.0   Begin by heading toward the metal gate and up Hunting Hollow Road (dirt). Just past the gate is a turnoff to Steer Ridge Road. Stay on Hunting Hollow Road.

0.7   A sign on the left directs you to Willson Camp via Lyman Willson Ridge Road. Pass through the gate and head up the singletrack. Ignore the seldom-used dirt road/trail just before the fence, about 200 feet up the trail. Go through the fence to continue on Lyman Willson Ridge Road. Ride or push steeply up through a forest of live oaks (bright green) and blue oaks (blue green). The poison oak can be very colorful in mid- to late summer.

This is a road? Lyman Willson Ride Road.

1.3 This is the last shade before a steep climb. If you find yourself looking down at the trail, watch for animal tracks in the dust: deer, coyote, bobcat, raccoon, pigs, foxes, jackrabbits.

1.4 The trail becomes narrower and leaves the top of the ridge to climb more gently among the trees.

1.6 The trail swings left and continues to climb.

1.7 Pass through a gate. If it's open, leave it open. If it's closed, leave it closed. (Cattle inhabit this area from late fall to early spring.) Look down into the canyon to see how far you've climbed.

2.0 The trail forks, but the two paths come back together on the other side of the knob. The right fork is easier.

2.3 The trail levels off. The grasslands allow for open vistas.

2.5 A small reservoir is on your left.

2.8 Trail junctions. At present they're unsigned, although the posts are in place. Turn right at the first fork to continue toward Willson's Ranch on The Bowl Road (singletrack).

3.0 A small spring-fed pond.

3.7 The sign says: WILLSON CAMP. An outhouse is available, but I hope you brought your own T.P.

3.8 You suddenly come across a graded dirt road in the middle of nowhere. This is Wagon Road. Turn left.

3.9	Multiple junction. You don't want the road to the extreme right. You don't want the road straight ahead. You don't want the road to the extreme left. Instead, you want to bear left onto the remaining road, which climbs gradually. This is an extension of Wagon Road.
4.2	Reach the high point of your ride.
4.8	You've just passed by a small reservoir and are facing a currently unsigned dirt road to your left. This is the beginning of the Grizzly Gulch Trail; take it. It starts off as a dirt road that follows a small seasonal creek gently downhill.
5.1	Ignore the wide singletrack that comes down on your left from Willson Peak, instead bearing right to stay on the Grizzly Gulch Trail.
5.4	Pass by another small reservoir.
5.6	Cross the small seasonal creek and enjoy the fact that the dirt road is looking more like a wide singletrack.
5.8	You plunge down into a creek bed—hopefully dry. Work your way downstream for 50 feet and the trail will reappear.
6.9	Another small reservoir.
7.1	A sign in the middle of nowhere directs people up to Kelly Lake, but continue straight and down on the Grizzly Gulch Trail.
8.1	Another sign in the middle of nowhere directs you up to Jackson Field, but continue straight and down on the Grizzly Gulch Trail, which now becomes a narrow singletrack. The first section is steep; after that the trail becomes quite playful and fun as it wanders down through an oak forest.
8.6	A sign directs you up the Anza Trail, but continue straight and down on the Grizzly Gulch Trail. Notice that these signposts look like they're made out of concrete; in fact, they're made from recycled plastic. Good idea!
8.9	Cross a large creek (or creek bed). This could be dangerous to cross after a major storm: Use caution.
9.3	Ignore the trail that heads up to the left. Bear right to continue downward. (The Grizzly Gulch Trail actually ends here; you've joined the Timm Trail.)
9.3 +	At the fork, take the right trail down to the picnic table and outhouse, then turn left onto the dirt road (a continuation of the Timm Trail) and ride a short distance to join Coit Road (dirt). Continue to ride downhill along Coyote Creek to the gate at the Coyote Creek entrance.
9.6	Pavement awaits you on the other side of the gate. It's all downhill beside a cool and shady creek back to your car.
11.7	Back in the parking lot.

Kelly Lake Loop

Location:	Coyote Creek entrance to Henry W. Coe State Park, about 1.5 hours south of San Francisco and 11 miles northeast of Gilroy.

See map on Page 48

Distance:	16.9-mile loop.
Time:	4.5 hours.
Elevation gain:	About 4,150 feet. Lowest elevation is 900 feet; highest elevation is 2,675 feet.
Tread:	Mostly singletrack, ranging from hard-packed and smooth to rough and rocky.
Aerobic level:	Strenuous!
Technical difficulty:	2–4 (mostly 3).
Highlights:	A long singletrack adventure through a secluded part of the park. Bike beside and through a creek in spring. Visit a lovely lake. Enjoy distant views from the top of Jackson Peak and a long downhill with two dozen switchbacks. No motorized vehicles are allowed on the trails.
Land status:	Henry W. Coe State Park.
Maps:	USGS Gilroy Hot Springs, Mount Sizer; free topographic maps are also available at the trailhead.
Access:	From Interstate 101 in Gilroy, take the Leavesley Road/California Highway 152 West exit. But instead of heading west on California Highway 152, head east on Leavesley Road. After 1.7 miles, turn left (north) onto New Road. After 0.6 mile, turn right (east) onto Roop Road. Follow Roop Road for 3.3 miles until it turns into Gilroy Hot Springs Road at the turnoff to Coyote Lake County Park. Continue on Gilroy Hot Springs Road for 5.5 miles until you reach the end of the road at the Coyote Creek entrance. An outhouse is available near the trailhead, but no water. No parking lot is available. Please park completely off the pavement along the

side of the road. Don't block the gate, and don't leave valuables in your car. If you must, make sure they aren't visible.

Notes on the trail: This isn't just a ride—it's an adventure! Be sure that you're prepared: Go with someone else or let someone know exactly where you'll be riding. Take extra water and food and something warm to wear in case you become injured and are forced to spend the night on the trail. Don't attempt this ride unless you're in excellent condition. Don't attempt this ride on a hot day.

To maximize the amount of singletrack on this ride, I've suggested that you ride up the lower switchbacks on the Anza Trail (singletrack), ride gently down the Anza Trail to Grapevine Spring, ride/push all the way up to Coit Route on the Grapevine and Coit Spring Trails (singletracks), glide down the Cross Canyon Trail West (singletrack) to the bottom of Kelly Cabin Canyon, ride/push up the Cross Canyon Trail East (singletrack), zoom down Coit Route (dirt road) to Kelly Lake, ride/push up Kelly Lake Trail (singletrack), Wasno Road (dirt road), and the Jackson Trail (double-track) to the top of Jackson Peak, and then meander down two dozen switchbacks along the Jackson and Anza Trails back to Coit Road. These trails are easily eroded. Please don't ride them when they are wet. Don't let your rear tire slide when descending or turning. Walk your bike through sections that you cannot ride without sliding. Ride or walk your bike over water bars, not around them.

The Ride

0.0 Pass through the gate at the Coyote Creek entrance (no sign is currently present). Start riding north on the dirt road.

0.1 A sign informs you that you're on Coit Road, heading for Coit Camp. That's the dirt road you want to be on. There's an outhouse above the sheltered picnic area. A notice on the bulletin board informs you that the wild pigs found in California are a cross between the feral pigs introduced by the Spanish in the 1700s and Eurasian wild boars introduced in the 1920s.

0.8 Reach the top of a hill.

1.0 A signed post on the right indicates that the Anza Trail to Grapevine Spring starts here. Turn right onto the Anza Trail. After

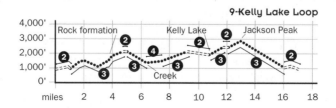

100 feet, turn left (turning right would take you to Woodchopper Spring) to continue on this newly rebuilt, narrow singletrack up the switchbacks under a canopy of bay and live oak trees.

1.9   As you ride along a grassy slope, you can see Coyote Creek way below you.

2.0   Unsigned intersection. To the right is the newly rebuilt Jackson Trail; you'll be returning on this trail at the end of the ride. For now, bear left to remain on the Anza Trail toward Grapevine Spring. Prepare for a wonderfully gentle and mellow descent on a narrow singletrack on the side of a grassy slope with constant views down into the canyon.

3.0   A sign in the middle of nowhere reads: ANZA TRAIL TO GRAPEVINE SPRING, 0.1 MILES. Follow that sign.

3.1   A dirt road swings down to the left toward Coit Road. Continue on the singletrack. A number of small springs are visible. Sections of this trail become quite steep; prepare to push.

3.4   Notice all the evidence of wild pigs rooting along the trail under the oak trees. This trail defines the phrase *narrow singletrack*. It's also quite rocky and technical in places.

3.8   A huge rock formation appears on your left. You're now climbing at the rate of 100 feet per 0.1 mile. That's steep!

4.1   Unsigned intersection. Take the left fork (the Coit Spring Trail) toward Coit Camp.

4.2   Signed intersection. The left fork would take you to Coit Camp; take the right fork straight up the hill (the Grapevine Trail) toward Coit Lake.

4.7   On the top of a grassy knoll, you hit a dirt road that has been blocked off to the left. Turn right. Notice the forest of blue oaks surrounding the grassy knoll, and Lick Observatory on top of Mount Hamilton many miles to the north.

4.7 +   Intersect Coit Route (dirt road). Moment of decision: You've climbed a total of 1,900 feet so far. If you continue on this ride, you'll need to climb another 2,250 feet. Once you ride down into the canyon, you're committed to continuing. There's no easy way to bail out. If you have any doubts in your mind, please go back the way you came, or bail out by turning left onto Coit Route at this point, and then turning left onto Coit Road toward Coit Camp. If you're certain that you have enough water, food, time, and energy, head across Coit Route to the Cross Canyon Trail West on the other side and enjoy the glide down to the bottom of Kelly Cabin Canyon on a medium-width singletrack through chaparral, followed by a forest of digger pines and oaks.

6.3   Arrive at the creek (or creek bed). The singletrack narrows and becomes much more technical as it runs along the creek, crosses the creek several times, and runs right up the creek bed itself in

Kelly Lake provides a splendid view.

places. You'll have lots of opportunities to rub up against poison oak and to acquire ticks along this section of trail.

7.4 The Cross Canyon Trail East crosses the creek one final time before heading steeply up and away from it on a wide singletrack. If there's any water remaining in the creek, I suggest you wash off any poison oak oils you may have acquired. You'll probably be riding up this portion in the afternoon. The trail will become quite exposed to the afternoon sun. Make sure you don't overheat by drinking lots of water, going slowly, and resting in the shade often if the weather is hot.

9.2 Turn right onto the Willow Ridge Crest Trail (dirt road). You're about to get a short break from climbing. Coit Lake is the body of water to your left.

9.7 Turn right onto Coit Route (dirt road) and coast down to Kelly Lake.

10.5 At the sign for Kelly Lake, grab your bike and carry it in the direction of the arrow up to the top of the dam. Enjoy the view of this natural-looking reservoir and don't look at the steep and loose trail heading up to the right of the lake. (I told you not to look yet!) Once you're fully rested, watered, fed, rejuvenated, and ready for another long climb, notice the steep and loose trail heading up to the right of the lake. Grab your bike and carry or push it up the beginning of the (unsigned) Kelly Lake Trail. Once you reach the top of the ridge, the medium-width singletrack will roller-coaster for a while.

11.6 Turn right onto the signed Wasno Road. (As in, there "was-no" road here until it was built.)

12.0 Turn left onto the Jackson Trail, heading toward the Coyote Creek entrance. The trail starts off as a dirt road and soon turns into a real doubletrack. It looks like service vehicles occasionally drive over the top of Jackson Peak to the spring, creating doubletracks. Look left as you climb. The Monterey Peninsula is clearly visible, and is that the ocean?

12.4 As you near the top of Jackson Peak, views to the north and east appear; you can see the Sierra Nevada on a clear day. Ignore the small singletrack that takes off on your right.

12.8 You did it! You're standing on top of Jackson Peak, with good views in all directions. See that deep canyon to the west of you? You'll now descend into it. Continue on the doubletrack as you head down through fields of green or golden grasses, depending on the season.

13.0 Ignore the Rock Tower Trail to Coit Camp and continue on the doubletrack.

13.0 + Ignore the Rock Tower Trail to Grizzly Gulch and continue on the doubletrack.

13.4 The first sign alerts you to the fact that a spring exists to your right. The second sign is currently incorrect! It should direct you to the Jackson Trail to the right—not straight ahead. You're now approaching the nicest part of this ride. The narrow singletrack descends two dozen switchbacks to the bottom of the canyon. Ride responsibly to preserve this wonderful trail.

14.6 Look out for some slippery roots on a left turn.

14.9 You're back at the intersection with the Anza Trail. Turn left and continue down the switchbacks.

15.8 A sign alerts you that Woodchopper Spring is straight ahead and the Coyote Creek entrance is to the right. Turn right.

15.9 You're dumped back onto Coit Road and are now faced with a slight insult—an uphill climb on the dirt road to the top of the hill. But turn left onto the dirt road and just keep thinking about how wonderful those switchbacks were. You'll find yourself at the top.

16.1 The top. Let 'er drift back to the gate.

16.9 If there's any water in the creek, it would be a good idea to wash your arms and legs to remove any poison oak oils. Check for ticks as soon as you can. Aren't you glad to be alive?

Frog Lake

Location:	Main entrance, Henry W. Coe State Park, about 1.5 hours south of San Francisco and 13 miles east of Morgan Hill.
Distance:	6.4 miles, out-and-back.
Time:	1 hour.
Elevation gain:	About 900 feet. Lowest elevation is 2,400 feet; highest elevation is 2,600 feet.
Tread:	Mostly singletrack, mostly smooth and hard-packed.
Aerobic level:	Easy.
Technical difficulty:	1–3 (mostly 3).
Highlights:	High-quality singletrack: narrow, mostly smooth and hard-packed, with gentle descents and ascents. Abundant wildlife, wildflowers in spring, large manzanita shrubs, and a pond. No motorized vehicles are allowed on the single-track.
Land status:	Henry W. Coe State Park.
Maps:	USGS Mount Sizer (the singletrack isn't shown). A lovely and complete map of the park is also available at headquarters.
Access:	To get to the main entrance, drive to Morgan Hill on U.S. Highway 101. Take the East Dunne exit and follow the signs for Henry W. Coe State Park. It's 13 miles of winding road and 2,600 feet of climbing from the freeway to "Coe." Parking is available adjacent to head-quarters for a nominal fee. Water and out-houses are available at headquarters and at the adjacent main campground. The campground is seldom full during the week, but reservations are suggested on weekends. No food is avail-able at headquarters.

Notes on the trail: After riding a short distance on a smooth dirt road, you'll turn onto a wonderful singletrack—Flat Frog Trail. (I don't know if

Frog Lake,
Middle Ridge Loop,
China Hole Trail

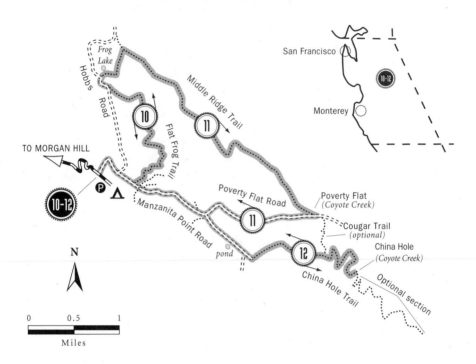

the name refers to the fact that the trail to Frog Lake is flat, or that some-one once encountered a flattened frog on the trail, but I suspect the for-mer.) There are just enough technical sections to keep you alert, but each is short and only slightly technical. For the most part, the trail is narrow, hard-packed, and smooth, and passes through a forest of ponderosa pines, live oaks, and large manzanita "trees." This is followed by a short section of steep uphill, rutted dirt road, and a shorter section of steep, downhill, eroded trail. The pond is best visited before August.

Although I've listed this ride as easy in terms of maximum aerobic level and total effort, it's not appropriate for first-time mountain bikers: The trail is narrow and technical in places. It is a great ride if you're feeling

Reflections on Frog Lake.

mellow, have little time to ride, or are ready for a "second ride." Since this is an out-and-back trip, be sure to look back at every trail junction so you'll know where to go on the return trip.

This trail is easily eroded. Please don't ride it when it is wet. Please don't allow your rear tire to slide when descending or turning. Walk your bike through sections that you cannot ride without sliding. Ride or walk your bike over water bars, not around them. Be alert for other trail users and yield them the right-of-way when you meet them.

The Ride

0.0 Headquarters. Ride north on the paved road for a short distance.

0.1 Take the paved road to the right. The sign reads: MANZANITA POINT ROAD. After a short distance, pass through a gate. The pavement soon ends.

0.5 Junction with Hobbs Road. Take the right fork to continue toward Manzanita Point.

0.7 Beginning of the Flat Frog Trail. There are three trails available; take the one on the far left. The sign simply states: FROG LAKE.

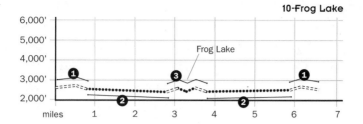

10-Frog Lake

1.6 Read the sign that declares: CAUTION, WALK YOUR BIKE. You're approaching a series of wooden steps. They're ridable for intermediate riders, but a mistake will result in a painful or fatal fall down a 75-foot cliff into a rocky creek bed. I walked, and suggest that you do, too.

2.5 Forest of manzanita "trees."

2.9 End of the Flat Frog Trail. Turn right onto Hobbs Road and climb or push steeply up.

3.1 At the sign for Frog Lake Camp, take this short, wide, steep, rocky, and rutted trail down to Frog Lake.

3.2 Frog Lake. In spring and early summer, this is a scenic and enjoyable pond. After having a snack or lunch, head back the way you came.

6.4 Back at headquarters (visitor center). Cold drinks are for sale inside.

Middle Ridge Loop

Location:	Main entrance of Henry W. Coe State Park, about 1.5 hours south of San Francisco and 13 miles east of Morgan Hill.	See map on Page 58
Distance:	10.7-mile loop.	
Time:	2.5 hours.	
Elevation gain:	About 2,500 feet. Lowest elevation is 1,300 feet; highest elevation is 2,800 feet.	

See map on Page 58

Tread:	Mostly singletrack, from smooth and hard-packed to rough and loose.
Aerobic level:	Moderate, with two long, strenuous climbs.
Technical difficulty:	2–4 (mostly 3).
Highlights:	Abundant, high-quality singletrack; technically challenging singletrack; abundant wildlife, including feral pigs; large specimens of manzanita, madrone, and ponderosa pine in the forest; a cool stream; abundant wildflowers in spring. Motorized vehicles are not allowed to use the singletracks.
Land status:	Henry W. Coe State Park.
Maps:	USGS Mount Sizer (not all trails are shown); a well-designed and complete map is also available at headquarters.
Access:	To get to the main entrance, drive to Morgan Hill on U.S. Highway 101. Take the East Dunne exit and follow the signs for Henry W. Coe State Park. It's 13 miles of winding road and 2,600 feet of climbing from the freeway to "Coe." Parking is available adjacent to headquarters for a nominal fee. Water and outhouses are available at headquarters and at the adjacent main campground. The campground is seldom full during the week, but reservations are suggested on weekends. No food is available at headquarters.

Notes on the trail: After riding a short distance on a dirt road, you'll turn onto a newly and well-built singletrack called the Flat Frog Trail. (See Ride 10.) From Frog Lake to the top of Middle Ridge, a singletrack is being rebuilt to incorporate more switchbacks and a lesser grade to make it more ridable and to decrease erosion. The Middle Ridge Trail is a primitive singletrack that's very narrow and well-preserved in most places. Unfortunately, because of its sandy nature and steep design in spots—and because some riders have been gouging out the trail by locking up their rear wheels—some sections are becoming eroded. Please don't ride it unless you can do so without locking up your rear wheels or are willing to walk your bike through the steep sections. Ride or walk over water bars rather than around them.

Middle Ridge is particularly impressive because of its huge manzanitas and colorful madrones. In midsummer you may spot madrones with old reddish brown bark toward the base, newer reddish orange bark peeling off in plates, and new greenish bark that's exposed. The Middle Ridge Trail delivers you to Poverty Flat, with a peaceful creek running through—a great place for a snack or lunch, and a rest.

There are three legal ways to get back to the visitor center. You can go back the way you came (this isn't a practical option, though it may be your only one if the creek is too high to safely cross), you can ride up the very steep and rocky Poverty Flat Road, or you may push your bike up the Cougar Trail (singletrack) to the China Hole Trail (singletrack). The China Hole Trail is well built and a pleasure to ride, but the Cougar Trail is too steep to ride; it's also surrounded by poison oak that reaches out to embrace you. This ride description assumes that you'll choose to bike up Poverty Flat Road. Perhaps by the time you read this, a trail will have been built from Poverty Flat to the beginning of the China Hole Trail. Check at headquarters before you begin the ride.

Finally, know that strenuous means strenuous. If your only aerobic activity is on weekends, you should not attempt this ride. The park rangers have seen so many people too exhausted to ride back up to the trailhead that they installed bike racks on their rescue vehicles! Be alert for other trail users and yield them the right-of-way.

The Ride

0.0   Headquarters. Ride north on the paved road for a short distance.

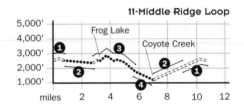

0.1   Take the paved road to the right. The sign reads: MANZANITA POINT ROAD. After a short distance, pass through a gate. The pavement soon ends.

0.5   Junction with Hobbs Road. Take the right fork to continue toward Manzanita Point.

0.7   Beginning of the Flat Frog Trail. There are three trails available; take the one on the far left. The sign simply states: FROG LAKE.

1.6   Read the sign that declares: CAUTION, WALK YOUR BIKE. You're approaching a series of wooden steps. They're ridable for intermediates, but a mistake will result in a painful or fatal fall down a 75-foot cliff into a rocky creek bed. I walked, and suggest that you do, too.

2.5   Forest of manzanita "trees." Notice how the trail is built narrowly so that water doesn't puddle up in the middle. Also, few trees or limbs had to be removed in its construction.

2.9   End of the Flat Frog Trail. Turn right onto Hobbs Road and climb or push steeply up.

3.1   At the sign for Frog Lake Camp, take this short, wide, steep, rocky, and rutted trail down to Frog Lake.

Drew on Middle Ridge Trail.

3.2 Frog Lake. In spring and early summer, this is a scenic and enjoyable pond. Cross the dirt dam, locate the sign TO MIDDLE RIDGE, and head up. Expect a steep climb. (At the time of this writing, this trail was being rebuilt with more switchbacks and a lesser grade.)

3.7 Arrive at the Middle Ridge Trail and turn right (south) onto it. This first part of the Middle Ridge Trail is narrow but gentle, filled with grasses and wildflowers in spring, and an absolute joy to ride!

4.3 The trail has been getting more extreme, with short steep climbs and descents. Gorgeous manzanita shrubs are appearing.

4.5 At the top of a steep climb, you'll see some of the largest manzanita shrubs in existence—they look more like trees. Ponderosa pines and California black oaks are cropping up.

5.0 Ignore the Fish Trail to the ranger station and continue straight on the Middle Ridge Trail.

5.7 This is the end of the climb for now. If you're feeling tired at this point, turn back: It's a long, steep climb out of the canyon below. After several gentle, fast miles, the trail now heads down through the forest on the east side of the ridge and grows steep, loose, rocky, twisty, narrow, and exposed. Please be willing to walk your bike whenever the trail gets too steep or technical for you—for the sake of both the trail and your health. Take some time to notice the madrone trees, whose leaves often form a soft covering on the trail.

7.1 Cross the stream, wash off the poison oak, and take a well-deserved rest. This is the Middle Fork of Coyote Creek. Notice the native sycamores. *Warning:* In winter and early spring, this stream may be dangerous to cross. If you have any doubts about crossing it, please push your bike back up to the top of Middle Ridge and return the way you came.

7.2 Cross the creek again and push your bike up to the dirt road. To get back to your car, take Poverty Flat Road to the right. It's a steep and rocky climb in any season, and a hot one in summer.

9.0 Junction with Manzanita Point Road, and the end of the steep uphill climb. Bear right and continue on the dirt road.

10.0 Junction with the Flat Frog Trail. Continue straight on the dirt road.

10.2 Junction with Hobbs Road. Bear left.

10.7 Back at headquarters.

Option: When you reach Poverty Flat Road (mile 7.2), turn left and go a short distance. Just before the road crosses the creek again, turn right onto the Cougar Trail, push your bike through poison oak 0.8 mile up to the China Hole Trail, travel up the China Hole Trail to Manzanita Point Road, and follow this road back to headquarters. This route involves the same amount of climbing but is slightly longer.

China Hole Trail

Location:	Main entrance of Henry W. Coe State Park, about 1.5 hours south of San Francisco and 13 miles east of Morgan Hill.
Distance:	10 miles, out-and-back.
Time:	2 hours.
Elevation gain:	About 1,900 feet. Lowest elevation is 1,200 feet; highest elevation is 2,600 feet.
Tread:	Mostly smooth, hard-packed singletrack.
Aerobic level:	Strenuous.
Total effort:	Moderate.
Technical difficulty:	1–3 (mostly 3).
Highlights:	A well-built, smooth, hard-packed, narrow singletrack that's enjoyable to ride both downhill and up; the feeling of seclusion at Coyote Creek; abundant wildlife including feral pigs, deer, and quail; wildflowers; views of the stream and canyon below. No motorized vehicles are allowed on the singletrack.
Land status:	Henry W. Coe State Park.
Maps:	USGS Mount Sizer (not all the trails are shown). A well-designed and complete map is also available at headquarters.
Access:	To get to the main entrance, drive to Morgan Hill on U.S. Highway 101. Take the East Dunne exit and follow the signs for Henry W. Coe State Park. It's 13 miles of winding road and 2,600 feet of climbing from the freeway to "Coe." Parking is available adjacent to headquarters for a nominal fee. Water and outhouses are available at headquarters and at the adjacent main campground. The campground is seldom full during the week, but reservations are suggested on weekends. No food is available at headquarters.

See map on Page 58

Notes on the trail: Don't attempt this ride unless you're in good aerobic condition: It's a long climb out of the canyon! I get almost spiritual pleasure riding on well-built singletracks through natural areas; I'd rather ride out and back on a singletrack than take a dirt road back—unless, of course, the singletrack is too steep to ride back. But the China Hole Trail is a delight to ride in either direction. Yes, you must take a dirt road (Manzanita Point Road) to the beginning of China Hole; still, it traverses an open ridge with good views of the area, and its descents and ascents are relatively gentle. You then begin the singletrack by riding through a forest of ponderosa pines, California black oaks, live oaks, and manzanitas; pop out onto the side of a chaparral-covered hill with views of the canyon below; and ride back into a forest before arriving at Coyote Creek. Although some of the turns are sharp, the trail is mostly smooth and hard-packed with no surprises. You feel quite isolated at the stream. Swimming holes are available early in the summer. (It gets pretty slimy late in the season.) If pumping back up the trail won't give you enough exercise or if your sense of adventure is strong, you may wish to continue on the China Hole Trail to the top of the next ridge (Mahoney Meadows) and back. It adds another 4.4 miles (2.2 miles each way) and 700 feet of climbing to this ride.

Since this is an out-and-back ride, be sure to look back at every trail junction to make sure you'll know where to go on the return trip! The only technical skill you'll need for this ride is the ability to ride on a narrow trail. If you cannot make the turns, simply walk your bike through them. This trail is easily eroded. Please don't ride it when it is wet or let your rear tire slide when descending or turning. Walk your bike through sections that you cannot ride without sliding. Ride or walk your bike over water bars, not around them. Be alert for other trail users and yield them the right-of-way.

The Ride

0.0 Headquarters. Ride north on the paved road for a short distance.
0.1 Take the paved road to the right. The sign reads: MANZANITA POINT ROAD. After a short distance, pass through a gate. The pavement soon ends.
0.5 Junction with Hobbs Road. Take the right fork toward Manzanita Point.

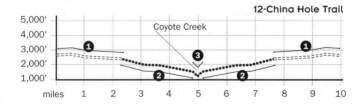

0.7 Junction with the Flat Frog Trail. Continue straight ahead on the dirt road.

1.6 At a dirt-road junction, bear right toward Manzanita Point.

2.1 Another dirt-road junction. Follow the sign for Manzanita Point by bearing left. You'll soon see a small reservoir on your right.

2.2 The dirt road forks. Take the left fork and notice the peeling manzanitas as you pass campsites 2 and 3.

2.3 Bear left past campsite 6.

2.4 Just past campsite 7 is a sign CHINA HOLE, 2.6 MILES and the beginning of the China Hole Trail. Pass through a forest of California black oaks, ponderosa pines, live oaks, tall grasses, and poison oak on a narrow, hard-packed singletrack.

2.6 Bear left at the fork. (The right fork goes back up into the campground.)

3.1 Read the sign describing prescribed fires as you leave the forest and enter chaparral. Notice the chamise with needlelike leaves and bunches of small white flowers, and the dead manzanita branches from the prescribed fires. Quail are abundant in the area.

3.5 Junction with the Cougar Trail. A sign directs you to China Hole, which is 1.5 miles to the right. As you glide down the singletrack, look into the canyon below to contemplate your destiny. Make sure you'll have enough energy to pump back up!

4.2 Constant vigilance is needed, because the trail is built on the side of a cliff. Stop and take a look at Coyote Creek below. You'll soon be there.

5.0 Junction with the Mile Trail: Continue straight for the remaining 50 yards of the China Hole Trail before arriving at the stream. *Warning:* This is the most technical portion of the China Hole Trail. It becomes steep and rocky. Use caution! In late spring and early summer, you might want to take a dip, or at least a splash in the creek. It gets warm, green, and slimy later in the season. Across the stream is a continuation of the China Hole Trail. It's a little narrower, steeper, and less well traveled than what you just rode down. A sign states: LOST SPRING TRAIL JUNCTION, 2.2 MILES. If you have the time and energy, ride up to this junction and back. Nothing is too steep to ride on the way back to headquarters, but some of the turns will be challenging for anyone. Enjoy the ride.

10.1 Back at headquarters.

Northern Coast Ranges

This section includes rides from San Francisco to the Oregon border.

Needless to say, the ecosystems change gradually throughout the coast ranges from south to north—in general, they become moister. Winter rains from Pacific storms increase significantly, with about 40 inches falling near San Francisco and more than 100 inches near the Oregon border. Summer fog often travels several miles inland, producing high winds, dripping trees, and cold temperatures, and supporting the growth of redwoods.

In many places valleys separate inland coast ranges from their coastal counterparts. These inland coast ranges seldom experience summer fog; they usually receive less winter precipitation and have significantly hotter summers than coastal ranges. Throughout the coast ranges, the closer you are to the ocean, the cooler will be the summer temperatures.

The wildflower season begins early in the coast ranges, with the first flowers appearing in January in the warmer areas, and the last flowers fading in August in moister areas. Grasses turn green as early as December and remain green until May in drier areas and until July in moister areas. California's coast ranges are known for their bright green color in winter and spring, and for their golden color during the summer and fall.

Poison oak is heavy in all regions, although the growth form changes from shrublike in the south to vinelike in the north. Ticks are also common throughout the coast ranges from early spring through summer.

North San Francisco Bay Area

North of San Francisco Bay, the coast ranges spread out over many miles, leading to diverse climates and vegetation. At the shoreline, the rainfall is low, summer fog is common, and grasslands prevail. In the mountains near the coast, the rainfall is quite high, summer fog is common, and coniferous forests—often redwood—prevail. Farther inland rainfall is low, summer fog is rare, summer temperatures can become quite hot, and chaparral and live oak forests are found.

These rides are arranged in a clockwise semicircle around the north bay. All are close to cities, and bike shops are plentiful. The trails are heavily frequented by a variety of trail users. Please ride in such a way that you don't catch them by surprise, and yield right-of-way by stopping and moving off the trail before they feel compelled to so do. These trails are also composed of easily eroded sediments. Please keep your rear wheel from sliding so you don't cause unnecessary erosion.

China Camp State Park

Location:	About 12 miles north of San Francisco, near San Rafael in Marin County, on a peninsula overlooking San Pablo Bay and San Francisco Bay.
Distance:	11.2-mile loop.
Time:	2 hours.
Elevation gain:	About 1,200 feet. Lowest elevation is 50 feet; highest elevation is 600 feet.
Tread:	Mostly smooth and hard-packed singletrack, with a few short rocky sections.
Aerobic level:	Moderate.
Technical difficulty:	2–3 (mostly 2).
Highlights:	Pristine forests of live oak, madrone, bay laurel, and redwood; wildflowers in spring; views of San Francisco Bay to the south and San Pablo Bay to the north; a historic site near the parking lot; miles of wonderful singletrack. No motorized vehicles are allowed on the singletracks.
Land status:	China Camp State Park.
Maps:	USGS San Quentin (the trails are not shown); state park topographic maps that show the trails are available for a small fee at the ranger station.
Access:	Approaching San Rafael on U.S. Highway 101, take the North San Pedro Road exit east. Follow this road east along the edge of San Pablo Bay for 5.5 miles until you encounter a sign for China Camp Village. Turn left into the upper parking lot. The trailhead is across the road from the entrance to the upper parking lot.

Notes on the trail: Most of this ride is on wide, smooth singletrack. A few sections are lightly to moderately technical. Long and legal singletracks are rare in Marin County, and these are sweet! They were built by the state park and by the Bicycle Trails Council of Marin as multiple-use trails. This is a good ride for those who feel confident in their mountain

China Camp State Park

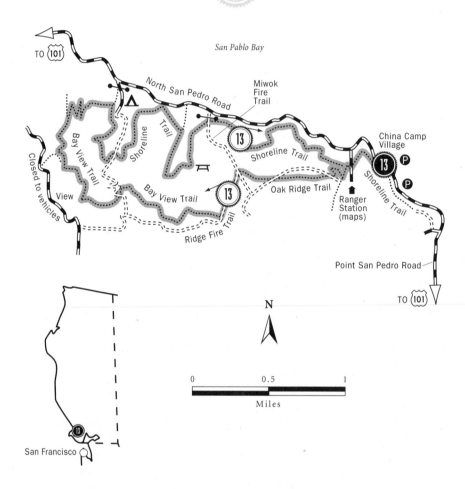

San Pablo Bay

TO 101

North San Pedro Road

Miwok Fire Trail

Shoreline Trail

Bay View Trail

Closed to vehicles

View

Bay View Trail

13

13

Shoreline Trail

Oak Ridge Trail

Ridge Fire Trail

China Camp Village

13

P

P

Shoreline Trail

Ranger Station (maps)

Point San Pedro Road

TO 101

N

0   0.5   1

Miles

San Francisco

13

biking skills and wish to venture out onto singletrack for the first time. China Camp State Park receives heavy use on weekends from mountain bikers, hikers, and equestrians, but it's quite empty on weekdays. The state park has been very supportive of the multiple-use concept; please maintain the respect that has developed between mountain bikers and the park by riding responsibly.

These trails are ridable for most of the year, but the lower portions become quite muddy for a few days following a heavy rain. Avoid riding on wet or muddy trails: It erodes them significantly. If you encounter mud, walk your bike through it. Summer varies from cool, foggy, and windy one day to hot, dry, and still the next. In general, summers at China Camp State Park are cooler than other inland areas but warmer and less foggy than coastal areas. My favorite season is springtime (April and May), because the hills are clothed in vivid green grasses and punctuated with wildflowers. A beautiful, forested walk-in campground is available (Back Ranch Meadows Walk-In Campground). It's less than 4 miles from civilization but feels quite isolated.

Drinking water, bathrooms with flush toilets, and an outdoor, cold shower are available at the historic site near the parking lot. (The shower feels particularly good after a ride on a hot day.) The historic site celebrates the Chinese immigrants who came to California during the gold rush, but stayed on to form a fishing village at China Camp. A descendant of the immigrants who still operates a fishing business also operates a small store selling drinks and sandwiches.

The Ride

0.0 The trailhead sign reads: VILLAGE TRAIL TO SHORELINE TRAIL, 0.1 MILES. This singletrack switchbacks up the hill to meet the Shoreline

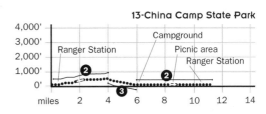

Trail. Notice the cow parsnips on the way up and enjoy the two sharp turns.

0.1 Turn right onto the Shoreline Trail. Enjoy the views of San Pedro Bay to your right and the large yellow flowers of mule's-ears on your left.

0.4 Arrive at the ranger station. Water and maps are available. Look across the paved road and you'll see the continuation of the Shoreline Trail. Get ready for two tight turns as the trail switchbacks up the hillside.

0.5 You'll be returning to this trail junction toward the end of the ride. I prefer to ride this loop clockwise. To do this, make a sharp left turn onto the Peacock Gap Trail.

0.6 Bear right onto the Oak Ridge Trail. The sign reads: TO MCNEAR'S FIRE TRAIL, 0.6 MILE. Get ready for three more tight turns.

1.2 Cross a dirt road (the McNear's Fire Trail) on the top of a ridge. The Oak Ridge Trail continues on the other side. You may want to stop shortly to enjoy the views of the Richmond/San Rafael Bridge, the Oakland Bay Bridge, the top of the Golden Gate Bridge, the city of San Francisco, and San Francisco Bay. This is a wonderfully narrow and smooth section of trail. Watch for deer.

China Camp State Park has nice singletrack.

1.7   Cross an old paved road (again, it's the McNear's Fire Trail) and continue to climb slowly on the Oak Ridge Trail through a dense forest on the other side of the ridge. The Oak Ridge Trail will dead-end onto the Miwok Fire Trail.

1.9   Turn left onto the Miwok Fire Trail and pedal or push steeply uphill for a few yards to the start of the Ridge Fire Trail. Turn right onto the Ridge Fire Trail. Watch for loose gravel on the short descent.

2.2   The sign reads: BAY VIEW TRAIL TO BACK RANCH FIRE TRAIL, 1.2 MILES. The Bay View Trail is a wonderful, gentle climb through a thick forest of bay, live oak, and madrone trees. (The madrone trees have reddish, peeling bark.)

3.4   It's tempting to ride straight through this trail junction and continue on the singletrack, but it quickly becomes an eroded and steep dirt road (the Back Ranch Fire Trail). Instead, turn left and climb up a short steep section of eroded dirt road to a continuation of the Bay View Trail.

3.5   You're situated next to a power-line tower, and the sign at the beginning of the singletrack reads: BAY VIEW TRAIL TO SHORELINE TRAIL, 2.4 MILES. Before leaving, check out the view of San Pablo Bay to the north. The next section of trail climbs steeply over loose rocks, reaches the high point of this ride, descends on a narrow and sometimes exposed singletrack, and traverses a grove of coast redwoods. Be aware that there is an extremely blind corner at the end of the grove.

4.1 Take the right fork just after the wooden bridge to continue on the Bay View Trail. Watch out for the short but steep and rocky downhill section, and the sharp right-hand turns after the wooden bridges. (If you have the time and energy, you might want to take the left fork to a view area and return. The left fork extends for about 0.25 mile to a closed paved road. Head up the paved road for another 0.25 mile to arrive at an old NIKE missile site, and a view of the entire north bay. *Warning:* This is a 500-foot climb.)

5.0 Take a sharp right turn to continue on the Bay View Trail. Several more sharp turns await you.

5.6 Turn right onto the Powerline Fire Trail for a few yards, then left onto a continuation of the Bay View Trail.

5.9 Make a sharp right turn onto the Shoreline Trail. The sign reads: SHORELINE TRAIL TO BACK RANCH FIRE TRAIL, 0.7 MILE. If you need water or want to bail out to the paved road, continue on the Bay View Trail for another 0.25 mile to its terminus.

6.7 Cross the Back Ranch Fire Trail and continue on the Shoreline Trail, which loops around the campground.

7.4 You've circled the campground; look across the meadow and parking lot to see where you were at mile 5.9. Wasn't that a lot better than just biking across the parking lot?

7.6 The Shoreline Trail contacts North San Pedro Road at this point. Continue on the trail. The sign reads: SHORELINE TRAIL TO MIWOK MEADOWS, 0.8 MILE.

7.9 The Bullethill Trail joins from the left. Continue on the Shoreline Trail along a small stream, through a dense live oak forest, over a small bridge, and to the parking lot for Miwok Meadows Group Day Use Area.

8.4 The sign near the rustic outhouses reads: SHORELINE TRAIL TO MIWOK FIRE TRAIL, 0.3 MILE. Take this dirt road to the next intersection.

8.7 Don't take the Miwok Fire Trail to your extreme right. To your left is a marsh, a good place for bird-watching. Take the Shoreline Trail to your right. The next 2 miles is one of my favorite sections of trail—it climbs and falls, winds back and forth, passes through open slopes with good views, wanders through dense forests and over small bridges, and makes you feel good to be alive!

10.5 All too soon you arrive at the intersection where you began the clockwise loop. Bear left to the ranger station and continue on the Shoreline Trail.

11.1 Turn left to return to the trailhead. If you want more singletrack or if you were having so much fun that you missed this turnoff, the Shoreline Trail continues for another 0.6 mile to the state park boundary. You can then return to this intersection or travel back to the parking lot on the paved road.

11.2 Trailtail! Now, wasn't that worth the drive? Don't forget to visit the village if you have time. If it's a hot day, I suggest taking advantage of the cold drinks at the store and the cold shower near the bathrooms.

Skyline Wilderness Park

Location:	In Napa, about 1.5 hours either northeast of San Francisco or west of Sacramento.
Distance:	7.4-mile loop.
Time:	2 hours.
Elevation gain:	About 1,600 feet. Lowest elevation is 200 feet; highest elevation is 1,000 feet.
Tread:	Singletrack, from smooth and hard-packed to rocky and loose.
Aerobic level:	Moderate, with one long, strenuous climb.
Technical difficulty:	3–4 (mostly 3).
Highlights:	Narrow singletrack, views of Napa Valley and the entire north bay area, wildflowers in spring and early summer, challenging technical uphill and downhill sections, lakes, rock gardens, bay forests, grassy knolls, manzanita groves. No motorized vehicles are allowed on the singletrack.
Land status:	Private nonprofit park on public land operated by the Skyline Park Citizen's Association.
Maps:	USGS Napa (the trails are not shown); a map of the trails is also available at the park entrance.
Access:	From the junction of Imola Avenue (California Highway 121) and Soscal Road (California Highway 29) in Napa, head east on Imola Avenue. (This junction is adjacent to Napa State Hospital.) Proceed 1.1 miles to 2201 Imola Avenue and turn right at the sign for Skyline Park. Leave your car here. Flush toilets, water, campsites, and a shady picnic table are available. The trailhead is near the large oak tree.

Skyline Wilderness Park

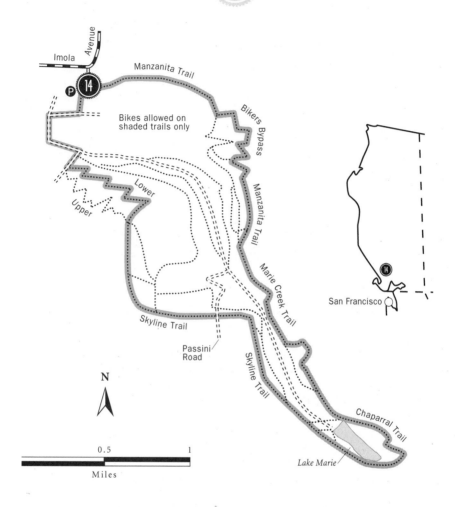

Notes on the trail: At the trailhead there is a sign that reads: WARNING: BEWARE OF RATTLESNAKES, WILD PIGS, POISON OAK, AND TICKS. (I suggest wearing long pants to avoid poison oak and thistles.) This ride also contains an abundance of narrow singletrack. The first portion involves a long climb to the top of a ridge, over a mixture of smooth and rocky singletrack. Intervening downhill sections contain challenging sharp turns. The descent from the ridge to the inlet of Lake Marie is steep. The Chaparral Trail on the far side of Lake Marie contains a very steep and rocky climb. The descent from the lake is also very steep with sharp switchbacks, rock gardens, and roots. The last portion of the ride contains several challenging technical maneuvers down rocky chutes, followed by log water bars around corners that can become quite slippery in wet weather. Variety is the theme of this ride, in terms of both ecosystems and terrain. The result is a feeling of having spent a wonderful few hours in nature, and of accomplishment after having successfully accomplished some of the technical challenges.

No riding is allowed on the trails within five days of a major winter storm. Some sections stay wet and muddy for longer. For the sake of the primo singletracks, please don't ride on them when they're wet or muddy. Some of the descents are quite steep. Walk your bike if you cannot ride it without sliding the rear wheel; ride or walk it over water bars rather than around them. Especially on weekends, watch carefully for other trail users. At all times, please take responsibility for not startling other trail users and yield the right-of-way to them by getting off the trail before they feel compelled to do so.

The Ride

0.0   Head along the fence to Skyline Park Social Center. At this point, a small sign will direct you to your right, past the botanical garden (which is worth a visit).

0.2   A tiny sign stating TO TRAILS leads you to a fenced corridor between two small lakes, across a paved road, and to another fenced corridor.

0.4   Follow the sign for the Skyline Trail by turning right.

0.5   Follow the sign for the Lower Skyline Trail by turning left. This trail is a very narrow singletrack surrounded by grasses, wildflowers, and thistles. Prepare to climb!

0.8   Experience the view of Napa Valley and get ready for some more steep climbing. Look out for thistles in grassy areas, followed by poison oak in forested areas.

1.2   Reach the top of the ridge.

1.5   Confusing junction. This is the end of the Lower Skyline Trail. Take the Bay Leaf Trail to the right for about 50 feet to another junction. This second junction is where the Upper Skyline Trail comes up from the right and the Skyline Trail takes off to the left. Turn left onto the Skyline Trail. Notice the blue marker for the

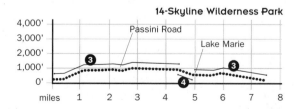

Mark negotiating a technical section in Skyline Wilderness Park.

Bay Area Ridge Trail. You'll be following these markers for a few miles until you pass the inlet creek to Lake Marie. *Warning:* You're approaching a short, tricky, rocky section.

1.7   Continue straight at this junction to stay on the Skyline Trail. You should be riding along the top of a ridge, with a rock fence on your right.

2.0   Continue straight at this junction to stay on the Skyline Trail. Get ready to climb steeply again. Bright yellow mariposa lilies, also known as sego lilies, are abundant along this trail in June.

2.3   This is a high point with views of Napa Valley. A steep downhill section with tight switchbacks is coming up.

2.4   Cross over Passini Road (eroded dirt) and continue steeply up on the Skyline Trail. If some of these uphill sections tempt you to ride downhill, just turn around and do it!

2.6   Confusing trail junction. The map provided at the entrance station is in error here and doesn't show this junction. The left (lower) fork leads to the Buckeye Trail; bikes are not allowed there. The Skyline Trail is the right (upper) fork. Start climbing! You soon travel alongside a barbed wire fence.

3.0   This is the highest point on the ride. The map shows a trail taking off at this point to an overlook. I found it to be overgrown with grasses, and the view of Mount Tamalpais and the north bay area to be limited. The Skyline Trail now drops down steeply through a series of tight switchbacks. Again, if you cannot ride without sliding your rear wheel, please get off and walk your bike.

3.1   Ignore the Buckeye Trail coming in from the left.

3.2   Do not head down to the Lake Marie Trail, but continue on the Skyline Trail.

3.3   Old House Site. Again, don't head down to the Lake Marie Trail; continue on the shady and cool Skyline Trail, perched on the side of a cliff with large ferns on your right and bay trees lining both sides.

3.4   Again, don't head down to the Lake Marie Trail. Continue on the Skyline Trail.

3.8   Cross the creek, proceed 100 feet to a junction with the Chaparral Trail, and turn left. The Chaparral Trail becomes steep and rocky as you climb above Lake Marie and descends quickly over loose rocks and roots.

4.4   Junction with the Marie Creek Trail. Take the right fork.

4.5   Go straight ahead on the Upper Marie Creek Trail and push your bike up through a steep rocky section. The rock garden beyond is quite ridable and fun: Head down through a series of very steep and very sharp zigzags on loose rock through a dense forest. Keep your rear tire from sliding as there is a lot of trail damage here.

4.9   Turn right onto the unsigned Marie Creek Trail and cross the creek twice.

5.4 Take the Manzanita/Toyon Trail by bearing right.

5.5 Bear right again to continue on the Manzanita Trail and enjoy the dense grove as you climb steeply. You'll also encounter chamise with small white flowers and needlelike leaves, and yellow sticky monkey flowers. (Monkey flowers are especially interesting because their lip-shaped cream-colored stigmas will close in front of your eyes if you tickle them with a piece of grass.) *Warning:* You will suddenly come upon a couple of technical sections on the Manzanita Trail on sharp downhill turns. If you get caught by surprise, shift your weight behind the seat, relax, and let your bike find its way through. If you make the mistake of grabbing the brakes, you might end up on your head!

6.1 Take the unsigned Manzanita Trail to the right. (The park map shows another trail taking off to Sugarloaf Mountain just prior to this point, but I haven't been able to locate it.) Climb briefly up to, and pass through, a portal in a rock wall. This trail then zigzags down over rocks and through a series of turns with water bars made from small logs. *Warning:* These water bars are slippery, even in dry weather! At one of the turns, an unsigned trail descends from the left. Continue to the right on the Manzanita Trail all the way back to the parking lot.

7.4 Arrive back at the parking lot. I would wash off the poison oak, if I were you.

Rockville Hills Community Park

Location:	About 1 hour from San Francisco Bay Area or from Sacramento on Interstate 80.
Distance:	7.9-mile loop.
Time:	2 hours.
Elevation gain:	About 1,550 feet. Lowest elevation is 100 feet; highest elevation is 550 feet.
Tread:	A little bit of everything—paved, graveled, rocky, smooth, loose, hard-packed, rutted, roots.
Aerobic level:	Moderate, with several strenuous climbs.
Technical difficulty:	1–4 (mostly 3).

Highlights:	Technical singletrack, wildflowers in spring, oak woodlands. No motorized vehicles are allowed.
Land status:	City of Fairfield, Rockville Hills Community Park.
Maps:	USGS Fairfield North; a free topographic map is also available at the trailhead.
Access:	From Interstate 80, take the Suisun Valley Road exit and head north. After passing Solano Community College, turn left onto Rockville Road. Go about 0.7 mile and you're there. No water or bathrooms are available at the parking lot.

Notes on the trail: I have conflicting feelings about listing this jewel. Lots of people already use this park in the late afternoon and evening, and on weekends. (It's close to a community college and to an urban area.) Therefore I hate to bring more people to it. Still, it contains such nice technical singletrack that I want to tell you about it. I do ask that you try to ride during the week; I've done so several times and rarely find any other trail users. I also ask that you treat the trails gently by preventing your rear wheel from sliding, by not riding on them when they're wet, and by riding or walking your bike over water bars, not around them. As always, ride in such a way that other trail users don't perceive you as a threat, and yield the right-of-way to them by getting off the trail before they feel compelled to do so.

The park includes oak woodlands, grasslands, chaparral, and abundant wildflowers in March and April. The trails are built on rock and hard-packed sand. Rock gardens provide technical challenges seldom encountered in the Bay Area. A free topographic map is available at the entrance, but it doesn't include all the trails within the park. I suspect that many are not official, so I've chosen a ride that includes only trails shown on the map. I've tried to show the nonofficial trails when possible to help orient you. The trails are not signed within the park, only on the map. With so many trails and no signs, it's a real challenge to do this ride. You need to keep a good sense of direction and to remember where you've been. Upper Lake is a good, recurring landmark. Fortunately, the park is small: The worst thing that can happen is that you arrive at another entrance (there are three). Although lots of poison oak grows within the park, you probably won't encounter it as long as you stay on the trail. Check yourself for ticks after the ride.

Rockville Hills Community Park

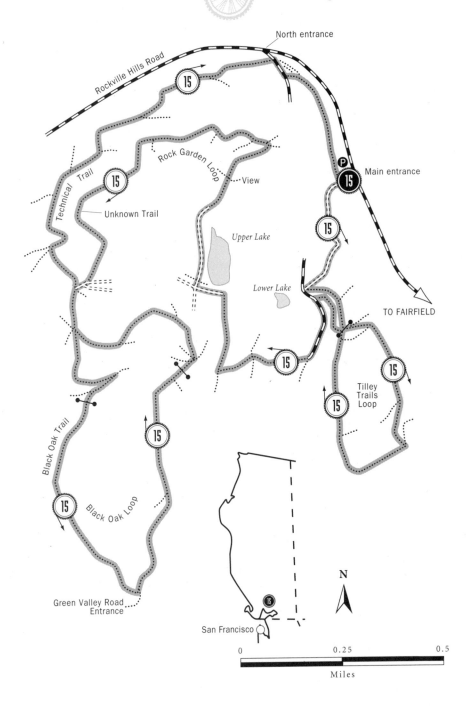

North entrance

Rockville Hills Road

Main entrance

Technical Trail

Rock Garden Loop

View

Unknown Trail

Upper Lake

Lower Lake

TO FAIRFIELD

Tilley Trails Loop

Black Oak Trail

Black Oak Loop

Green Valley Road Entrance

San Francisco

N

0   0.25   0.5

Miles

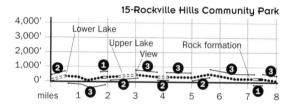

The Ride

0.0 Begin by riding up the dirt road, while ignoring the singletracks that take off on the right and left.

0.4 Intersection with a paved road. Turn left. (To your right is Lower Lake, which may or may not have water in it, depending on the season.)

0.4 + Take the first singletrack on your left, about 100 feet from the last intersection.

0.5 Take the second singletrack on your left.

0.6 Remember this spot: You'll be returning here at mile 1.8 and taking the eroded trail up to the right. For now, pass through the gate and take the eroded trail down.

0.6 + Ignore the singletracks coming in from both sides and blow straight through the intersection.

0.7 Ignore the trail that sweeps down to the right.

0.9 Crest the hill. Ignore the trail that comes down from the right and bear left.

1.0 Another fork. Bear left again.

1.1 A view of Solano Community College is below you. Begin a short, rocky class 4 section.

1.2 Trails take off in every direction. The trail to the far left loses a lot of altitude, so I chose to take the trail to the far right. *Warning:* A class 4 right-hand turn is approaching. Look out for the 3 Rs: roots, rocks, and ruts!

1.3 Ride along a fence, but be careful, because it's topped with barbed wire, and the trail is fairly narrow and technical and very close to the fence.

1.4 The trail pulls away from the fence and climbs gently uphill along a seasonal creek inhabited by lizards and chubby meadow mice in midsummer.

1.6 Ignore the trail that comes down from the right and head straight.

1.8 Major intersection: Turn left.

Riding on slickrock in Rockville Hills Community Park.

1.8 +	Back at the gate that you passed through at mile 0.6. You've just finished the Tilley Trails Loop. Pass through the gate again and bear left, up the eroded trail and across a small bridge.
1.9	You're back on the paved road. Turn left.
2.0	The pavement ends, and the trail forks. Take the trail to the right and pass over the wooden bridge.
2.1	Ignore the small singletrack taking off to the left and continue on to the intersection with the wide singletrack. Turn left.
2.2	The wide singletrack swings right.
2.5	Turn left onto the dirt road and begin to ride around Upper Lake.
2.5 +	At the signpost for Green Valley, turn right onto another dirt road to continue around the lake.
2.5 ++	Blow through this intersection and continue straight on the dirt road.
2.5 +++	Take the right fork to continue around the lake. Ignore the many singletracks that take off; stay on the dirt road.
2.8	The dirt road narrows to a singletrack and crosses under some high-voltage lines.
2.9	Confusing intersection: Head for the view rocks. Take a well-deserved rest and have a snack. Go back to the intersection when you're ready. Instead of turning left, under the high-voltage lines, bear right and head down the rocky and bumpy singletrack. Hang on!
3.0	Ignore the singletracks that head off to the right. Don't head down a trail that loses a lot of altitude. You want to remain on top of the cliff.
3.2	You should be passing through a grove of manzanita shrubs and under high-voltage lines at this point.
3.2 +	Ignore the minor singletrack on the left and take the major singletrack on the right.
3.4	Ignore the small singletrack coming in from the left and continue on the gentle, smooth, rolling singletrack overlooking a residential area.
3.6	Look out for the low limb! (You're now riding on the "Unknown Trail.")
3.7	Two dirt roads come down from the left. One dirt road heads off to the right. You've completed the Rock Garden Loop. Turn right. Singletracks come and go; just stay on the dirt road.
4.0	The dirt road turns into a singletrack at this intersection. Go straight through. (The steep and wide trail heading down to your right is the beginning of the Technical Trail, which you'll be taking later.)
4.1	The trail coming down from the left is the Mystic Ridge Trail, which you'll be taking later. Blow straight through this intersection.

4.1 +	Take the left fork and travel down the narrow singletrack.
4.1 ++	Take the left fork up.
4.4	Cross the small bridge and turn right onto the Black Oak Trail.
4.4 +	Take the left fork and ride up.
4.5	Pass through the gate.
5.0	This is mostly a hard-packed, class 2 surface. Don't let your speed exceed your visibility! This section of trail isn't only fast but also close to a residential area and another park entrance. Cross under high-voltage lines and meet a trail coming up from the right. Turn left onto this trail. The bad news is that you're climbing on a south-facing slope with no shade. The good news is that this slope is filled with wildflowers in March and April. The bad news is that it's probably not March or April.
5.2	Ignore the singletrack coming in from the left.
5.5	Top of the ridge. Ignore the singletrack going over to the power-line tower. Continue straight.
5.6	Carry your bike through the gate. Don't turn left onto the Mystic Valley Trail. Instead, continue straight for another 100 feet to the power-line tower. Don't turn left onto the steep, eroded single-track; instead, turn left a few feet beyond this trail and beside the power-line tower. This is the Mystic Ridge Trail. Views of Upper Lake soon appear.
5.7	Arrive at the top of the ridge and bear right to continue on the Mystic Ridge Trail. Enjoy the open views from the top of the ridge.
5.8	Ignore the small singletrack taking off on the right.
5.9	Bear right at the fork.
6.1	If you can't ride this downhill section without sliding, please get off your bike and walk it down. Turn right onto the wide single-track. (You were here at mile 4.0.)
6.2	Another major intersection that you've been at before. Notice the wide singletrack heading left and down and then turning right. Take it, but be ready to get off, because it soon leads to a class 4 chute that only the best riders will be able to handle without chewing up the trail. You're entering the Technical Trail, which skirts the northwest periphery of the park.
6.3	Two singletracks enter from the left. Take the one to the right. The Technical Trail is basically a class 3 trail, although there are a number of short class 4 sections.
6.5	Ignore the singletrack taking off to the left.
6.5 +	Ride along the fence until you come to a fork. Then take the right fork, away from the fence.
6.7	Ignore the singletrack taking off to your right and prepare to ride steeply down. Get your weight back!
6.7 +	Take the left fork heading down.

6.8 Ride along the fence with a BEWARE OF DOG sign.

6.9 Ride along a modern barbed-wire fence.

7.1 Ride up to a weird rock formation, then down steeply and back up to a hidden continuation of the Technical Trail behind the manzanita shrubs.

7.2 Take the left fork.

7.2 + Take the left fork.

7.3 You're now at the North Entrance. Take the paved road to the right and head uphill, passing several singletracks that head left.

7.4 Take the old paved road to the left. Swoop down until you hit a barbed-wire and rock fence. Turn right and ride along the fence. Ignore the singletracks coming down from the right.

7.5 You're passing through an old rock quarry on a slickrock surface. Watch out for other trail users as you ride back to your car on the smooth, fast singletrack.

7.9 Back at the car.

Santa Rosa/Clear Lake Area

This region is just far enough away from the bay and coast that it seldom benefits from the moderating effects of the ocean. The lower altitudes, such as Annadel State Park, can be very hot in summer; higher altitudes like Boggs Mountain can be very cold in winter. Unfortunately, these are the only two sites in this area with significant high-quality singletrack. Fortunately, the trails in each are abundant and great! Campgrounds are available at or near each of these locations. Annadel State Park is close to an urban area; Boggs Mountain State Demonstration Forest is quite remote.

Annadel State Park— Ledson Marsh

Location:	In Santa Rosa, off Interstate 101, about 1 hour north of San Francisco.
Distance:	12.7-mile loop.
Time:	2.5 hours.
Elevation gain:	About 1,950 feet. Lowest elevation is 300 feet; highest elevation is 1,300 feet.
Tread:	Smooth dirt road, rocky dirt road, smooth singletrack, rocky singletrack.
Aerobic level:	Moderate, with one long, strenuous climb.
Technical difficulty:	2–3 (mostly 3).
Highlights:	Wild turkeys; wonderful singletrack that has been recently rebuilt; a marsh with rushes, waterfowl, and endangered red-legged frogs; a variety of wildflowers from March to June. Annadel is the most pristine and diverse example of a native oak woodland in the entire state. No motorized vehicles are allowed on the trails.
Land status:	Annadel State Park.

Annadel State Park—Ledson Marsh, Annadel State Park—Lake Islanjo

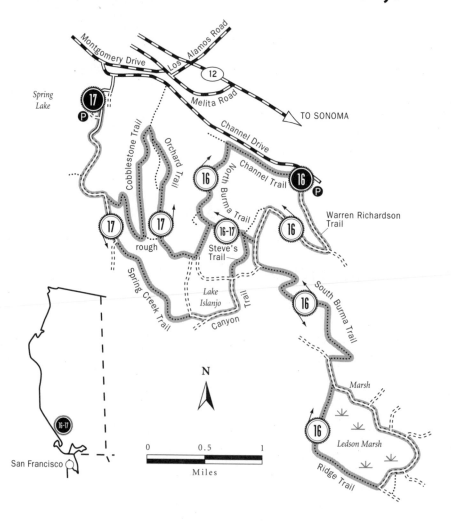

Montgomery Drive

Los Alamos Road

12

Melita Road

TO SONOMA

Spring Lake

17
P

Channel Drive

Cobblestone Trail

Orchard Trail

16

Channel Trail

North Burma Trail

16
P

17

17

rough

16-17

Steve's Trail

16

Warren Richardson Trail

Spring Creek Trail

Lake Islanjo

Canyon Trail

16

South Burma Trail

16

Marsh

Ledson Marsh

Ridge Trail

16-17

San Francisco

N

0   0.5   1
Miles

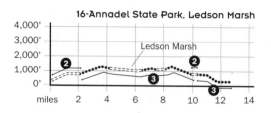

16-Annadel State Park, Ledson Marsh

4,000'
3,000'
2,000'
1,000'
0'

Ledson Marsh

2   2

3

3

miles   2   4   6   8   10   12   14

Maps: USGS Santa Rosa, Kentwood. A beautifully drawn topographic map is also available at the park entrance for a nominal fee.

Access: From Interstate 101 in Santa Rosa, take the California Highway 12 exit toward Sonoma. After a sharp right-hand turn, drive 3.6 miles and turn right onto Los Alamos Road, then right onto Melita Road. Notice the sign for Annadel State Park. Turn left onto Montgomery Drive, then left onto Channel Drive. At the sign for Annadel State Park and Spring Lake Park, head for Annadel. Along the way you'll pass through a gate where you'll be asked to self-register for a nominal fee. This gate is open between 9:00 A.M. and sunset. The parking lot is at the end of the pavement. Bathrooms are available at the parking lot, but no drinking water.

Notes on the trail: Although it's possible to ride all the singletracks here in one long and strenuous trip, I've chosen to split them into two rides, each with a desirable destination. This ride takes you up a dirt road (the Warren Richardson Trail) to the beginning of a lovely twisty singletrack (the South Burma Trail) that used to be a dirt road. The singletrack in turn takes you through a Douglas fir forest to a dirt road (the Marsh Trail), which leads to large Ledson Marsh, filled with rushes higher than your head. This marsh supports waterfowl as well as the endangered red-legged frog. Picnic tables are available at the marsh as well as in several locations along the way. A dirt road (the Ridge Trail) that's regenerating into a rocky, technical singletrack leads you back to the South Burma Trail, which you now get to ride downhill. Finally, you return to your car via a playful downhill singletrack (the North Burma Trail) and a rolling singletrack (the Channel Trail).

Because it's so close to Santa Rosa, this park gets a lot of use—especially on weekends. I advise riding it during the week and being extra careful not to catch other trail users by surprise. You'll be riding on easily eroded volcanic soils. Late winter and early spring are the seasons when an endangered species of newt chooses to mate. Please be careful not to run over them as they slowly waddle across the trails. Summer days are usually very hot at Annadel. Get an early start and take lots of water. Poison oak is abundant, but the trails are wide enough that you probably won't come into contact with it. And finally, ride only on signed trails. If a trail doesn't have a sign, then it's not legal for anyone to use. The Mounted Assistance Unit—an official volunteer horse and bike patrol group—is usually (especially on weekends) available to answer your questions and to assist you if you need help. More trail building is planned in the future. The land manager requests that you call ahead during the winter months: Some of the newer trails are closed during the wet season to prevent damage.

The Ride

0.0   Take the horse trail out of the parking lot. This is the Warren Richardson Trail (dirt road).

0.1   Ignore Steve's Trail—no bikes are allowed on it.

0.8   Bear to the right at the fork in the dirt road.

0.8 +   Take the right fork to remain on the Warren Richardson Trail. Climb through a cool Douglas fir and California redwood forest.

1.2   The dirt road levels off a little. Look for California black oaks with their large indented leaves.

1.5   Ignore the Louis Trail and continue on the Warren Richardson Trail, which is still a dirt road.

1.9   The North Burma Trail (singletrack) takes off to the right. You'll return to this point later and take this singletrack then. For now, continue on the dirt road.

2.1   Leave the Warren Richardson Trail and turn left onto the South Burma Trail (singletrack). Get ready to climb for a long time through a forest of Douglas firs.

2.5   It's hard to believe that this used to be a dirt road. What a nice singletrack it makes now!

3.5   Picnic table under a big Douglas fir at the top of the ridge. This is the top of the climb. If you don't want to drop down and climb back up again, you can skip ahead to mile 8.5, and turn around—but you'll miss the marsh and rock garden.

3.7   Watch for wild turkeys in this region.

4.2   Arrive in Buick Meadow at the junction with the Marsh Trail (dirt road). Take a break on the bench, if you wish. Watch for jackrabbits, which are abundant here. Turn left onto the dirt road.

4.5   Trail junction and picnic table. Turn left to remain on the Marsh Trail. (You'll later be riding down the other fork to return to this spot.)

4.9   Bear right at the junction with the Two Quarry Trail to remain on the Marsh Trail.

5.3   Arrive at a lush, green marsh, with rushes higher than your head. This is a great place to watch for birds. The strange-looking plastic birdhouses attached to the trees were placed here by Boy Scouts as nesting sites for wood ducks.

5.4   Bear right at the junction with the unsigned trail coming in from the left to continue around the marsh.

5.6   Read the display about the red-legged frog, and have a picnic at the table, if you wish.

5.9	Ignore the Pig Flat Trail (dirt road) and continue on the Marsh Trail, which narrows to a wide singletrack.
6.1	Ignore the unsigned singletrack that takes off to the right.
6.2	One moment you feel far from civilization; the next you find yourself riding along a fence with houses on the other side. The old dirt road now becomes a rock garden with a singletrack meandering through the rocks, and the Marsh Trail turns into the Ridge Trail
6.6	A sign in the middle of nowhere states: no camping, no motor vehicles, no dogs. But you knew that, didn't you?
7.0	Ignore Steve's Trail, which takes off to the left (no bikes allowed), and head downhill on the wide singletrack that was once a road. Note that this section of Steve's Trail is presently being rebuilt for use by mountain bikes. By the time you do this ride, you may be able to take Steve's Trail and turn right onto Marsh Trail to return to the beginning of the South Burma Trail.
7.6	You're now back on the Marsh Trail (dirt road). Turn left.
7.9	Turn right onto the South Burma Trail (singletrack). After a small climb, you get to ride this trail downhill.
8.5	At the top!
9.9	Wasn't that a fun singletrack? Turn right onto the Warren Richardson Trail (dirt road).
10.2	Now you get to take the North Burma Trail (singletrack) to your left
10.3	Ignore the Louis Trail taking off to the right.
10.7	Ignore the Live Oak Trail taking off to the left.
10.8	The North Burma Trail has been fairly flat so far, but now it begins to drop.
11.1	This is a beautiful trail, hard-packed and swooping between rocks, up and down as well as back and forth. Ignore the singletrack coming in from the left and bear right to continue on the North Burma Trail. This trail was designed to be fun without speed, but don't forget to ride responsibly.
11.6	Cross over a seasonal creek and keep going.
11.8	Turn right onto the singletrack just before the pavement. This is the Channel Trail, with a mixture of smooth and rocky sections. It's just technical enough to keep you on your toes, and hopefully off your face.
12.3	The going gets confusing and eroded as you hit the Quarry Picnic Area. It's probably best to hit the pavement, ride past the picnic area, and jump back onto the Channel Trail.
12.7	Back at the parking lot. Wow, all that great singletrack in Santa Rosa?

Annadel State Park— Lake Ilsanjo

Location:	In Santa Rosa, off Interstate 101, about 1 hour north of San Francisco.
Distance:	10.3-mile loop.
Time:	2 hours.
Elevation gain:	About 1,150 feet. Lowest elevation is 350 feet; highest elevation is 900 feet.
Tread:	Mostly singletrack, a combination of smooth and hard-packed, and rocky.
Aerobic level:	Moderate, with one long, strenuous climb.
Technical difficulty:	1–3 (mostly 3).
Highlights:	A beautiful swimming lake (reservoir, actually); turkeys foraging around the lake; and a lot of nice, lightly to moderately technical singletrack. Annadel is the most pristine and diverse example of a native oak woodland in the entire state. No motorized vehicles are allowed on the trails.
Land status:	Spring Lake County Park and Annadel State Park.
Maps:	USGS Santa Rosa, Kentwood. A beautifully drawn topographic map is available at the park entrance for a nominal fee.
Access:	From Interstate 101 in Santa Rosa, take the California Highway 12 exit toward Sonoma. After a sharp right-hand turn, drive 3.6 miles and turn right onto Los Alamos Road, then right onto Melita Road. Notice the sign for Annadel State Park. Turn left onto Montgomery Drive, then left onto Channel Drive. At the sign for Annadel State Park and Spring Lake Park, head for Spring Lake Park by turning right onto Violetti Road. Enter the park, pay a nominal fee, and drive to the parking area near the concession stand. (You'll need to vacate the

See map on Page 88

parking lot before sunset or risk having your car locked in for the night.) Water and bathrooms (and food and drinks) are available. This ride starts as a paved bike path to the right of the concession stand. Ride very slowly to avoid running into kids and dogs as you pass through the picnic area.

Notes on the trail: Although it's possible to ride all the singletracks here in one long and strenuous trip, I've chosen to split them into two rides, each with a desirable destination. This ride takes you up to Lake Ilsanjo on a gradual singletrack that passes along a creek under a canopy of bay trees. You'll circle the lake on dirt roads, then return via a series of beautiful and varied singletracks.

Because it's so close to Santa Rosa, this park gets a lot of use—especially on weekends. I advise riding it during the week and being extra careful not to catch other trail users by surprise. You'll be riding on easily eroded volcanic soils. Late winter and early spring are the seasons when an endangered species of newt chooses to mate. Please be careful not to run over them as they slowly waddle across the trails. Summer days are usually very hot at Annadel. Get an early start and take lots of water. Poison oak is abundant, but the trails are wide enough that you probably won't come into contact with it. If you enjoy lake swimming, bring a swimsuit. And finally, ride only on signed trails. If a trail doesn't have a sign, then it's not legal for anyone to use. The Mounted Assistance Unit—an official volunteer horse and bike patrol group—is usually (especially on weekends) available to answer your questions and to assist you if you need help. More trail building is planned in the future. The land manager requests that you call ahead during the winter months: Some of the newer trails are closed during the wet season to prevent damage.

The Ride

0.0 Follow the paved bike path through the picnic area, being careful to avoid hitting kids and dogs. Walking your bike through this section might be a good idea.

0.3 The paved bike path swings to the right at this point. Bear left onto another paved bike path.

0.4 The pavement becomes dirt and gravel.

0.5 Ride around the gate. A sign alerts you to the fact that the bike trail you're on is part of the Bay Area Ridge Trail system.

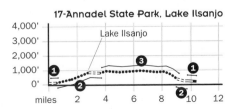

17-Annadel State Park, Lake Ilsanjo

0.8 Ignore the trail on the right coming from a residential area.

1.1 Junction of the Rough Go Trail and the Spring Creek Trail. Bear right to take the Spring Creek Trail, which at this point is a dirt road. This is a major passage into Annadel State Park. Please be extra alert for, and considerate of, other trail users by stopping and moving off the trail when you meet them.

1.2 A trail comes in from the right, across a dam. Continue straight.

1.3 Enter Annadel State Park.

1.6 Junction of the Canyon Trail and the Spring Creek Trail. Take the Spring Creek Trail (singletrack) to the left. Travel uphill on this medium to wide singletrack along a creek and under a canopy of bay trees.

2.3 Come out of the trees and cross a (usually) dry creek.

2.8 The trail becomes very exposed to the sun as it approaches Lake Ilsanjo. An access has been cut through the rushes near the picnic table to the left of the dam in case you want to go for a swim. Turn right onto the Rough Go Trail (dirt road) and ride across the dam.

2.9 Join the Canyon Trail by bearing left to continue around the lake. don't turn off onto any unsigned singletracks; they're not legal. Watch for wild turkeys feeding in the moist areas adjacent to the lake. Ride through a mixed woodland composed of Douglas firs, madrones, live oaks, and bay trees.

3.2 Continue on the dirt road past the outhouse.

3.5 Arrive at a major intersection. Cross over the Warren Richardson Trail (dirt road) and take Steve's S Trail (singletrack) straight ahead. It starts off wide as it skirts the meadow but narrows as it enters the forest.

3.9 A view down into a long meadow presents itself. The trail begins to playfully zigzag around large boulders.

4.2 Turn left to join the North Burma Trail (singletrack).

4.5 The trail reaches a crest and then frolics downhill between more large boulders to its junction with the Live Oak Trail.

4.9 Turn left onto the Live Oak Trail. Travel through fields of false lupine (yellow flowers) up onto a ridge with live oaks. This singletrack zigzags both up and down, and back and forth.

5.4 Cross a wooden bridge.

5.7 Pop out of the forest and into a meadow at the junction of the Live Oak Trail with the Rough Go Trail. Turn right to join the Rough Go Trail.

6.0 Turn right onto the Orchard Trail. This is a wonderfully narrow singletrack that climbs steeply up to the junction with the Orchard Trail Alternate.

6.5 Continue straight on the Orchard Trail.

6.7 There's a vernal (springtime) pond on your left.

6.9 Ride through a dense, cool Douglas fir forest.

7.1 Notice the rare native bunchgrasses growing on the forest floor. Most of California's native bunchgrasses have been either grazed out of existence or outcompeted by introduced species.

7.1 + Ignore the Orchard Trail Alternate and continue on the Orchard Trail.

7.2 Turn left onto the Cobblestone Trail.

7.2 + Turn left onto the Cobblestone Alternate Trail to enjoy a cool passage through a bay forest lined with wood ferns and sword ferns.

7.3 Turn left onto the Cobblestone Trail.

7.4 This junction is currently unsigned. Bear right to remain on the Cobblestone Trail. The first part of Cobblestone is smooth; the later part involves riding over—guess what?—cobblestones. All of this singletrack is wide, approaching dirt-road status near the end.

8.2 Turn right onto the Rough Go Trail. This is a perfect example of how to build a singletrack that's fun but not fast. Basically smooth, it has enough rocks and zigzags built in to keep all trail users traveling at about the same speed.

9.1 Ignore the unnamed singletrack taking off to your right. Continue straight toward the wooden bridge.

9.2 Cross the wooden bridge and turn right onto the Spring Creek Trail (dirt road). This should look familiar.

9.9 The dirt and gravel road turns into a paved road.

10.0 Swing to the right onto a bike path with a yellow stripe down the middle and pass between a lake and a swimming pond. Kids and dogs are running all over the place. Please ride very slowly, or walk your bike.

10.3 Back to the concession stand and parking lot. Ice cream, anyone?

Boggs Mountain Demonstration State Forest

Location:	Boggs Mountain Demonstration State Forest is at least 2.5 hours north of San Francisco, near Calistoga.
Distance:	12.5-mile loop.
Time:	3 hours.
Elevation gain:	About 1,800 feet. Lowest elevation is 2,800 feet; highest elevation is 3,600 feet.
Tread:	Mostly singletrack, from smooth and hard to rocky and loose.
Aerobic level:	Moderate, with several strenuous climbs.
Technical difficulty:	3–4 (mostly 3).
Highlights:	Miles of wonderful singletrack—much of it seldom traveled—through forests of ponderosa pines, California black oaks, Douglas firs, dogwoods, maples, and wildflowers. This is a great place to get away from people. No motorized vehicles are allowed on the singletracks.
Land status:	Boggs Mountain Demonstration State Forest.
Maps:	USGS Whispering Pines (the trails are not shown). A local contour map that shows the trails is also available at the entrance.
Access:	Probably the hardest part about Boggs Mountain is getting there. From Calistoga, take California Highway 29 to Middletown, then California Highway 175 to Cobb; proceed 1.3 miles past Cobb and turn right onto an unsigned road (Road 500) at a sign that reads: STATE FIRE STATION. Continue on Road 500 past the sign for Boggs Mountain Demonstration State Forest; past the office, parking, heliport, and bathroom; and past end of the pavement, until you reach the junction with Road 200 at Calso Camp (1.7 miles from California Highway 175). The ride begins here. No water is available at the trailhead.

Boggs Mountain
Demonstration State Forest

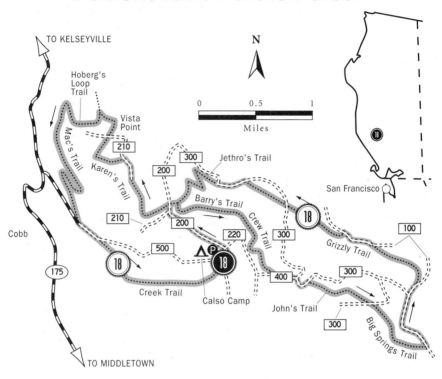

Notes on the trail: Since Boggs Mountain is so far away from major cities, you might want to camp here. No water is available, but the campground is in the middle of a ponderosa pine forest reminiscent of Yosemite Valley. All that's missing is the river and the 3,000-foot vertical granite walls. Unless you happen to arrive on a weekend when a bike race is scheduled or during deer-hunting season, you won't see many people, and might even have the place to yourself. But you still need to be alert for other users, and to yield the right-of-way to them when you meet them.

This area doesn't have fantastic views, but it does feature miles of slightly to moderately technical narrow singletracks meandering up and down and back and forth through dense forests. The trail system is complex. I've chosen a figure-eight double loop that includes 90 percent of the available singletracks. You can do this as one continuous ride from Calso Camp, or as two rides, each from Calso Camp. The best times to visit Boggs Mountain are spring (April through June) and fall (September and

October). Wildflowers and dogwoods are in bloom in the spring, and temperatures are cool to warm. Dogwoods and big-leaf maples are in color in the fall, and temperatures are cool to warm. It can be quite hot here in summer, and quite cold in winter. Snow can even cover the trails in midwinter! Still, Boggs Mountain provides some of the finest singletrack riding in California.

The Ride

0.0 Begin by riding up Road 200.

0.1 Junction with Road 201. Bear left to stay on Road 200. Notice how similar the forest is to that in Yosemite Valley: ponderosa pines, California black oaks, and Douglas firs.

0.6 Bear right to remain on Road 200. In about 100 feet you'll see a singletrack crossing the road. Take Berry's Trail to the right.

0.7 Take the right fork at this junction. (The left fork is Jethro's Trail. You'll be climbing back up to this point later in the ride.) The right fork is a continuation of Berry's Trail. It starts out with a steep and rocky downhill, and turns into a narrow, little-used, exquisite trail.

1.0 Cross over the dirt road and keep going on Berry's Trail.

1.4 Berry's Trail becomes the Crew Trail at this point. Notice the abundant and colorful manzanita plants. *Warning:* Several roots and rocks are coming up, providing good opportunities for face plants.

1.7 As the trail dips down into a dry creek bed, notice the native bunchgrasses. Once abundant in California, they've become rare by being overtaken by nonnative grasses and grazed by cattle.

1.9 This is the end of the Crew Trail and the junction with Road 400. Turn left onto Road 400.

2.0 Road 300 comes up from the left. Bear right onto Road 300.

2.2 John's Trail is a hard-to-spot singletrack taking off to the right; its small sign is barely visible. A keep-your-weight-behind-the-seat downhill is approaching. Several impressive madrone trees can be seen along the way.

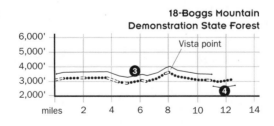

3.0 This is the end of John's Trail and the junction with Road 600. Turn left and immediately begin looking to your right for the beginning of the Big Springs Trail, which you take. There are some steep sections along this trail, and also some beautiful banked, downhill-swooping switchbacks.

3.7 Reach Big Springs and the end of the Big Springs Trail. Even though the water is cold and clear, a sign reads: NON-POTABLE WATER. Charlie's Trail is coming down from the right. Take Road 100 to the left. Get ready for some fast downhill riding complete with speed bumps (water bars, actually).

4.3 Road 300 takes off to the left. Bear right to stay on Road 100. Immediately begin looking for the Grizzley Trail taking off to the left. A small sign may or may not be there. (From the spelling, I suspect that this trail is named not for the bear, but probably for a person.) This trail passes by dogwood trees (blooming white in May and turning red in October) and big-leaf maples (turning yellow in October).

5.0 You're temporarily dumped onto Road 100.

5.1 After passing over a bridge, turn left onto the Grizzley Trail again. There are some challenging rocky sections and steep climbs ahead—as well as more dogwoods.

5.9 Cross Road 300 and continue on the Grizzley Trail.

6.2 You're dumped back onto Road 300. Watch for a singletrack taking off to your left at mile 6.4.

6.4 Although there's no sign, this is the beginning of Jethro's Trail. If you find yourself pushing your bike up a steep climb to a water tank, you're on the right trail. You'll begin riding again just before the tank, but the next 0.5 mile is mostly uphill.

6.9 An unnamed and unmapped trail turns sharply left and down here. Bear right and continue to climb on Jethro's Trail.

7.2 This is the end of Jethro's Trail and the junction with Berry's Trail. This should look familiar. Bear right onto Berry's Trail.

7.3 Berry's Trail ends at Road 200 and Karen's Trail begins on the other side. At this point, you can continue with the ride or take a break by turning onto Road 200 and coasting back to your car. Take Karen's Trail to continue the ride. Get ready for some climbing!

7.7 Karen's Trail dumps you out on the beginning of Road 210, which climbs steeply through rocks to the top of a ridge.

8.0 A view area on the right (Vista Point) is a great place for lunch. Karen's Trail takes off to your left and becomes narrow, smooth, fast, and fun. Watch out for a small log across the trail followed by several quick turns.

8.4 The trail crosses Road 210 at this point and becomes the Boggs Ridge Trail (no sign).

9.1 Trail junction. Both trails go to the same place. The Hobergs Loop Trail to the left is 0.9 mile long, with a short climb and a long descent. The Hobergs Loop Trail to the right is 0.6 mile long, with a shorter descent. I've chosen the left fork, which is longer and wilder; the right fork goes past the backyards of houses with barking dogs.

10.0 At this point the Hobergs Loop Trail continues to your right, but you want to bear left onto Mac's Trail.

10.2 Mac's Trail meanders through a stump forest—trees that have been thinned to provide enough light, moisture, and nutrients for others.

10.6 A sharp downhill left turn into a manzanita shrub. If you don't turn sharply enough, you'll have an intimate and perhaps painful relationship with this shrub. Past this point there's a steep and rocky downhill section, and then a smooth section down to the office/bathroom/parking lot/heliport area.

10.8 End of Mac's Trail at the office (et cetera) area. Turn left onto Road 500.

11.1 You want to turn right off Road 500 and onto the Creek Trail, but it's very difficult to find. The Creek Trail takes off to the right just after Road 520 forks off to the left. A tiny sign marks the beginning of this wonderful, narrow, winding, technically challenging trail. For a short distance, it joins an old dirt road, but it quickly takes off again as a singletrack.

11.6 Houghton Creek: sugar pines, Douglas firs, huge ferns, wild grapes, horsetails, dogwoods, alders, hound's-tongue, trilliums. Cross the creek and look for a trail heading upstream. The remainder of the Creek Trail climbs steeply and is quite rocky in places, but it takes you along the creek through beautiful, shady fern gardens. Beginning and intermediate riders should expect to walk/push their bikes through some of the steeper and rockier sections—but then, what's the hurry?

12.5 You reach the end of the Creek Trail back at the junction of Road 500 and Road 200, and your car.

North Coast Redwood Parks

This is the land of frequent and heavy winter storms and summer fog—perfect conditions for redwood forests.

Unfortunately, there aren't many singletracks open to mountain bikes up here. Those that are tend to be steep and very technical. Thus I've included only one ride here—but it incorporates a significant segment of narrow singletrack, is incredibly scenic, and passes through old-growth redwood forests. It's well worth the long drive.

Because of the lingering moisture from the large and frequent winter storms, and because of the moisture arriving from the frequent summer fog, trails don't dry out until summer, and wildflowers bloom late into the season. Summer temperatures range from hot to cold, depending on whether the fog is in. During foggy times the trees drip constantly; take rain gear.

Campgrounds are available in and near this park, and motels and bike shops are located in Arcata and Eureka.

Prairie Creek Redwoods State Park

Location:	About 1 hour north of Eureka, on U.S. Highway 101.
Distance:	19.0-mile loop.
Time:	4 hours.
Elevation gain:	About 1,300 feet. Lowest elevation is 50 feet; highest elevation is 800 feet.
Tread:	Paved road, gravel road, dirt road, doubletrack, smooth singletrack, and short sections of rocky singletrack.
Aerobic level:	Strenuous.
Technical difficulty:	1–3.
Highlights:	Lush old-growth redwood groves, herds of elk, coastal marshes and sandy beaches, fern-lined

waterfalls. No motorized vehicles are allowed
on the trails.

Land status: Prairie Creek Redwoods State Park.

Maps: USGS Fern Canyon, Orick. A detailed and
beautifully drawn local topographic map is also
provided by the state park.

Access: From Eureka, travel about 50 miles north on
U.S. Highway 101 and take the exit for Prairie
Creek Redwoods State Park and Newton B.
Drury Scenic Parkway. After 4.2 miles, turn
left toward the visitor center and park beside
the tollbooth. A beautifully drawn topographic
map is available both at this tollbooth and in
the visitor center. Water and flush toilets are
also available.

Notes on the trail: Only a small part of this ride is on singletrack, and
some of it is on paved and dirt roads, but the entire ride passes through an
extremely scenic area. One section of trail is a doubletrack through a lush
dense forest. Another segment—a primitive singletrack struggling to avoid
being overtaken by grasses at the edge of a coastal marsh—takes you along
the base of a rocky bluff with views of small waterfalls framed in five-finger ferns. Still another section of singletrack passes through a grove of giant
redwoods. Expect to see elk browsing in the meadows and marshes at the
base of the bluffs. As tempting as it may be, please don't approach them!

The ride begins at the visitor center. There is both a day-use parking
area and a campground (by reservation only) available there. But if you're
planning on camping, don't mind driving a few miles on a dirt road, and
enjoy the beach, you may wish to camp at the Beach Campground (first-
come, first-served) and begin the ride from there. Although it rarely
snows, the winters here can be longer than in other areas of California.
Trails may not dry out enough for riding until June, and may become too
wet by late October. Please avoid riding on wet or muddy trails, and carry
your bike over muddy sections, particularly on the Coastal Trail. Fog is
common during the summer. When the fog is in, temperatures will be in
the 50s, it may be windy, and the trees may drip. Bring appropriate clothing. Wildflowers bloom here throughout the summer, with shows of
Shasta daisies during June. This may be one of the most wild and beautiful places in the world. UNESCO has designated it a World Heritage Site.

The Ride

0.0 Head south from the visitor center on a paved road passing along
the edge of the meadow and leading to the Elk Prairie Campground. Bear left at the campground to continue riding along the
edge of the meadow.

Prairie Creek Redwoods State Park

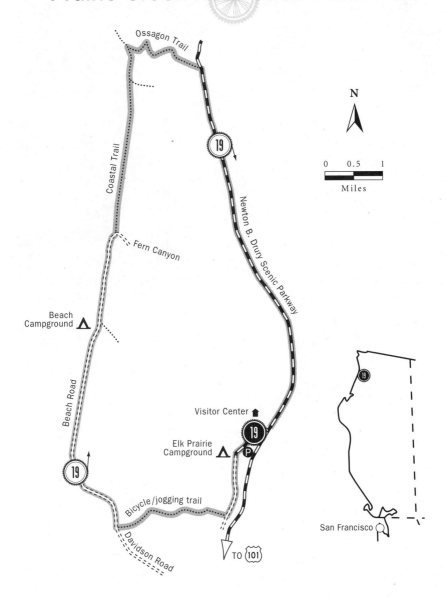

Ossagon Trail

Coastal Trail

19

Newton B. Drury Scenic Parkway

N

0   0.5   1
Miles

Fern Canyon

Beach
Campground ⛺

Beach Road

Visitor Center 🏠

19

Elk Prairie
Campground ⛺ P

19

19

San Francisco

Bicycle/jogging trail

Davidson Road

⬇ TO 🛡101

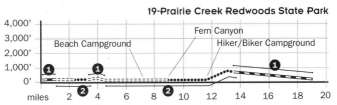

19-Prairie Creek Redwoods State Park

Beach Campground

Fern Canyon

Hiker/Biker Campground

4,000'
3,000'
2,000'
1,000'
0'

miles   2   4   6   8   10   12   14   16   18   20

A wide singletrack through redwoods in Prairie Creek Redwoods State Park.

0.7 Metal gate. The pavement ends here, and the road turns into a doubletrack along the edge of the meadow.

1.0 Enter a beautiful forest of redwoods and ferns. The ground cover has reduced the dirt road to a wide singletrack.

1.1 Metal gate and Creek Trail junction. A yellow sign with a sketch of a jogger points the way to the wide dirt road.

1.5 Another yellow sign with a jogger instructs you to veer right and begin to climb on a doubletrack. Buttercups, foxgloves, and ferns are abundant.

2.5 Pass beside a stream with alders and big-leaf maples. Redwood sorrel with three leaflets and light purple flowers forms a dense ground cover, crowding the trail into a singletrack.

3.5 The pristine singletrack meets up with a dirt road open to motorized vehicles. Turn right and join them.

4.0 This is the high point in the road. Coast down to the beach.

4.3 Pass by the sign for Gold Bluffs Beach. Notice the skunk cabbage in the bog on your right—look for its huge leaves and large stalks with clusters of yellow flowers. It's related to taro in Hawaii, and was prepared and eaten in the same way by Native Americans.

6.4 You're biking along the base of Gold Bluffs. Listen carefully to the sound of the surf bouncing off the cliff. Start watching for elk. Remember to fight the urge to approach them. A large bull elk with a full rack of antlers can be dangerous—especially during the fall mating season.

6.6 The stunted trees around you are Sitka spruces. Although common in Oregon, they're unusual in California, and don't occur south of here.

7.0 Beach Campground. Water and bathrooms with flush toilets are available. Ignore the turnoff to the Miner's Ridge Trail and continue on Beach Road.

7.4 Watch for wild roses.

8.8 This is the end of the dirt road (and the motorized vehicles) and the beginning of the Coastal Trail. You'll encounter many other trail users; please be very considerate of them. When you reach the turnoff for Fern Canyon, find a good place to hide your bike or lock it to a tree and take a detour up the canyon. This is a spectacular canyon with vertical walls covered in five-finger ferns. After exploring this canyon, return to your bikes and look for a sign that reads: OSSAGON TRAIL, 2.7 MILES. This trail is a true singletrack with grasses coming right up to the trail, some roots and rocks to climb over, some willows to duck under, and some Sitka spruces to squeeze around.

10.0 Listen for a waterfall—find it, if you wish.

10.1 Take a short hike to the base of Gold Dust Falls. This is a good waterfall to stand under on a hot day. Like the other waterfalls along this trail, it's bordered by ferns.

10.2 Another waterfall. Shortly past this point are some wooden bridges and a technical maneuver at the junction with the West Ridge Trail. Continue on the Coastal Trail. A sign directs you to continue to the Butler Creek Trail Camp.

11.5 Navigate some technically tricky places. At this point, the Coastal Trail heads left and the Ossagon Trail heads right. Take the Ossagon Trail.

11.6 The trail seems to dead-end at a hiker/biker campground. Head for the first picnic table, though, and you'll see it veering off to the right. What a wild area!

11.8 Climb steeply through a dense Sitka spruce forest.

12.1 Please walk the steps going down. If you try to ride around them, you risk widening and eroding the trail.

12.4 The singletrack widens to a doubletrack with walls of ferns as high as your head.

12.7 The trail narrows again to a singletrack.

13.0 Don't take the small singletrack to your left. Stay on the more traveled singletrack.

13.1 Enter a pristine old-growth redwood grove on a gravel singletrack that gives you good traction. Hikers may be present so descend slowly.

13.4 Intersect the Newton B. Drury Parkway. Turn right onto this paved road and glide back to the visitor center through miles of old-growth redwoods. You're sharing this road with motorists who are often looking at the impressive trees rather than watching for bikers. Please ride in single file carefully and watchfully.

19.0 Arrive back at the visitor center with vivid memories of the last few hours.

Southern Cascades and Northern Sierra Nevada

The Cascade Range is a series of volcanoes that extends from Washington to northern California. In California the range is represented by two large volcanic peaks, Mount Shasta and Mount Lassen, and many smaller volcanic peaks. Near Mount Shasta the Cascade Range blends in with the coast ranges, and the Klamath River cuts a canyon all the way to the Pacific. South of Mount Lassen the Cascades blend in with the northern Sierra Nevada. The northernmost extent of the Great Central Valley is at the bases of Mount Shasta and Mount Lassen.

The Sierra Nevada is the longest continuous mountain range in the continental United States, as well as the highest. It extends for more than 200 miles and reaches altitudes above 14,000 feet. The Sierra Nevada is also known for its lakes and granite. Because it has been heavily glaciated, its granite is exposed in many places, and many lakes have been formed. Although the Downieville and Lake Tahoe regions contain the highest concentrations, singletracks are available for riding throughout these mountains. Since the Sierra is so long, I've divided it in half. This section considers the Sierra Nevada north of Yosemite National Park.

Most of the higher altitudes of both the southern Cascades and the northern Sierra Nevada are contained in national parks and wilderness areas, which don't allow mountain bikes on their singletracks. Most other singletracks are open, however. One important exception is the Pacific Crest Trail.

These mountains are known for their heavy snowfall at altitudes above 7,000 feet, fairly warm winters and hot summers at lower altitudes, cold winters and warm summers at high altitudes, and dry summers at all altitudes. You can ride as soon as the snow has melted, through the summer, and into fall with little or no rain. Trails in the foothills are ridable year-round, but you're encouraged to let them dry out for a few days after major winter storms. On the other hand, the snow might not melt out at the higher altitudes until mid-July or even August. Below 4,000 feet poison oak, ticks, and rattlesnakes are abundant. Above these altitudes poison oak becomes nonexistent, and ticks and rattlesnakes grow rare. Mountain lions follow the herds of deer into the high country in summer and into the foothills in winter. Lion attacks on humans are exceedingly rare, but if you're approached by a mountain lion, stand tall, hold your bike between you and the animal, and slowly back away. In the unlikely event that you're attacked, use your bike as a shield and fight back aggressively. Bears may also be encountered at higher altitudes. If you catch one by surprise, stop and wait for it to leave the area. If you find yourself between a mother and her cub, slowly back away until they are rejoined and have left the area.

The ecosystems are quite variable, depending on proximity to the ocean, latitude, and altitude.

Mount Shasta Area

North of Mount Shasta lies a huge region in the northwest corner of California that contains the Red Butte, Siskiyou, Marble Mountain, and Trinity Alps Wilderness Areas, along with the Salmon and Klamath Rivers. Unfortunately, trails within the wilderness areas are off-limits to bikes. The Pacific Crest Trail also passes through this region, and it too is off-limits to bikes. Singletracks leading to the wilderness areas are usually open, but they tend to be very short, very steep, or not well maintained. I found only one short singletrack that was appropriate, near Fort Jones. This trail leads beside a stream through a cool forest of ponderosa pines and Douglas firs to the boundary of the Marble Mountains Wilderness Area; it's snowed in during the winter. Camping is available near the trailhead, and motels and a bike shop can be found in Yreka.

South of Mount Shasta you'll find the lower-altitude Whiskeytown-Shasta-Trinity National Recreation Area; there are legal singletracks at Shasta and Whiskeytown Lakes. Although winter here sometimes brings snow, it usually melts within a few days. Spring offers pleasant temperatures, dry trails, and wildflowers. Summers are hot; you may want to ride in the morning or evening. Fall again brings pleasant temperatures. Do not ride the trails when they are wet, as the soils are easily eroded. Campgrounds, bike shops, and motels are available in or near Redding.

The trails at Shasta Lake are well planned, well built, and well signed. All are depicted on a free map that's available at the visitor center. Shasta Lake is a reservoir. It fills in late winter or early spring, and begins to empty in summer. The lake is most scenic when it's full. Otherwise a desolate "bathtub ring" is formed below the high-water level.

The trails at Whiskeytown Lake are more subtle, and usually follow old logging roads or ditches. They are simply marked with carsonite posts with the word TRAIL and an arrow. Some of these trails are not shown on the free map available at the visitor center. Some are also poorly maintained, and may change from year to year. Fortunately, John Shuman's guidebook *Mountain Biking Whiskeytown* (second edition) is available in local bike shops and at the visitor center.

Kelsey Trail

Location:	About 1 hour west of Yreka. Yreka is about 4 hours north of Sacramento on Interstate 5.
Distance:	7.7 miles, out-and-back.
Time:	2 hours.
Elevation gain:	About 1,700 feet. Lowest elevation is 2,150 feet; highest elevation is 3,500 feet.
Tread:	From smooth and hard-packed to loose and rocky.
Aerobic level:	Moderate, with one long, strenuous climb.
Technical difficulty:	2–3 (mostly 3).
Highlights:	A nice singletrack alongside a cascading creek leading to the boundary of a wilderness area. No motorized vehicles are allowed on the singletrack.
Land status:	Klamath National Forest.
Maps:	USGS Scott Bar; a forest service map is also available at the forest service office in Fort Jones.
Access:	From Yreka on Interstate 5, take California Highway 3 south for 15 miles to Fort Jones. (This is your last chance to buy food.) Just outside the city limits, turn right (north) onto Scott River Road. Drive for 17.5 miles, cross the bridge over the Scott River, and park at the Bridge Flat Campground. An outhouse is available, but no water. Water is available at the Indian Scotty Campground, 3 miles back.

Notes on the trail: This is the only singletrack I could find in the entire Yreka/Klamath River/Salmon River area that's open to bikes, ridable by bikers with intermediate technical skills, and of significant length. The Klamath National Forest publishes a pamphlet titled *Great Mountain Biking Routes,* but it lists only dirt roads and paved roads—not significant chunks of singletrack. Fortunately, this is a great little trail, mostly ridable in the uphill direction and entirely ridable downhill. It follows Kelsey Creek up to the boundary of the Marble Mountain Wilderness Area. (Bikes are not allowed past this point.) Views of the stream, cascading in May and

Kelsey Trail

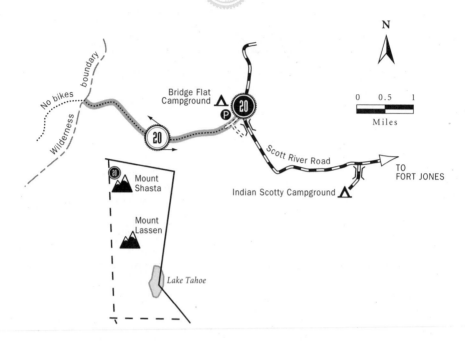

June and lined with big-leaf maples, are constant and impressive. Riding downhill with the water cascading below is especially thrilling. Lots of hikers and horses frequent this trail, especially on weekends. Please ride in such a way that you don't threaten or surprise them. Yield them the right-of-way when you meet them. Let the trail dry out thoroughly in spring (May to June) before riding on it. Poison oak is abundant, but the trail is wide enough that you probably won't touch it.

The Ride

0.0 Begin by riding up the unsigned dirt road along Kelsey Creek, across the paved road from your car.

0.4 Fork. Continue straight, along the right side of Kelsey Creek.

0.6 On your right is a sign for the Kelsey Trail. The singletrack begins here.

0.9 Trail junction: Bear left to continue on the Kelsey Trail.

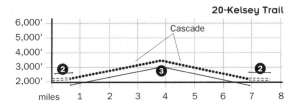

1.2   Travel through a forest of California black oaks, Douglas firs, and big-leaf maples on a narrow and sometimes rocky singletrack, with the sound and sight of Kelsey Creek cascading below you.

1.9   If you're riding in May or June, you may get to see the large white flowers of dogwoods. In fall the fruits and leaves are bright red.

2.1   Madrones and live oaks are growing in this drier section. It gets pretty cliffy in places. Though your instincts tell you otherwise, keep your weight on the *downhill* side of your bike to stay on the trail. If you begin to hug the uphill side, you'll slide down for sure.

2.6   Bracken ferns and bright blue lupines decorate the trail.

2.9   The creek is forced over a ledge and funneled down a channel, creating an impressive cascade.

3.0   The trail begins to zigzag up.

3.2   Cross a small seasonal creek and look left for a view of some of the peaks in the Marble Mountain Wilderness Area.

3.3   The trail is cut through rock that appears to be granitic.

3.5   The trail is getting more rocky and technical.

3.8   Sign for the Marble Mountain Wilderness Area. Notice the claw marks: Bears have tried to rip the sign off. You're not allowed to ride into the wilderness area. Turn around and descend.

7.7   Back at your car. There's a beautiful swimming hole under the bridge.

Bailey Cove Loop

Location:	Shasta Lake, about 3 hours northwest of Sacramento, on Interstate 5.
Distance:	3.1-mile loop.
Time:	45 minutes.
Elevation gain:	About 200 feet. Lowest elevation is 1,250 feet; highest elevation is 1,250 feet.
Tread:	All hard-packed, sometimes smooth and sometimes rocky.
Aerobic level:	Easy.
Technical difficulty:	3.
Highlights:	You'll enjoy almost constant views of Shasta Lake on this well-built trail with some lightly to moderately technical challenges. No motorized vehicles are allowed on the trail.
Land status:	Whiskeytown-Shasta-Trinity National Recreation Area.
Maps:	USGS O'Brien (the trail is not shown). A nice map of the entire recreation area is also available at the visitor center south of Shasta Lake on Interstate 5.
Access:	About 17 miles north of Redding on Interstate 5, take the Shasta Caverns Road exit and head east. At the sign for Bailey Cove, turn right. At the stop sign, turn left into the day-use area parking lot. A bathroom and water are available, and there's a campground nearby.

Notes on the trail: This ride takes you around a knoll just above Shasta Lake's high-water level. There's a lot of poison oak, but the trail is usually wide enough that you won't rub up against it. You'll probably hear the screaming of an osprey overhead, because they tend to nest here. I've ranked this a class 3 trail: Some parts are cliffy, others rocky and rooty, and it's just darn tricky in places. If you're not a good technical rider, please walk

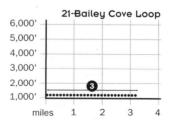

Bailey Cove Loop, Waters Gulch Trail

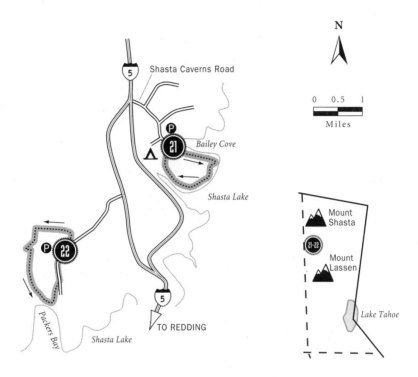

N

Shasta Caverns Road

5

P

21

Bailey Cove

Shasta Lake

0   0.5   1
Miles

Mount
Shasta

21-22

Mount
Lassen

Lake Tahoe

P

22

5

TO REDDING

Packers Bay

Shasta Lake

your bike through the tricky sections, both to save you some discomfort and to save the trail from unnecessary damage. Since this trail is so close to the picnic area and campground, it receives heavy use from hikers. Please keep this in mind when your visibility becomes limited so that you don't catch them by surprise. When you meet other trail users, yield them the right-of-way.

The Ride

0.0 Ride into the picnic area on the inconspicuous path. At the last picnic tables, bear left onto the conspicuous singletrack at the sign for Bailey Cove Loop. Ride through a forest of California black oaks and Douglas firs.

1.1 You're passing through a forest of knob-cone pines. Notice that the cones don't fall off the tree, but instead become embedded within the trunk as it grows. They'll remain embedded until the tree is eventually burned.

1.2 Ride through a canopy of manzanitas.

1.7 Wild grapevines are growing into the oak trees and trying to take over the trail in places.

2.0 This side is very exposed to the afternoon sun: Plan not to be here on a hot afternoon.

3.1 Back at the car. This ride is so short that you might as well ride it again in the other direction!

Waters Gulch Trail

Location:	Shasta Lake, about 3 hours northwest of Sacramento, on Interstate 5.
Distance:	4.1-mile loop.
Time:	1 hour.
Elevation gain:	About 600 feet. Lowest elevation is 1,275 feet; highest elevation is 1,500 feet.
Tread:	Mostly singletrack, sometimes smooth and sometimes rocky.
Aerobic level:	Easy.
Technical difficulty:	1–3 (mostly 3).
Highlights:	A nice singletrack passing through a forest and along the bank of Shasta Lake. No motorcycles are allowed on the singletrack.
Land status:	Whiskeytown-Shasta-Trinity National Recreation Area.
Maps:	USGS O'Brien (the trail is not shown); a nice map of the entire recreation area is also available at the visitor center south of Shasta Lake on Interstate 5.
Access:	From the south, about 17 miles north of Redding on Interstate 5, take the Shasta Caverns Road exit, head west under the freeway, imme-

See map on Page 113

diately get back on the freeway heading south, and take the exit for Packers Bay Road. From the north, about 16 miles north of Redding on Interstate 5, take the exit for Packers Bay Road. At mile 1.2 on Packers Bay Road, turn right into the parking area for the Waters Gulch Trailhead. No facilities exist.

Notes on the trail: This ride takes you from the top of a ridge down to Shasta Lake, along the lakeshore for a bit, then back up the ridge. The final climb back up to your car is along Packers Bay Road. There's a lot of poison oak, but the trail is usually wide enough that you won't rub up against it. I've ranked this a class 3 trail: Parts are cliffy, others rocky and rooty, and it's just darn tricky in places. If you're not a good technical rider, please walk your bike through the tricky sections, both to save you some discomfort and to save the trail from unnecessary damage. This trail receives heavy use from hikers. Please keep this in mind when your visibility becomes limited so that you don't catch them by surprise. When you meet other trail users, please yield them the right-of-way. Several small ditches have been cut across the trail to drain water away; as you approach each one, pull up, and you'll ride right over it.

The Ride

0.0 Begin by pedaling through a California black oak forest. The trail is very obvious.

0.3 Descend through a Douglas fir forest.

0.4 Reach a steep downhill section. If you cannot ride this without sliding your rear wheel, please get off and walk. And while you're walking, take a look at the small waterfall below you.

0.6 Bench (for tall people).

1.0 Wander just above the high-water mark.

1.2 Ride around an old mudslide.

1.4 Notice the ponderosa pine growing on a rocky knob that becomes an island at high water. In midsummer you should be able to walk out to this "island" for a good view of the lake. Now start climbing!

1.7 A steep climb through an area that's quite exposed to the sun. This is not a good place to be on a hot afternoon.

2.1 You're approaching a fun swooping-downhill section.

2.7 Nasty (rocky) dry creek crossing. Just after this, turn right onto the Fish Loop.

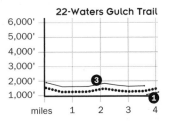

2.9 Another exposed, southwest-facing slope.

3.1 The lake comes into view again. From now on you'll come across more trail users. Please ride slowly to the end of the singletrack.

3.4 End of Fish Loop. Ride along the edge of the parking lot until you reach Packers Bay Road, then carefully ride along the edge of the road back to your car.

4.1 Back at the car.

Option: After completing the above ride, you can take the short trail to Packers Overlook. This mostly class 2 singletrack climbs steadily for 0.4 mile and 250 feet to a rock wall. It takes only about 15 minutes to ride up and back.

Clikapudi Trail

Location: Shasta Lake, about 3 hours northwest of Sacramento, on Interstate 5.

Distance: 7.3-mile loop.

Time: 1.5 hours.

Elevation gain: About 700 feet. Lowest elevation is 1,275 feet; highest elevation is 1,500 feet.

Tread: Mostly smooth and hard-packed, with infrequent but regular technical sections.

Aerobic level: Easy, with several moderate climbs.

Technical difficulty: 3.

Highlights: A nice singletrack with good views of Shasta Lake. No motorized vehicles are allowed on the singletrack.

Land status: Whiskeytown-Shasta-Trinity National Recreation Area.

Maps: USGS Bella Vista (the trail is not shown); a nice map is also available at the visitor center.

Access: On Interstate 5 from Redding, drive about 10 miles to the Mountain Gate/Wonderland Boulevard exit onto Old Oregon Trail toward the east. (Take the first right to the visitor center for a free map and return, if you wish.) At mile 2.8, turn left onto Bear Mountain Road to head

Clikapudi Trail

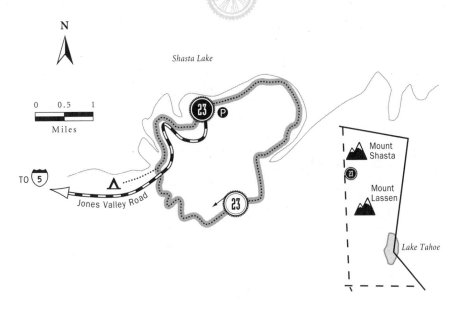

for Jones Valley. At mile 8.7 is a stop sign; turn left onto Backbone Road. At mile 9.6 a sign reads: ENTERING NATIONAL RECREATION AREA, SHASTA LAKE. Turn right at mile 9.8 onto Jones Valley Road. At mile 9.9, head for Jones Valley campgrounds; pass the campgrounds and continue until you reach the Jones Valley Boat Ramp parking area at mile 12.2. A bathroom and water are available. The trail begins where the road meets the parking lot, at the Jones Valley Boat Ramp National Recreation Area sign.

Notes on the trail: This ride takes you along the lake just above the highwater level, then up to the top of a ridge and back down to the lake. There's a lot of poison oak, but the trail is usually wide enough that you won't rub up against it. I've ranked this a class 3 trail: Parts are cliffy, others rocky and rooty, and it's just darn tricky in places! If you're not a good technical rider, please walk your bike through the tricky sections, both to save you some discomfort and to save the trail from unnecessary damage. Don't take shortcuts. This trail receives heavy use from hikers. Please keep this in mind when your visibility becomes limited so you don't catch them by surprise. Yield the right-of-way to other users.

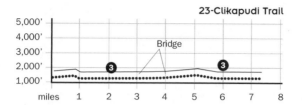

The Ride

0.0 Begin by riding through a forest of knob-cone pines at the Jones Valley Boat Ramp National Recreation Area sign. Notice that their cones don't fall off, but instead become slowly embedded in the branches as the tree grows. They'll remain embedded until released by fire.

0.7 Don't take the shortcut to the right—it's causing lots of erosion. Notice the forest of blue oaks, with their bluish green leaves.

1.0 A rocky, technical downhill. Get your weight behind the seat, or just get off and walk down.

1.2 Another rocky, technical section.

1.8 Another rocky, technical section.

2.2 Ride through a forest of tall manzanita shrubs.

3.1 A big bridge over a small seasonal creek.

3.4 Ride through a shady and cool Douglas fir forest.

3.5 Join an old, eroded dirt road for about 100 yards, then climb up onto a singletrack on the right. Be careful; this trail is easy to miss.

3.9 Turn right onto a dirt road, bike past a fence enclosing Native American artifacts (don't disturb them), and then jump back onto the singletrack as it takes off to the right.

4.0 Another big bridge over a small seasonal creek.

4.1 Cross a dirt road to the singletrack on the other side.

4.3 Turn left onto the dirt road and look for another dirt road taking off on the right.

4.5 The dirt road narrows to a wide singletrack.

4.6 The wide singletrack becomes a narrow singletrack. Begin to climb steeply.

5.1 The top of the hill!

5.4 When you hit the paved road, look to your right. You'll see a TRAILHEAD sign about 200 feet away. Watch for cars, too.

5.6 At the singletrack intersection, go right. (The left fork comes up from the campground—a good option if you're camped there.)

6.2 In late summer the poison oak becomes quite beautiful in here, with bright red and purple leaves, and white berries.

7.3 Arrive at a dirt road. Look to the right and you'll see the parking area with your car. That's all there is, folks!

Clear Creek Vista Trail

Location:	On California Highway 299 near Redding, about 2.5 hours northwest of Sacramento.
Distance:	5.8 miles, out-and-back.
Time:	1 hour.
Elevation gain:	About 550 feet. Lowest elevation is 1,300 feet; highest elevation is 1,500 feet.
Tread:	Mostly hard-packed.
Aerobic level:	Easy, with one moderate climb.
Technical difficulty:	2–3 (mostly 2).
Highlights:	An old mine that is being renovated, some sweet singletracks, several challenging switchbacks, lots of blackberries to eat in midsummer. No motorized vehicles are allowed on the singletracks.
Land status:	Whiskeytown-Shasta-Trinity National Recreation Area.
Maps:	USGS Whiskeytown (not all the trails are shown); a nice map is also available at the visitor center.
Access:	From Interstate 5 in Redding, head west on California Highway 299 for 15 miles. Turn left toward Oak Bottom and stop at the pay station to purchase a day pass. Go back to the highway and turn left. Drive for another 2 miles and turn left onto Carr Powerhouse Road. This ride begins at the other side of the bridge over Clear Creek. There's room to park there, or you can drive to the picnic area and ride back to this point. The picnic area has water and bathrooms.

Notes on the trail: Many hikers use this trail; use caution. Ride slowly, especially when your visibility is limited. Yield the right-of-way to other trail users by stopping and moving off the trail. You also need to keep your weight back on the class 3 section to prevent your rear wheel from sliding and digging up the trail—or walk your bike down this section. Ride or walk your bike over water bars rather than around them. Be aware that it

Clear Creek Vista Trail

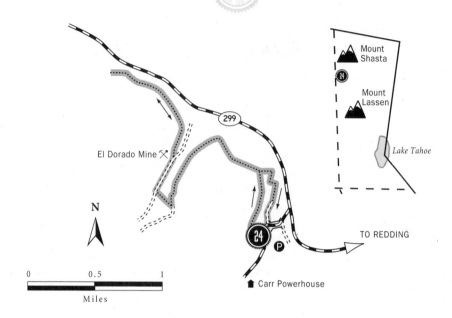

can get very hot up here in the afternoon during summer. There's lots of poison oak, but the trail is wide enough that you probably won't hit it. This trail is open year-round, but please let it dry out for a few days after a storm. This trail is unofficially known as the El Dorado Mine Trail.

The Ride

0.0 Ride down the pavement toward the picnic area.

0.1 Turn right onto the singletrack and ride up through digger pines and California black oaks, followed by a pure stand of manzanita.

0.5 Leaf-covered trail through a shady live oak forest.

0.6 It looks like the trail was built in the bottom of a small ditch!

0.8 Ignore the singletrack coming in from your extreme right for now. (You'll take it on the return trip.)

1.1 The trail narrows and becomes rockier and looser.

1.7 Intersection with a dirt road. Turn sharply right to continue on the singletrack. The narrow trail descends steeply to a stream. Keep your weight back far enough that your rear wheel doesn't slide—or get off and walk your bike down.

2.1 Cross the stream and turn right onto the dirt road. Stop and take a look at the old mine and stamp mill. Hopefully by the time you

ride this, the El Dorado Mine will be restored and available for you to experience.

2.1 + The sign reads: TOWER'S IRRIGATION DITCH. Take this wide single-track. You can stop to pick ripe blackberries, if you wish.

2.3 Walk your bike up and down the steps. Don't ride around them.

2.6 Pass by the grave site.

2.9 The trail dead-ends at the creek (or creek bed). Notice the small diversion dam that used to supply water to the irrigation ditch. Now turn around and head back. If you're riding this trail in mid-summer, you can eat your way back to the mine.

3.7 Cross the creek and get ready to push your bike up this class 3 section, unless you're a very strong climber.

4.1 At the top of the hill, return the way you came by making a sharp left-hand turn.

5.0 This time, take the left fork. Ride down switchbacks through a ponderosa pine forest.

5.5 The singletrack dumps you out onto a dirt road. Follow it downhill, back to your car.

5.8 Short, but sweet!

Recliner Loop

Location:	At Whiskeytown Lake, 10 miles west of Redding and about 3 hours north of Sacramento.
Distance:	7.0-mile loop.
Time:	2 hours.
Elevation gain:	About 2,000 feet. Lowest elevation is 1,150 feet; highest elevation is 2,450 feet.
Tread:	Dirt roads and singletrack, from hard-packed sand to loose, broken shale.
Aerobic level:	Moderate, with one long, strenuous climb.
Technical difficulty:	2–3.
Highlights:	Downhill singletrack, a granite-enclosed stream, bright red Indian pinks and scarlet monkey flowers. No motorcycles are allowed on the trails.
Land status:	Whiskeytown Lake National Recreation Area, National Park Service.
Maps:	USGS Igo (not all the trails are shown on this map).
Access:	From Interstate 5 in Redding, take California Highway 299 West toward Weaverville and follow it through Redding. At 10.3 miles from Interstate 5, turn left onto J. F. Kennedy Memorial Drive. The sign will direct you to the Visitor Center/Vista Point. Purchase a day pass at the visitor center and fill up with water. You might also wish to pick up a free map. Continue driving on J. F. Kennedy Memorial Drive toward the dam. When you reach the dam, turn left onto Paige Bar Road. (If you find yourself driving across the dam, you've gone too far.) Drive another 1.2 miles and turn right onto Peltier Valley Road (dirt). (If you don't want to drive your car down the dirt road, you can park in the lot opposite the turnoff and ride your bike down.) Drive 0.5 mile down the dirt road, cross a one-lane bridge over Clear Creek, and park in the lot to your right. This

Recliner Loop Ride

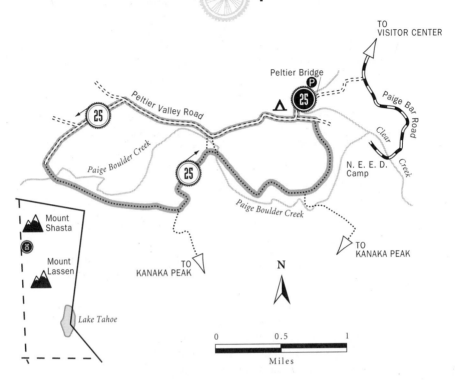

parking lot is shaded and is located beside a creek so that you can wash off after the ride. An outhouse is available, but no water. Nearby is a peaceful and lovely campground filled with canyon live oaks, dogwoods, big-leaf maples, huge grapevines, lots of blackberries, and the continual sound of Peltier Creek. If you wish to camp here, you must drive back to the park headquarters and register for the site.

Notes on the trail: Even though this ride involves a long climb on a dirt road, it seems to incorporate the best downhill singletrack in the area. The very beginning of the singletrack is sketchy. Only those with advanced technical skills will be able to ride this section without tearing up the trail. The rest of us should just walk our bikes down to the creek. Springtime creek crossings could be interesting—and even dangerous—but during the summer months, it's quite easy to jump from rock to rock. There's evidence of heavy equestrian use on these trails. Please keep this in mind when approaching sections with limited visibility. When you encounter

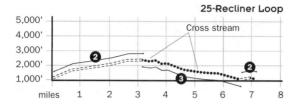

other trail users, please yield to them. If you approach other trail users from behind, slow down, alert them to your presence, give them adequate time to move off the trail, and pass them slowly.

The Ride

0.0 Start by climbing steeply west on Peltier Valley Road.

0.1 Take the right fork.

0.9 Top out temporarily, then glide down to and across a small creek. Notice the bright red Indian pinks blooming along the sides of the road.

1.0 About 75 yards after crossing the creek, notice the trail on your left. A sign states: TRAIL, NO MOTORCYCLES. This ride is in the shape of a backward B. The dirt road you're on will take you up the side of the B. Continue to climb straight ahead on the dirt road through a forest of ponderosa pines and Douglas firs.

2.1 Reach the top of a saddle, turn left onto a narrow and seldom-used dirt road, and ride around the gate. A sign reading TRAIL will direct you.

2.5 Mount Lassen may be visible in the distance. Mints with bright blue-purple flowers line the road.

2.7 Take the left fork and climb up the loose rocks. (No one will notice if you have to push your bike up this hill. Walking helps stretch your calves and returns blood to the body parts you've been sitting on.)

2.8 Enjoy the short reprieve from climbing.

3.2 Take the singletrack that drops off to your left. This is easy to miss. If you accidentally continue straight, the dirt road will quickly turn into a singletrack, the singletrack will dissolve into nothing, and you'll reach a stream. While you're here, you might as well enjoy the stream cascading down through a granite-lined ravine. Now go back 100 yards and look for the singletrack that you should be on. If the stream is too high to safely cross, please turn back! If not, cross over to the other side, and ride/push your bike up the steep singletrack. Notice the bright scarlet monkey flowers growing alongside the stream.

On Recliner Loop in the Mount Shasta area.

3.6 The quality of the trail increases as the sweet singletrack begins to head downhill. Watch for equestrians and hikers.

3.8 Junction with the Kanaka Peak Loop Trail. Turn left onto this old dirt road, which has narrowed to a wide singletrack.

4.7 Just before you hit the creek, take the small singletrack to your right. (On the other side of the creek is the dirt road where you were standing back at mile 1.0. You've completed one semiloop of the B and are beginning the second.)

4.8 Pass around the gate.

5.0 Cross the creek by hopping from rock to rock—unless it's springtime. Then you'll need to carefully forge your way through the water. If you were able to make the last creek crossing, you should be able to make this one. Again, notice all the scarlet monkey flowers in summer as you cross.

5.4 A carsonite post reminds you that you're on the trail. Ignore the tiny trail that drops off to your left.

5.5 Lift your legs to avoid the blackberries.

5.5 + Take the left fork, away from Kanaka Peak.

5.8 You're faced with a simple choice: Trail 1 to the left, or Trail 2 to the right. What could be simpler? Actually, I've tried both, and found Trail 1 (Satan's Crack) to be more to my liking. The end of the other trail (Shin Bone Alley) is a bit too sketchy for me. Take Trail 1 (left turn) and descend down into a canyon filled with dogwoods and wild grapevines. Watch your speed as you approach spots with limited visibility.

6.5 Don't take the little singletrack to your right. Instead, continue straight.

6.7 Turn left onto the dirt road and begin to climb.

6.8 Pass through the brown gate, bear right onto Peltier Valley Road, and glide back down to your car.

7.0 Back at the parking lot. Now aren't you glad you parked beside the stream?

Land Luge Loop

Location:	At Whiskeytown Lake, 10 miles west of Redding and about 3 hours north of Sacramento.
Distance:	7.6-mile loop.
Time:	1.75 hours.
Elevation gain:	About 1,000 feet. Lowest elevation is 1,000 feet; highest elevation is 1,175 feet.
Tread:	Mostly smooth, hard-packed singletrack, with one short stretch of technical, rocky singletrack.
Aerobic level:	Moderate.
Technical difficulty:	2–3.
Highlights:	A long nontechnical section of lugelike trail contained within an old ditch, followed by a short technical section of trail perched above a beautiful stream.
Land status:	Whiskeytown Lake National Recreation Area, National Park Service.
Maps:	USGS Igo; most, but not all, of these trails are shown on the free map available at the visitor center.
Access:	From Interstate 5 in Redding, take California Highway 299 West toward Weaverville and follow it through Redding. At 10.3 miles from Interstate 5, turn left onto J. F. Kennedy Memorial Drive. The sign will direct you to the Visitor Center/Vista Point. Purchase a day pass at the visitor center and fill up with water. You might also wish to pick up a free map. Continue driving on J. F. Kennedy Memorial Drive toward the dam. When you reach the dam, turn left onto Paige Bar Road. (If you find yourself driving across the dam, you've gone too far.) Drive another 1.2 miles and turn left into the parking area. An outhouse is available, but no water. The ride begins at the northern end of the parking area.

Land Luge Loop

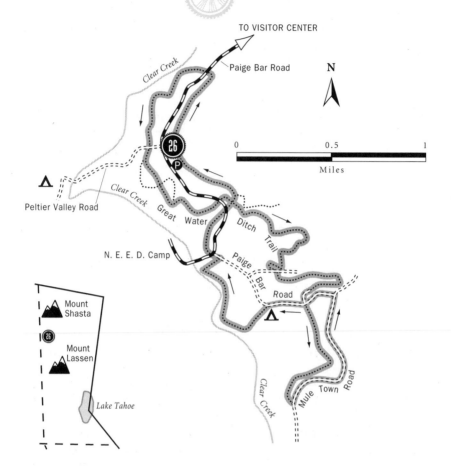

TO VISITOR CENTER

Clear Creek

Paige Bar Road

N

0   0.5   1

Miles

26

P

Clear Creek

Peltier Valley Road

Great Water Ditch Trail

N. E. D. Camp

Paige Bar Road

Mount Shasta

26

Mount Lassen

Lake Tahoe

Clear Creek

Mule Town Road

Notes on the trail: A lot of this trail is singletrack, much of it traversing an old ditch, which is appropriately called the Great Water Ditch Trail. The name of the ride is also appropriate, because you spend much of your time riding in the bottom of the old ditch, which looks like a luge. This "luge" section is almost flat, but the ride starts out with a series of short steep climbs and descents, and ends with a technical and scenic romp above Clear Creek. (You can bypass the technical section, if you wish.) Some of these trails are quite popular with equestrians and hikers. Please look ahead for other trail users, slow down when visibility is limited, and yield to them by stopping and moving off the trail. If you're approaching from behind, please slow down, let them know you're there, and wait patiently until they can safely move off the trail.

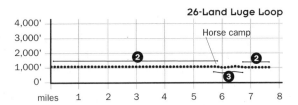

The Ride

0.0 At the north end of the parking area, a carsonite post marks the beginning of the ride. Get ready for a series of steep and short climbs and descents.

0.4 If you don't have the advanced technical skills that allow you to ride down this steep section without sliding your rear tire, please get off and walk your bike down. Carefully cross the road (Paige Bar Road) to the singletrack awaiting you on the other side. This is the beginning of the Great Water Ditch Trail. For the next few miles, you'll be riding in and out of it. Notice the large manzanita shrubs with peeling purple bark.

0.6 The tall skinny pines with cones that remain attached are knobcone pines.

1.3 Pass over the dirt road (Peltier Valley Road) and continue on the other side.

1.4 Major trail junction. Either trail will get you there, but I found the left fork to be less eroded and steep than the right one.

1.7 You're faced with a steep, downhill, eroded section. A small trail takes off on your left, but unfortunately leads out to the road. To avoid a section of asphalt, then, walk your bike down the eroded section. The blackberries get a little personal at the bottom, but they make great eating in summer!

1.9 Blow right through the large intersection to continue on the singletrack. At the second intersection, turn right onto the dirt road and look for the singletrack taking off on your left.

2.1 Carefully cross the paved road (Paige Bar Road). A sign with a sketch of a hiker and a horse mark the beginning of the next segment of trail. (Bikes are allowed, but this is a major hiking and equestrian trail.)

2.3 Turn right onto this trail. You're now back in the ditch.

2.3 + Turn right onto the Clear Creek Canal Trail, which on the map is called the "Great Water Ditch Trail."

3.0 I imagine a flume used to carry water across this ravine, but you get to hike your bike down into it and up the other side.

3.1 Back in the ditch.

3.5 Pass by a concrete retaining wall.

3.7 Cross over the dirt road and continue on the other side.

4.7 Cross over the gravel road (Paige Bar Road) and take the Clear Creek Miner's Ditch Trail, which on the map is still the "Great Water Ditch Trail." The forest is composed almost entirely of knob-cone pines.

4.9 After miles of riding in the ditch, you finally leave it by heading steeply down a rocky chute to the dirt road. This is becoming torn up so if you can't ride down it without sliding, walk your bike down. Turn left and ride up the dirt road (Mule Town Road).

5.2 Turn left onto the gravel road (Paige Bar Road), toward the dam.

5.4 Cross the trail you were on a few minutes ago and continue on the gravel road.

5.6 Ride straight through the horse camp, heading for the small dirt road on the other side of the campsite in front of you. This will quickly turn into a singletrack. Get ready to use your technical skills on this trail. (If you don't have strong intermediate technical skills, I suggest you turn right onto the gravel road and rejoin the ride when you reach the pavement.) When the trail turns to the right, stop for a view into the canyon below.

6.0 Either fork will take you to the right place, but the left one takes you down to Clear Creek.

6.1 Deep and cold swimming holes and a sandy beach await you. You now need to push or carry your bike up through a rocky section for about 100 yards.

6.2 The trail remains fairly technical.

6.3 The trail tops out and you see the N.E.E.D. camp below. It's downhill now, so get your weight back and be ready to abort if you cannot ride without sliding.

6.5 Cross a seasonal stream and head upstream on the small single-track.

6.5 + Turn left onto the dirt road (Paige Bar Road).

6.6 Cross over the paved road (Paige Bar Road) to the wide singletrack on the other side.

7.0 Carefully cross the paved road (Paige Bar Road) to the singletrack on the other side, and turn left (north). This is the last leg of your journey.

7.6 Arrive at the parking area a bit too soon!

Mount Lassen Area

This is volcano country. Volcanic soils are very porous and therefore tend to dry out quickly after summer rains and after the winter snow melts, but they're also soft and easily eroded. It's imperative that you ride gently on these trails by keeping your rear tire from sliding on descents and on turns. These are rocky trails as well; please don't ride off the trail to avoid rocks or water bars. If you cannot ride what you encounter, get off and carry your bike over the obstacles.

Hikers and equestrians may not be used to encountering mountain bikers on these trails. Travel very slowly when your visibility is limited so that you don't surprise them, let them know that you're approaching them, and yield the right-of-way when you meet them. If you're the first mountain biker they've met, your friendly attitude will set the scene for positive future encounters.

This is a beautiful and wild area. Please enjoy it thoroughly while keeping it that way.

Spencer Meadow Loop

Location:	Near Lake Almanor and Lassen Volcanic National Park, on California Highway 36, about 3 hours northeast of Sacramento and about 2 hours north of Lake Tahoe.
Distance:	12-mile loop.
Time:	3.5 hours.
Elevation gain:	About 2,410 feet. Lowest elevation is 4,875 feet; highest elevation is 6,500 feet.
Tread:	Smooth to rocky, mostly soft.
Aerobic level:	Strenuous.
Technical difficulty:	3–4 (mostly 3).
Highlights:	A wonderful wilderness feeling while riding through forests and beside meadows, views of the canyon below and the distant volcanic peaks above, and a chance to spend some time

on the edge of a large, green meadow near the boundary of Lassen Volcanic National Park.

Land status: Lassen National Forest.

Maps: USGS Childs Meadows, Reading Peak.

Access: From the intersection of California Highway 89 and California Highway 36 at the southwest corner of Lake Almanor, drive 18 miles west to the parking area for Spencer Meadows National Recreation Trail. From Chico, drive 52 miles on California Highway 32 to its junction with California Highway 36. Turn left and drive 7.4 miles to the parking area for Spencer Meadows National Recreation Trail. From Red Bluff, drive 53 miles on California Highway 36 east to the parking area for Spencer Meadows National Recreation Trail. No water or bathrooms are available at the parking area.

Notes on the trail: The volcanic soils here dry out quickly after a rain and after the snow melts, but they don't pack well, leaving them highly vulnerable to erosion from sliding tires. Please don't ride this trail unless you're able and willing to prevent your tires from sliding. Watch for bears; I saw a beautiful cinnamon-colored one! Watch also for other trail users, because many backpackers and equestrians use these trails. Ride slowly enough that you don't catch them by surprise, and yield the right-of-way if you meet them.

The current forest service map shows only one trail leading to Spencer Meadows, but there are actually two. Canyon Route leads along the top of a canyon with constant views into the canyon below and of the volcanic peaks above. Meadows Route leads along the top of the ridge past several meadows. I did the ride in a clockwise direction, going up Canyon Route and coming down Meadows Route. Although there's less than 3,000 feet of climbing in this ride, I've classified it as strenuous because of its technical nature. I guarantee you'll feel as though you've climbed much more than 3,000 feet!

The Ride

0.0 Begin to ride up through a forest of incense cedars, ponderosa pines, and white firs. (You have 2 miles of constant climbing, so you might

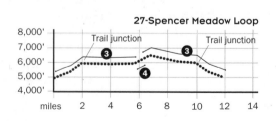

27-Spencer Meadow Loop

ing, so you might

Spencer Meadow Loop

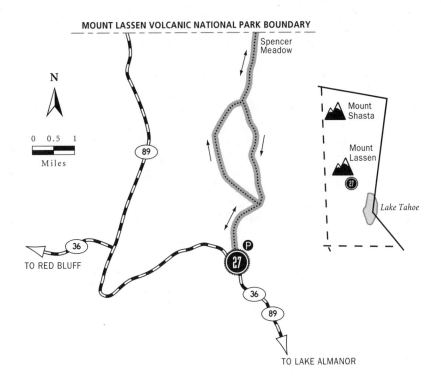

as well look at the trees.) The strongest riders may be able to ride it all. The rest of us can alternate between walking and riding.

0.1   A beautiful example of a mature ponderosa pine with yellow-orange bark. It doesn't look like this area has been logged.

0.5   The huge cones—they're more than a foot long—belong to sugar pines.

1.3   You're passing some exposed volcanic rock. The mosses are quite green at the beginning of summer, but become red toward season's end.

1.5   A small stream is on your left.

1.7   Pass through a forest of pure white firs with grayish white bark, and then a rocky section.

1.9   The stumps tell you that this area has been logged.

2.0   A bridge of rocks just before a trail junction. (Notice the beautiful bleeding heart to the left of the last rock.) Turn left to take Canyon

Canyon overlook from the Spencer Meadow Loop.

Route. The trail goes down a little at first, through a ghostly forest of crowded white firs with dead lower branches that seem to reach out for you.

2.1 You're passing through shrubs of huckleberry oaks.

2.4 A sign for the canyon overlook lets you know you can get off your bike and walk out to the rock outcropping for a spectacular view of the canyon below.

2.7 The trail is becoming playful, meandering up and down and alternating between class 3 and class 4.

3.1 Views down into the canyon are becoming more frequent.

3.5 Notice the well-built raised trail passing through the small meadow. Also notice the corn lilies, which are more closely related to lilies than to corn.

3.6 A small stream passing through a meadow.

4.1 A beautiful view into the canyon below and the volcanic peaks beyond. If you don't feel like riding the whole loop, this makes a good destination. It's also a good place to have a snack.

4.2 Some downhill sections are coming up. Prepare to keep your weight far back.

5.0 The trail passes through a rock garden. Stay off the brakes or you'll end up riding on your nose!

5.5 You'll hear a creek on your left as you begin a class 4 section. The trail becomes very rocky and sometimes overgrown.

6.0 The trail smooths out a little and returns to class 3.

6.6 Fork in the trail. Turn left to head for Spencer Meadow. (You'll return to this point after visiting the meadow, taking the other fork.)

6.7 Spencer Meadow. Drop your bike and walk down to the edge of the meadow. If you're lucky enough to arrive when it's not mosquito season, sit down and enjoy the view of the large, green meadow. You may have noticed that the boundary of Lassen Volcanic National Park is just 0.75 mile farther. Unfortunately, there's nothing more scenic than what you're looking at now. Turn around and head back.

6.8 Trail junction. This time, take Meadows Route by heading left. *Warning:* There are lots of water bars approaching—both log water bars and rock water bars. You're also approaching some steep downhill sections.

10.1 Arrive back at the junction with Canyon Route. Ride over the rock bridge and get ready to ride down for 2 miles. The trail is much narrower on the way down than it was on the way up. Keep your speed down to avoid riding off the trail and to avoid surprising other trail users and bears.

12.0 Back at your car.

Trail Lake Trail

Location:	Near Lake Almanor on California Highway 36, about 3 hours northeast of Sacramento and about 2 hours north of Lake Tahoe.
Distance:	7.9 miles, out-and-back.
Time:	2 hours.
Elevation gain:	About 1,050 feet. Lowest elevation is 6,300 feet; highest elevation is 6,500 feet.
Tread:	Mostly rocky.
Aerobic level:	Easy with several moderate climbs.
Technical difficulty:	3–4 (mostly 3).
Highlights:	You'll ride along the boundary of the Caribou Wilderness Area to a small, shallow lake in the middle of a forest.
Land status:	Lassen National Forest.

Maps: USGS Red Cinder, Bogard Buttes.

Access: Drive 6.8 miles east of the Almanor Ranger Station in Chester on California Highway 36, then turn left onto an unsigned road opposite the turnoff to Lake Almanor Peninsula East Shore. After 1 block you'll reach a T intersection with a sign for Forest Service 10. (Bears love to chew and tear up wooden signs, so it may or may not be there.) Turn left. (From now on you'll be trying to stay on Forest Service 10.) At 0.5 mile turn right. At the intersection at 4.1 miles, keep going straight. At 4.9 miles, bear right at the T. At 6.8 miles, bear right at the fork. At 7.4 miles, go straight through the junction. At 10.0 miles, the pavement stops: Continue straight ahead (toward Echo Lake). At 10.6 miles, leave Forest Service 10 by going straight onto 30N64, a well-maintained dirt road. At 11.2 miles is a sign on the right for Echo Lake. Park off the road near the intersection or drive the short distance into the Echo Lake campground and park there. A bathroom is available at the Echo Lake campground, but no water.

Notes on the trail: This trail is right on the boundary of the Caribou Wilderness Area, but it stays outside the wilderness and so is legal to ride. Unfortunately, it has eroded badly in sections. The good news is that those sections are so rocky that no further erosion should take place. Nevertheless, ride carefully to avoid eroding the remaining sections of good trail. This trail also requires fast judgments as to what you are and are not capable of riding. When in doubt, err toward the cautious side. This trail is used by hikers and equestrians in addition to mountain bikers. Please ride in such a manner that you don't surprise others, and please yield to other users. Trail Lake is an attractive lake to visit, but it's a bit shallow and mucky to swim in. On the other hand, Echo Lake looks like a great swimming spot.

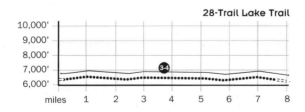

Trail Lake Trail

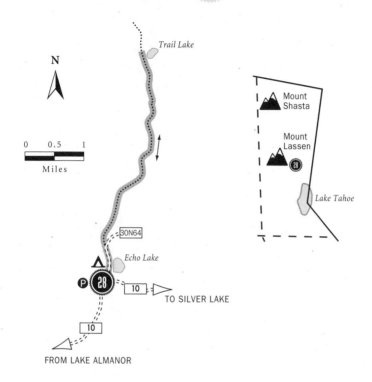

The Ride

0.0 Start by riding north on the dirt road through a lodgepole pine forest.

0.3 A sign on your left indicates the beginning of the Trail Lake Trail. There's even a picture of a bike on the tree, so you know that you and your bike are welcome here.

1.7 Pass through a pure fir forest with nuthatches whining above you.

2.1 Rock garden.

2.2 Ride through a pure lodgepole pine forest.

2.3 Another rock garden is followed by a surprisingly smooth section.

2.4 A meadow filled with bright green corn lilies.

2.5 Another section that is perfect if you're a "rock person."

3.7 To your left is a National Forest Wilderness Area sign.

3.8 The dried-up pond through which you're riding is not the lake. Have faith.

3.9 Arrive at Trail Lake. Hopefully you've come at a time when the mosquitoes are not dominant! A lot of the sections that weren't ridable on your way in, may be ridable on your way out.

5.3 Keep your weight back so you don't slide.

7.5 Turn right onto the dirt road and head back to your car.

7.9 Back at your car. If it's hot, consider going for a swim in Echo Lake.

Bucks Creek Loop Trail

Location:	About 3 hours northeast of Sacramento, 1 hour east of Oroville, and 2 hours north of Lake Tahoe, on Bucks Lake Road.
Distance:	4.3-mile loop.
Time:	1 hour.
Elevation gain:	About 400 feet. Lowest elevation is 5,200 feet; highest elevation is 5,500 feet.
Tread:	Varies from nonexistent to hard-packed.
Aerobic level:	Easy, with several moderate climbs.
Technical difficulty:	1–3 (mostly 3).
Highlights:	A well-built but seldom-used singletrack loop passing through numerous flower-filled meadows. No motorized vehicles are allowed on the trail.
Land status:	Plumas National Forest, Bucks Lake Recreational Area.
Maps:	USGS Bucks Lake, Haskins (the trails are not shown). A good topographic map of the area titled "Bucks Lake & Wilderness" is published by Bob Reedy (P.O. Box 21-4152, Sacramento, CA 95821), and is available locally.
Access:	Take California Highway 162 from Oroville. Continue as it turns into Oroville-Quincy Road. Drive for a total of 47 miles until you reach Bucks Lake. Turn left at the RESORT AREA sign.

Bucks Creek Loop Trail

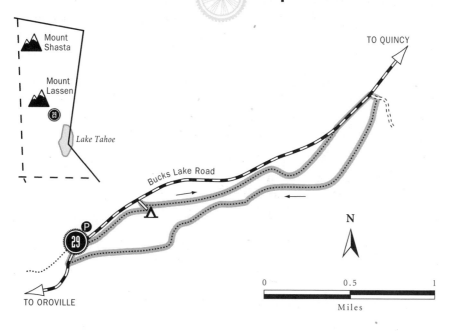

You're now on Bucks Lake Road (Forest Service Road 414). Continue 2.4 miles to the trailhead sign for Bucks Creek Trail; park next to this sign, on the north side of the road. This ride begins south of the road, on the left side of the bridge. Look for a small trail passing between cut logs, and blue signs with black arrows. No water or bathrooms are available at the trailhead, but you'll find both as you pass through the Whitehorse Campground 0.2 mile up the trail.

Notes on the trail: Three trails start near this bridge. The Bucks Creek Trail starts on the north side of the road, where you parked. (See the option at the end of the ride description.) The two arms of the Bucks Creek Loop Trail are located on the south side of the road, on each side of the bridge. You'll be going upstream on the left side of Bucks Creek (the less traveled side) and returning on the right side (the more traveled side). And when I say that the left side is less traveled, I mean you won't be able to see the trail at times; you'll be navigating from one small blue sign with an arrow to another (unless the trail is cleared by the time you ride this). If you don't feel comfortable traveling on faint trails, you can ride both up and down the trail on the other side of the creek.

Whichever way you go, the theme of this ride is wildflower-filled meadows, one after another! This is also one of the few singletracks I've encountered where little signs with a picture of a bike are attached to trees. I felt very welcome. Thanks, people! But this trail also belongs to hikers and equestrians. Please be on the lookout, and yield if you encounter them.

The Ride

0.0 Find the beginning of the trail and follow it through meadows filled with wildflowers, including tall yellow groundsels.

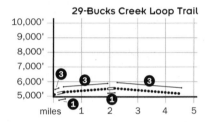

0.2 You suddenly encounter asphalt. This is the Whitehorse Campground. Follow the blue sign to the right and ride past the bathroom to the pay station. Turn right at the pay station and follow the road around until you reach campsite number 15. Quietly work your way to the rear of the campsite, and you'll notice the singletrack on the other side of a small creek. Unfortunately, this small creek is at the bottom of a ravine. Using your ingenuity, get yourself and your bike to the other side. Now concentrate on locating cut logs and blue signs in order to stay on the trail.

0.9 You're passing through a ghost forest of lodgepole pines. As a result of the added sunlight, the forest floor has become filled with lupines, and the trail is overgrown and inconspicuous.

1.0 A dead snag contains a blue sign with an arrow that points left. But in fact the trail continues almost straight ahead of you and then passes to the right of the chaparral-covered knoll. (You might not be able to see the trail; just have faith that you're close to it.)

1.1 You're now climbing up onto a knoll covered with buckbrush, a spiny plant that you don't want to get too close to.

1.2 Confusing spot! You're close to the road. A barricade to keep motorized vehicles out is on your left. Blue signs are everywhere with arrows pointing in all directions. Continue parallel to the barricade, around the buckbrush, toward the "parting of the trees."

1.3 Head for the three large volcanic boulders on your left. If you look closely, you can see some beautiful trail work—a raised trail—as it passes through (under) a meadowy area. Just past the meadowy area is a barricade of branches, which guides you to the left. Look ahead to see a blue sign with an arrow, and a white post in the distance. Head for the white post.

1.4   The trail seems to come to an end, but if you look ahead you can see another small blue sign with an arrow. Head for it any way you can.

1.9   Arrive at the back of a sign that reads BUCKS CREEK CROSS COUNTRY SKI AND MOUNTAIN BIKE TRAIL. At this point, ride on the asphalt road in the same direction you've been going (uphill).

2.1   Turn right onto the dirt road. Notice the bright purple fireweed.

2.2   On your right is a much more distinct trail than you've been riding on. Go for it!

2.6   You're far enough from the road that it seems very wild.

2.8   The tall, bright pink flowers are spirea, in the rose family; smell them. The tall blue flowers are monkshood. Orange tiger lilies also appear.

3.2   Cross a small creek.

4.1   Ride through another section where the flowers are as high as your head, parting them gently as you pass through.

4.3   Back to the bridge.

Option: The Bucks Creek Trail across the road extends for only 1.9 miles before entering the Bucks Wilderness Area. Still, this 1.9 miles is a beautiful stretch of singletrack that wanders along the shoreline of Bucks Lake. Although this lake is a reservoir, scenic slabs of granite and sandy beaches are uncovered as the water recedes. Aspens and wildflowers line the trail.

Feather Falls Trail

Location:	About 1 hour east of Oroville and 2 hours northeast of Sacramento.
Distance:	9.7 miles, out-and-back.
Time:	2 hours.
Elevation gain:	About 1,550 feet. Lowest elevation is 1,950 feet; highest elevation is 2,600 feet.
Tread:	All singletrack, mostly wide, smooth, and hard-packed.
Aerobic level:	Moderate.
Technical difficulty:	2–4 (mostly 2).
Highlights:	Besides being an extremely well-built trail passing through a very diverse and beautiful forest, this leads you out to the fourth tallest waterfall in the United States.
Land status:	Plumas National Forest.
Maps:	USGS Brush Creek, Forbestown.
Access:	At Oroville, take the California Highway 162 exit and head east. At about mile 8, turn right onto Forbestown Road. Drive for 6.0 miles on Forbestown Road and turn left onto Lumpkim Road at the sign for Feather Falls. Drive for 11.1 miles on Lumpkim Road and turn left onto an unnamed road at the sign for Feather Falls Trail. Drive to the end of the road (1.7 miles) and park. A campground with water and bathrooms is located at the trailhead.

Notes on the trail: This trail travels through an extremely diverse forest: ponderosa pines, California black oaks, canyon live oaks, Douglas firs, dogwoods, California nutmegs, incense cedars, madrones, bays, big-leaf maples, tanbark oaks. You'll ride beside many granitic boulders and outcroppings, ending with an impressive view of Feather Falls. This trail is extremely well built. It's a bit too wide and smooth for my preferences, but perfect for riders in good physical condition who lack intermediate technical skills. Still, a class 3 climb awaits the more technically inclined at the end of the Upper Trail, and a class 4 descent to the overlook will

Feather Falls Trail

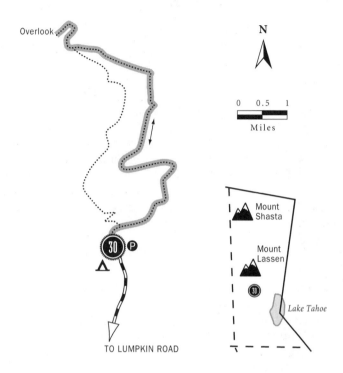

Overlook

N

0   0.5   1

Miles

Mount
Shasta

Mount
Lassen

30

Lake Tahoe

TO LUMPKIN ROAD

challenge almost any rider. This trail is used mostly by hikers. I recommend not riding it on a weekend. Even during the week, please ride slowly, watch ahead for other trail users, and slow down considerably when visibility becomes limited. Please yield to other trail users when you encounter them. The ride is basically downhill to the waterfall. The area often sees snow, but it melts away fairly early in spring; look for the trail to be dry by early May. The best time to see the dogwoods in bloom and the waterfall at its highest is between May 15 and June 15.

The Ride

0.0   Begin to ride downhill on the wide, smooth, and hard-packed trail. Please resist the urge to ride fast, watch for other users on the trail, and slow down when visibility becomes limited.

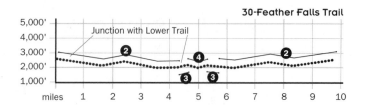

30-Feather Falls Trail

Junction with Lower Trail

5,000'
4,000'
3,000'
2,000'
1,000'

miles 1 2 3 4 5 6 7 8 9 10

0.3   Junction of the Lower Trail and the Upper Trail. The Lower Trail was closed at the time of this writing.

0.5   A very large Douglas fir.

0.7   Dogwoods, giant chain ferns, scarlet monkey flowers.

1.2   A new bridge is currently being built.

1.7   Stop at the bridge over Frey Creek to enjoy the cascade. Notice the tanbark oaks with their large, dark green, shiny, serrated leaves. Get ready for a climb!

2.4   Manzanita and canyon live oaks-a much drier habitat. Read the display about the Bald Mountain pluton of granitic rock that was responsible for the terrain you see today. Watch your speed on the upcoming descent.

3.3   As you cross the seasonal creek, notice the spicebushes with wine-colored flowers.

4.3   Junction with the Lower Trail. Turn right to continue toward Feather Falls. The trail shortly becomes class 3. I don't know how they got it here, but someone in the past brought in some cement. Ride or walk up on the combination of rocks and cement.

4.6   A sign tells you about the Middle Fork of the Feather River.

4.7   Trail junction. Ignore the steps leading up to your right. Follow the sign for the overlook, leading you down and to the left. From here to the overlook, the trail is basically class 4. All but the most advanced technical riders will need to walk most or all of it. If you're riding and come across another trail user, please get off; the trail is narrow.

4.8   Overlook. (No comments from me are necessary.)

4.9   Back up to the trail junction.

5.0   You're back at the sign discussing the Middle Fork of the Feather River. Now begins the class 3 downhill. There's sand on the cement; it's very slippery. Slow down, put all your weight on your left pedal, lean your bike to the right, and move your weight back.

5.2   Trail junction. I took the Upper Trail back to the car. If it's open, you may wish to try the more challenging Lower Trail.

9.2   Regardless of which route you took, you end up here.

9.6   Back at the car.

Feather Falls is a great bonus to this great ride.

Downieville Area

Downieville is located in the bottom of the North Yuba River canyon, at an elevation of about 2,900 feet and surrounded by steep hills, streams, and rivers. Several high-quality singletracks end in or near town. Few trail users are around during the week, but motorcycles, mountain bikes, equestrians, and hikers are common on weekends. At all times, you should slow down considerably when approaching sections with limited visibility, and yield to hikers and equestrians. Remember also that uphill riders have the right-of-way over downhill riders. I've noticed that many mountain bikers are locking up their rear wheels and eroding the trails badly. Please keep your weight back or walk your bike down sections that you can't ride without sliding.

The town of Downieville is only a couple of blocks long, but it contains motels, a grocery store, restaurants, a bakery, a saloon, a hardware store, a post office, a medical clinic, a gas station, and a bike shop with a mechanic, maps, parts, rentals, and shuttle service. A public rest room is located at the community center, and water is available at the small park beside the pizzeria. In addition, there are many campgrounds, motels, bed-and-breakfast places, and resorts within a few miles of Downieville.

Downieville is located right at the snow line. Expect the trails above to be snowed in during the winter. The Bullards Bar Trail and North Yuba Trail might be free of snow between winter storms, but allow them to dry for a few days after each storm. The order of melt-out in the spring is: Bullards Bar Trail, North Yuba Trail, First Divide Trail, Halls Ranch/Fiddle Creek Trails, Downie River Trail, Second Divide Trail, Third Divide Trail, Downie River Trail, Downieville Downhill (via Butcher Ranch, or Pauley Creek, or Big Boulder Trails), and Chimney Rock/Empire Creek Trails. The latter trails usually melt out between mid-May and mid-June. All the rides that I've described are set within the Tahoe National Forest. I appreciate their progressive view of allowing mountain biking on most of their trails. We can show our appreciation by minimizing our impact and conflicts while riding, and by writing them to thank them or by stopping by a ranger station to thank them in person.

There are many singletracks open to mountain bikes in the Lakes Basin above Downieville (Plumas National Forest), and the area is incredibly beautiful, but I've found the trails to be too technical for me (mostly class 4).

The town of Downieville is very supportive of mountain biking. Please reciprocate by supporting their businesses.

Bullards Bar Trail

Location:	Intersection of Marysville Road and California Highway 49, about halfway between Nevada City and Downieville, about 1.5 hours northeast of Sacramento.
Distance:	17.5-mile loop.
Time:	3 hours.
Elevation gain:	About 1,800 feet. Lowest elevation is 2,100 feet; highest elevation is 2,700 feet.
Tread:	Mostly singletrack, mostly smooth and hard-packed; some dirt and paved roads.
Aerobic level:	Moderate.
Technical difficulty:	1–3 (mostly 3).
Highlights:	A narrow, exposed, and recently constructed singletrack contouring around the edge of a reservoir; streams surrounded by ferns and big-leaf maples; shady forests; dogwoods and wildflowers blooming in spring; dogwoods and big-leaf maples in color in fall.
Land status:	Tahoe National Forest.
Maps:	USGS Camptonville, Challenge (trails not shown); the best map is "Downieville, California, published by TerraPro GPS Surveys Limited," available locally.
Access:	From Nevada City, drive north on California Highway 49. From Downieville, drive southwest on California Highway 49. From Marysville, drive east on Marysville Road. This ride begins at the Mountain Store, on the corner of Jaynes Lane and Marysville Road, 0.2 mile west of California Highway 49. Parking is available near the store. Please purchase something from the owner and ask for permission to park there. The parking area isn't shaded but provides a convenient access to the ride. (If you wish to drive up the dirt road to mile 1.6 in order to park in the shade, you can do so, but you'll have an extended climb at the end of

the ride.) I usually do this ride on the way to or on the way back from Downieville.

Notes on the trail: This is the lowest-elevation ride in the Downieville region. Therefore it experiences the least amount of snow, and is often snow-free when other trails are covered. The trail can become quite muddy after large or frequent Pacific storms. The corollary to this is that it can be quite hot during the summer: hot enough for me to suggest that you avoid riding in the middle of a summer afternoon.

Most of this ride passes through a shady forest of ponderosa pine, incense cedar, and Douglas fir. Poison oak lines most of it. Dress accordingly; you won't be able to avoid brushing up against it. In cooler, shady areas dogwoods are in bloom in May and in color in October. The ridge is open and faces the west in several places, making it quite hot in summer.

The ride begins with a long downhill. After reaching the reservoir level, you'll roller-coaster on narrow, exposed singletrack steeply up and down for several miles. Even though you're basically following the reservoir level, the short climbs add up substantially, making this ride more strenuous than you might think. You'll then climb to the top of the ridge and contour along it on your way back to your car. If you become tired or run short on time, there are several trails and roads that you can use to shorten the ride.

In spring and early summer, the reservoir is full and scenic. Because of the amounts and kinds of sediments carried by the North Yuba River into the reservoir, the color of the water is a striking creamy emerald blue. But in mid- to late summer the level falls, exposing an unattractive "bathtub ring." Many hikers use these trails. Please slow down considerably when your visibility becomes limited and yield the right-of-way to other trail users.

The Ride

0.0   Head east on Old Camptonville Road as you ride out of the parking lot.

0.1   Junction. Bear left to remain on Old Camptonville Road.

0.5   The pavement turns to dirt.

0.6   The road swings sharply to the left.

0.8   Ignore the dirt roads that take off on your left.

1.6   The pavement begins again. Look for a sign on your left that reads: BULLARDS BAR TRAIL. This trail is maintained by Bicyclists of Nevada County for hikers, mountain bikers, and equestrians. Motorized vehicles are not allowed. This trail heads downhill on old dirt roads that are being converted to singletracks for the next 2.7 miles. Please slow down when approaching spots with limited visibility to avoid surprising other trail users—or rattlesnakes.

1.8   Cross an old dirt road.

Bullards Bar Trail

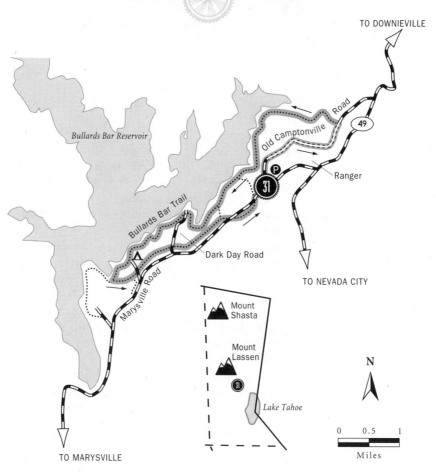

TO DOWNIEVILLE

Bullards Bar Reservoir

Old Camptonville Road

49

Ranger

P 31

Bullards Bar Trail

Dark Day Road

TO NEVADA CITY

Marysville Road

Mount Shasta

Mount Lassen

31

Lake Tahoe

N

0   0.5   1
Miles

TO MARYSVILLE

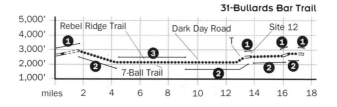

31-Bullards Bar Trail

Rebel Ridge Trail

Dark Day Road

Site 12

5,000'
4,000'
3,000'
2,000'
1,000'

1

3

2

T

1   1   1

2   2   2

7-Ball Trail

miles   2   4   6   8   10   12   14   16   18

3.7 At this junction, ride straight ahead (west), toward Dark Day Road. From now on you'll have numerous views of the reservoir, and numerous wildflowers in spring and early summer.

4.3 Lake level. The trail becomes narrow and exposed and begins to roller-coaster steeply up and down. Fortunately, the surface is mostly smooth and hard-packed.

5.4 Lovely creek.

6.0 Shady creek crossing.

6.2 Trail junction. If you wish to shorten the ride, you can ride up the Rebel Ridge Trail to Marysville Road and back to your car. If not, continue around the reservoir.

7.7 Stream crossing with ferns and big-leaf maples. Shortly thereafter you'll reach a junction with the 7-Ball Trail. Again, if you wish to shorten the ride, just head up the 7-Ball Trail to Marysville Road and back to your car. If not, continue around the reservoir.

9.0 The trail becomes wider and less cliffy, but ride slower, because you're nearing civilization.

10.0 Parking lot, drinking water, and bathroom. The trail continues on the other side of the parking lot. If you wish to shorten the ride, take Dark Day Road to Marysville Road and back to your car.

10.2 You're spit out onto a paved road among campsites. Look to your right and you'll see a sign reading: TRAIL .1 MILE. Follow this paved road, watching your left for a sign to Bullards Bar Trail. Follow the trail signs at the next two trail junctions. Many big-leaf maples and ferns grow along this section of trail.

12.8 The Schoolhouse Trail comes in from the left. Turn left to take this trail and begin a long uphill climb to the top of the ridge.

13.0 The trail dead-ends at a T. Turn left onto the well-traveled trail and continue to climb.

13.5 Enter the campground at site 12 beside a water faucet. Turn right and follow the paved road out of the campground to its junction with Marysville Road. The singletrack begins on your left at a sign that reads: DARK DAY ROAD ½ MILE.

13.9 The trail makes an abrupt left turn into the campground, passes along its edge on an old dirt road, narrows to a singletrack, and crosses a paved road (Dark Day Road) at 14.0 miles.

14.0 Continue riding on the 8-Ball Trail on the other side of the paved road.

15.9 A trail heads down from the right. Bear left and follow the old paved road through the gate.

16.0 Junction with the 7-Ball Trail. Bear right on the dirt road. Continue straight as you reach the pavement.

16.1 Carefully cross Marysville Road and ride east on the shoulder.

16.5 A new trail takes off on the right just past a large knotty-pine gate marking the entrance to someone's private property. (At present, this trail is not signed.)

16.8 Jump back onto the asphalt just before Old Toll Road, and jump back onto the singletrack shortly thereafter.

17.5 Arrive back at your car. I suggest you purchase something from the store and thank the owner for letting you park.

North Yuba Trail

Location:	About 8 miles west of Downieville on California Highway 49, about 2 hours northeast of Sacramento and about 2 hours northwest of Lake Tahoe.
Distance:	16.2 miles, out-and-back.
Time:	3 hours.
Elevation gain:	About 2,600 feet. Lowest elevation is 2,400 feet; highest elevation is 2,800 feet.
Tread:	Wide singletrack, ranging from smooth and hard-packed to loose and rocky.
Aerobic level:	Moderate.
Technical difficulty:	2–3 (mostly 3).
Highlights:	Any singletrack is a highlight in and of itself, but this newly built trail is perched on a cliff above the North Fork of the Yuba River. In May and June this river is a cascade of whitewater. Dogwoods adorn the trail, blooming white in spring and turning red in fall. You cross several streams, each surrounded by bigleaf maples and ferns. No motorized vehicles are allowed on the trail.
Land status:	Tahoe National Forest.
Maps:	USGS Goodyears Bar (this trail is not shown). The best map is "Downieville, California, published by TerraPro GPS Surveys Limited," available locally.
Access:	From the west, after crossing the bridge over the North Yuba River on California Highway 49, travel about 3 miles to the Rocky Rest Campground. From the east, after passing

Noah negotiating a turn on North Yuba Trail.

Downieville, travel about 8 miles to the Rocky Rest Campground. Park next to the outhouse. The trailhead begins at the wooden bridge over the river. Water is available at the entrance to the campground.

Notes on the trail: As you can tell by the elevation gain, this trail roller-coasters up and down a lot! The upper end of the trail is only 400 feet higher than the lower end, but you really have to work to gain those 400 feet. This also means that you get to enjoy a lot of downhill riding in both directions. Each part of the trail is equally but uniquely beautiful. The trail stays high above the rushing river and travels through coniferous forests, broad-leaved forests, and rock gardens; over small streams; and beside small waterfalls. Dogwoods and wildflowers are in bloom in May and June. Dogwoods, big-leaf maples, and poison oak are in color in October. The last zigzags back to the trailhead are particularly fun, but be careful, because a lot of hikers use the lower end of this trail. In fact, I encourage you to ride carefully on all parts of this trail: There's not much room for error, and it's a long tumble down to the river. Don't forget that other trail users have the right-of-way. It's impossible to get lost on this trail, because there are no trail junctions along it. This trail is often open when others are snowed in, but please let it dry out for a few days after a storm, to prevent damage to sections that become muddy. When descending steeply, keep your weight back to prevent your rear wheel from sliding, or dismount and walk your bike down.

North Yuba Trail, Halls Ranch/Fiddle Creek Trails

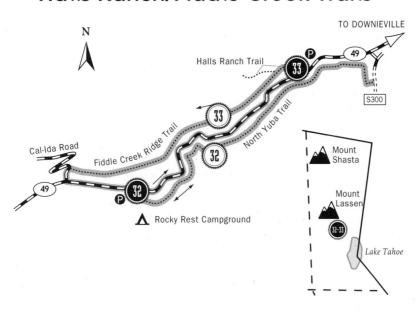

32-North Yuba Trail

The Ride

0.0   Ride over the wooden bridge to begin the North Yuba Trail, and enter a dense Douglas fir forest with big-leaf maples, dogwoods, and poison oak.

0.7   Cross the bridge over Humbug Creek and prepare for steep climbs, followed by steep descents.

3.5   Cross the bridge over St. Catherine Creek. Notice that whenever the trail cuts into the mountain to cross a creek, the environment becomes increasingly green.

7.2 Ride down hellishly steep switchbacks in this region. Notice the trail work. Concrete blocks were brought in to stabilize and protect wet areas. A raised trail was built through a small meadow.

8.1 Junction with Road S300 (dirt). Turn around to enjoy this trail in the other direction. (You'll be surprised how different the scenery is on your return trip.)

16.2 Arrive back at the trailhead.

Options:

1. If you prefer to return a different way, you can turn left onto Road S300, then left onto California Highway 49 at the small community of Goodyears Bar, and ride back down to the trailhead. The total distance is 15.7 miles for this loop.

2. This ride may be combined with Ride 33, Halls Ranch/Fiddle Creek Trails, to form a long, strenuous loop. Turn left onto Road S300, then left onto California Highway 49 at the small community of Goodyears Bar, and ride 1 mile down to the beginning of the Halls Ranch Trail. This expanded loop should take between 4 and 5 hours.

Halls Ranch/Fiddle Creek Trails

Location:	About 4 miles west of Downieville on California Highway 49, about 2 hours northeast of Sacramento, and about 2 hours northwest of Lake Tahoe.
Distance:	14.5-mile loop.
Time:	3 hours.
Elevation gain:	About 2,700 feet. Lowest elevation is 2,850 feet; highest elevation is 4,335 feet.
Tread:	Mostly narrow and hard-packed singletrack, with some paved road to return to the trailhead.
Aerobic level:	Moderate, with several long, strenuous climbs.
Technical difficulty:	1–3 (mostly 3).
Highlights:	Views of the Sierra Buttes to the east and the North Yuba River canyon below. Challenging, narrow, hard-packed singletrack passing over ridges and through dense forests.

See map on Page 153

Sean enjoying a smooth section of Halls Ranch/Fiddle Creek Trails.

Land status:	Tahoe National Forest.
Maps:	USGS Goodyears Bar (not all the trails are shown). The best map is "Downieville, California, published by TerraPro GPS Surveys Limited," available locally.
Access:	The Halls Ranch Trailhead is located on the north side of California Highway 49 across the street from the Halls Ranch Trailhead/Indian Rock Picnic Area, about 7 miles east of the North Yuba River bridge and about 4 miles west of Downieville.

Notes on the trail: Although you can opt to be shuttled from the single-track trailtail back to the singletrack trailhead to avoid riding on a paved road, the distance on the road is short enough, the climbing small enough, and the scenery impressive enough to ride this as a loop. And although you'll have to ride or push up the steepest part of the trail, you'll also enjoy a maximum of downhill. (Some riders call the first section the "Hurting Trail.") The good news is that you'll ride or push through a forest of ponderosa pines and live oaks—much like what you'd find on the Upper Yosemite Falls Trail in Yosemite Valley—and see more and more impressive views on the way up.

After gaining 1,500 feet in 1.9 miles, the trail levels off and reaches a view rock. As the Halls Ranch Trail heads north, continue west on the Fiddle Creek Trail, which roller-coasters for a while through dense fir forests before zigzagging downhill to Cal-Ida Road. A short stretch of pavement brings you back to your car. This trail is not as heavily used as other trails in the region, providing you with a wonderful wilderness experience.

The lack of regular use also means that wildlife—including rattlesnakes—is encountered more often. One rider I know came across a rattlesnake coiled in the middle of the trail, ready to strike. Fortunately, he was able to move his leg quickly out of the way so that the snake struck the bike instead. Be careful! And although few people use this trail, hikers, equestrians, motorcyclists, and other mountain bikers may be around. Please remember this when you approach sections with limited visibility. When you do encounter other trail users, please stop and move off the trail. Sections of these trails can become quite muddy after a storm. Let them dry out before using them to avoid damaging them.

The Ride

0.0 Begin by winding up through a forest of Douglas firs and canyon live oaks.

1.0 Intermediate riders are probably walking at this point. Stronger riders are still riding.

33-Halls Ranch/Fiddle Creek Trails

1.5 The trail becomes steeper and looser, limiting riding to the strongest.

1.9 Arrive at the top of the hill and enjoy the relatively easy riding surrounded by views.

2.5 Junction with Halls Creek Trail. Go straight—not right! You're now diving down through a dense forest of firs. After all that uphill, enjoy this.

3.6 Just when you're really loving the downhill, you'll meet a steep uphill, followed by a steep downhill on loose rocks.

3.8 Another steeper uphill challenges you prior to a series of downhill zigzags.

4.3 Another steep climb greets you as the trail zigzags up the hill.

4.5 A short downhill is followed by a short climb.

4.9 The trail levels off, leading to a long and well-earned downhill.

5.4 The downhill becomes steeper. Be careful.

5.8 Views of the North Yuba River canyon are visible, but you should probably stop riding to look at them!

6.5 The trail surface is hard-packed dirt with some loose rocks. It could get quite muddy when wet. Prepare for some challenging downhill switchbacks.

7.0 The smooth and hard-packed singletrack passes through a dense forest and is followed by another climb.

7.4 This last descent before the paved road is especially enjoyable in spring when the dogwood trees are in bloom, and in fall when the California black oak trees are turning yellow and orange and the dogwood trees are turning red.

8.2 You're all too soon dumped out onto the paved Cal-Ida Road. Turn left and ride a short distance to California Highway 49. Turn left to ride back up to your car, or turn right to visit a small grocery store/cafe and then return to your car. Be sure to ride single file: The road is narrow, with fast-moving trucks.

14.5 Back at the car.

Option: This ride can be combined with Ride 32, North Yuba Trail, to form a long, strenuous loop. Turn into the Rocky Rest Campground, ride across the bridge, and take the North Yuba Trail up to Road S300. Then turn left and ride about 1 mile to California Highway 49, turning left again to glide 1 mile back down to your car. This expanded loop should take between 4 and 5 hours.

Chimney Rock/Empire Creek Trails

Location:	Ride or shuttle from downtown Downieville on California Highway 49, about 2 hours either northwest of Lake Tahoe or northeast of Sacramento.
Distance:	21.7 miles point-to-point from the "Bee Tree," with a shuttle from Downieville. (Add 8 miles if you're riding a loop from Downieville.)
Time:	3 hours. (Add another 2 hours if you're riding a loop from Downieville.)
Elevation gain:	About 2,200 feet. Lowest elevation is 2,900 feet; highest elevation is 7,000 feet. (Add another 3,200 feet of climbing if you're riding a loop from Downieville.)
Tread:	Dirt road and singletrack, varying from smooth and hard-packed to loose and rocky.
Aerobic level:	Moderate, with one long, strenuous climb.
Technical difficulty:	2–3 (mostly 3).
Highlights:	Incredible views from the top of a volcanic ridge, wonderful singletrack, thick forests with brilliant green ground cover, wilderness.
Land status:	Tahoe National Forest.
Maps:	USGS Downieville. The best map is "Downieville, California, published by TerraPro GPS Surveys Limited," available locally.
Access:	Most people ride this point-to-point from the junction of Cal-Ida Road (dirt) and Saddleback Road (dirt) to Downieville. An ordinary car can make it up to the end of Cal-Ida Road. Four-wheel-drive vehicles can make it up to this point via Saddleback Road. Shuttles are available from Downieville. But it's also possible to ride this as a loop from Downieville. If you choose to do so, pick a cool day: Climbing steadily from 2,900 feet to 7,000 feet when it's hot out can destroy the strongest of mountain

Chimney Rock/Empire Creek Trails

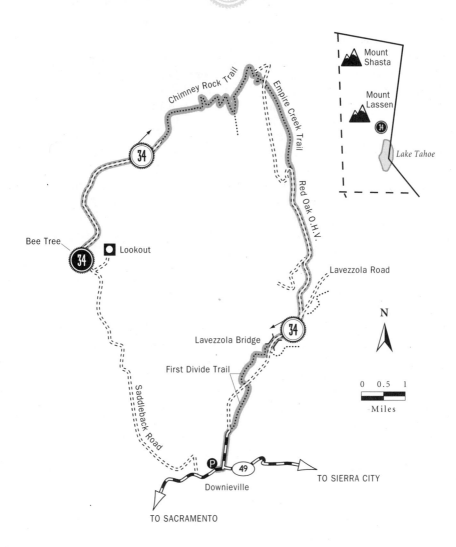

Mount Shasta

Mount Lassen

Lake Tahoe

Chimney Rock Trail

Empire Creek Trail

Red Oak O.H.V.

Bee Tree

Lookout

Lavezzola Road

Lavezzola Bridge

First Divide Trail

Saddleback Road

N

0   0.5   1
Miles

P

49

Downieville

TO SIERRA CITY

TO SACRAMENTO

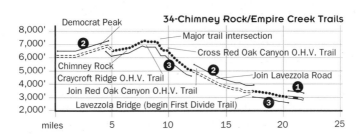

34-Chimney Rock/Empire Creek Trails

Democrat Peak

Major trail intersection

Cross Red Oak Canyon O.H.V. Trail

Chimney Rock

Craycroft Ridge O.H.V. Trail

Join Red Oak Canyon O.H.V. Trail

Lavezzola Bridge (begin First Divide Trail)

Join Lavezzola Road

8,000'
7,000'
6,000'
5,000'
4,000'
3,000'
2,000'

miles   5   10   15   20   25

bikers! Saddleback Road begins just outside the western city limits of Downieville on California Highway 49. Cal-Ida Road begins about 12 miles west of Downieville on California Highway 49.

Notes on the trail: The singletrack in the middle of this ride is only 7 miles long, but what a singletrack! It climbs up onto a ridge among strange volcanic formations and views to the very edge of the earth; descends steeply down a series of switchbacks on a loose and rocky surface; and finally descends slowly through thick, moist forests with vivid green ground covers on a smooth and hard-packed surface. This is a ride for someone who really enjoys the wilderness. You're ultimately dumped out onto Lavezzola Road, and take the First Divide Trail into Downieville.

Even though this ride involves a shuttle, it's still strenuous. Do not attempt it unless you're in good physical condition. Intermediate riders should be able to ride most of it, advanced riders all of it; it's not appropriate for beginners. Please be on the lookout for other trail users when riding so as not to catch them by surprise. Yield to them by stopping and moving off the trail.

The Ride

0.0   At the junction of Cal-Ida Road (dirt) and Saddleback Road (dirt), begin (or continue) by riding north on Saddleback Road.

0.2   Junction with the dirt road to Saddleback Mountain Lookout. I've heard that a spring exists a short distance up this road, but I haven't checked it out. If you rode up from Downieville, it would be a good idea to fill up. Just past this junction is an old dead snag referred to as the "Bee Tree" and a great view to the northwest.

1.4   Fork in the road (sharp left). Go straight. There should be a sign here for the Chimney Rock Trail, but it sometimes ends up in the bushes.

2.5   Fork in the road. Turn right, up the hill.

3.1   Ignore the dirt road coming in from the right and continue straight. A sign can be seen in the distance that reads: CHIMNEY ROCK TRAIL.

3.1 +   Ignore the small dirt road heading off to the left at the sign and bear right.

4.1   Democrat Peak is on your left. It's composed of columns of basalt and was once the "plug" of a volcano.

4.6   Beware of a steep downhill section with loose rocks—a perfect endo setup.

5.1   Sign for the Chimney Rock trailhead. This marks the beginning of the singletrack—and it's a great one, narrow, rocky, exposed in places. Switchback up through a dense white fir forest.

Sean hammering up the trail of Chimney Rock/Empire Creek Trails.

5.8   The trail leaves the forest and enters chaparral with huckleberry oak, bitter cherry, and views toward the northwest.

6.0   A beautiful view with a small, rocky pinnacle that you can easily climb to the top of.

6.4   Chimney Rock rises out of the ground to your left. The trail now roller-coasters along the top of a volcanic ridge with views in all directions. This is a wild and beautiful place. The trail surface varies from hard-packed to rocky to loose volcanic debris.

7.6   Beginning of the "Pain and Suffering Switchbacks." Because of the steepness and loose volcanic debris, this is a push-up for most people. You'll soon be riding down into the forest, so enjoy the open views.

8.2   Don't turn right onto the Craycroft Ridge OHV Trail. Instead, turn left to continue on the singletrack. Don't be alarmed that the trail is heading northeast, away from Downieville.

9.1   Major trail intersection: Follow the sign for the Empire Creek Trail (sharp right) and get ready for some steep and hairy switchbacks. The volcanic debris in this portion of the trail seems to grab at your front wheel. Keep your weight back to avoid endos.

9.6   The trail becomes smooth and hard-packed at the bottom of the switchbacks.

9.7   Cross the Red Oak Canyon OHV Trail and continue on the Empire Creek Trail.

10.9	It's very moist and green in this section, with lots of ferns and some mud.
11.0	Cross a series of small streams.
11.8	Glide down through the trees with good visibility, hard-packed trail, and green ground cover. Life is beautiful!
12.1	You're abruptly thrown out onto a dirt road. Bear left (downhill) on Empire Creek Road.
12.6	Cross a large creek.
16.1	Lavezzola Road (dirt). You're just 0.2 mile southwest of the Third Divide Trail. Turn right onto Lavezzola Road, watching carefully for motorized vehicles.
16.3	Pass by the end of the Third Divide Trail on your left and keep riding down Lavezzola Road.
17.4	At the bridge over Lavezzola Creek, turn right into the primitive campground, then turn left onto the (presently unsigned) upper section of the First Divide Trail, which follows the path of an old water flume. (If you're tired of riding singletracks, you can just follow Lavezzola Road back into town.)
19.2	Pass through the opening in the fence, and cross Lavezzola Road (don't forget about the loaded logging trucks). The lower portion of the First Divide Trail starts off as a dirt road. (Again, if you're tired of singletracks, just turn right and follow Lavezzola Road back into town.)
19.4	A small sign on a tree alerts bikers to turn right onto the singletrack at this point. If you miss this turnoff, you'll end up in a mining camp, and a dog will probably chase you back up to it anyway.
20.8	Bottom of the First Divide Trail. After you stop hyperventilating from the exhilarating ride and fantastic scenery, turn left onto Main Street and ride back across Hospital Bridge into downtown Downieville. (You're expected to stop at every stop sign and will be cited and fined if you don't.)
21.7	Back in Downieville! (I sure hope you don't have to ride back up Saddleback Road to retrieve your car. I did that . . . once.)

Divide Loop

Location:	Downtown Downieville on California Highway 49, about 2 hours either northwest of Lake Tahoe or northeast of Sacramento.
Distance:	16.0-mile loop.
Time:	3 hours.
Elevation gain:	About 2,600 feet. Lowest elevation is 2,900 feet; highest elevation is 4,600 feet.
Tread:	Mostly hard-packed singletrack, sometimes rocky and technical; there are short sections of dirt road and a short section of paved road.
Aerobic level:	Moderate, with one very long, strenuous climb.
Technical difficulty:	1–4 (mostly 3).
Highlights:	Mature pine forests, dogwoods, roaring streams, fun descents, and absolutely divine singletrack.
Land status:	Tahoe National Forest.
Maps:	USGS Downieville (not all the trails are shown). The best map is "Downieville, California, published by TerraPro GPS Surveys Limited," available locally.
Access:	Arrive in Downieville via California Highway 49 from Lake Tahoe or from Nevada City. Parking is limited in downtown Downieville. (which is only 2 blocks long). It's best to park at Cannon Point, 0.25 mile west of town. A clean bathroom is available at the community center. Water is available at the small park next to the pizzeria.

Notes on the trail: It's rare that you can ride from the center of town on some of the finest singletrack available into true wilderness—and return in a few hours. This is one of those rides. You'll climb out of town through a forest on a lightly technical singletrack overlooking a roaring stream, ride a short distance on a dirt road, climb on a moderately to highly technical singletrack built on the side of a cliff (again overlooking a roaring stream), descend on a fast and wide singletrack, and descend on a singletrack back into town. Besides the roaring streams, you'll pass through forests con-

Divide Loop, Downieville Downhills

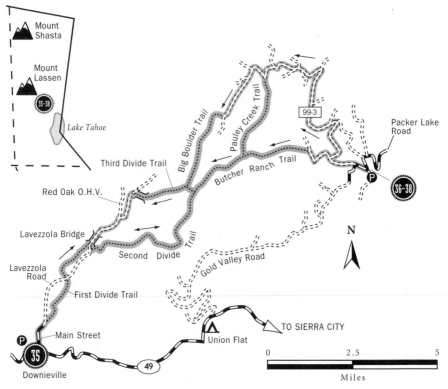

sisting of ponderosa pines, incense cedars, white firs, and dogwoods. (The dogwoods are in bloom in May, and in color in October.) This ride, in contrast to many rides in the Downieville region, requires no shuttle, and can be done in spring when the high country is still covered with snow. In an average year this route should be free of snow from early April to late November. A variety of users are on these trails: equestrians, hikers, backpackers, motorcyclists, and other mountain bikers. Please be aware of the trail in front of you and use conservative judgment when visibility is limited. Yield the right-of-way to other trail users by stopping and moving off the trail when you meet them.

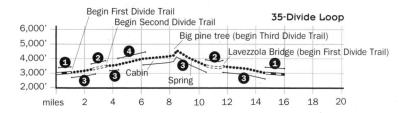

Begin First Divide Trail
Begin Second Divide Trail
Big pine tree (begin Third Divide Trail)
Lavezzola Bridge (begin First Divide Trail)
Cabin
Spring

6,000'
5,000'
4,000'
3,000'
2,000'

miles 2 4 6 8 10 12 14 16 18 20

The Ride

0.0 Ride from the center of town by heading east on Main Street and crossing Hospital Bridge.

0.9 Turn right onto the lower portion of the First Divide Trail just after the last building on Main Street, and near the intersection of Hummingbird and Lavezzola Roads. The trail passes along a fence and quickly begins to climb steeply. Expect descents as well as climbs on a smooth to rocky singletrack. Some spots are very exposed, both to the sun and to the raging creek in the canyon below. You're suddenly dumped out onto a small dirt road. Turn left and climb up this dirt road to another dirt road—Lavezzola Road.

2.5 Turn right onto Lavezzola Road. Ride this road with care, because it's heavily used by motorized vehicles, including loaded logging trucks. Carefully continue to the top of the ridge.

3.6 Turn right onto the Second Divide Trail just after the crest of the hill. Beware of the poison oak that lines this trail. In general, if it's green, let it be.

4.2 The Second Divide Trail turns into a narrow, rocky, exposed singletrack built on the side of a cliff. Pauley Creek is roaring below, especially during May and June. You encounter a number of steep, technical climbs and descents. Don't hesitate to walk your bike, because a mistake could result in a long and damaging fall into the canyon and stream below.

4.4 Ignore the primitive singletrack that heads off to the right. A sign reads: THIRD DIVIDE, 3 MILES.

5.6 Ride through a forest of white firs, California black oaks, dogwoods, and incense cedars. In spring and fall this section of trail may be covered with oak leaves.

5.9 Attack an incredibly steep uphill. The good news is that it's short.

6.1 The trail flattens out for a while.

6.8 Bike quietly by the mining cabin so that you don't disturb the residents, and get ready to do more climbing, some of it on the edge of a cliff.

8.2 Bravely face some of the steepest climbing that you'll ever encounter. (There are many advantages to pushing your bike: You rest your behind; you straighten out your body; you stretch your calf muscles; and you get to enjoy the scenery. Just keep telling yourself that!) Ignore trails that head off to the right in this region—they head for mining claims.

8.3 Hug the huge and beautiful pine at the top of the climb. This is a fine example of a mature ponderosa or Jeffrey pine (the cones appear to be that of a ponderosa, but the bark looks more like Jeffrey). You're now standing on the lower portion of the "Downieville Downhill." Turn left onto the Third Divide Trail and ride up a short distance to the high point of this ride.

8.5 Before you descend this smooth, fast section, think about a few things. Is there enough visibility to be going this fast? Are your skills sharp enough to be going this fast? What will it feel like to fall going this fast? What will it feel like to hit a tree going this fast? Ride accordingly. Lots of trail users frequent this trail and hate being surprised by fast-moving bikes. (The small singletrack that heads off to the right a short distance below this point is the end of the Big Boulder Trail; see Ride 38.)

9.2 Reach a spring. The wide trail now gets narrow. It also begins to swoop and zigzag. The trail surface becomes rockier and the visibility lessens.

10.4 Cinder blocks have been placed on this steep downhill to increase traction. Keep your weight back and brake lightly for a successful trip down.

10.6 The Third Divide Trail dead-ends onto Lavezzola Road (dirt). Turn left and begin to return toward Downieville, watching carefully for motorized vehicles.

11.7 At the bridge over Lavezzola Creek, turn right into the primitive campground, then left onto the (presently unsigned) upper section of the First Divide Trail, which follows the path of an old water flume. (If you're tired of riding singletracks, you can just follow Lavezzola Road back into town.)

13.5 Pass through the opening in the fence, and cross Lavezzola Road (don't forget about the loaded logging trucks). The lower portion of the First Divide Trail starts off as a dirt road. (Again, if you're tired of singletracks, just turn right and follow Lavezzola Road back into town.)

13.7 A small sign on a tree alerts bikers to turn right onto the singletrack at this point. If you miss this turnoff, you'll end up in a mining camp, and a dog will probably chase you back up to it anyway.

15.1 Bottom of the First Divide Trail. After you stop hyperventilating from the exhilarating ride and fantastic scenery, turn left onto Main Street and ride back across Hospital Bridge into downtown

Downieville. (You're expected to stop at every stop sign and will be cited and fined if you don't.)

16.0 Arrive back at the center of town a much richer and dirtier person than when you left.

Option: The First, Second, and Third Divide Trails can be ridden as part of the Downieville Downhill (see the following three rides).

Downieville Downhill via Butcher Ranch Trail

Location:	Ride or shuttle from downtown Downieville on California Highway 49, about 2 hours either northwest of Lake Tahoe or northeast of Sacramento.
Distance:	13.7 miles point-to-point. (Add 18 miles if you're riding from Downieville to form a loop.)
Time:	2 hours. (Add 2 hours if you're riding from Downieville to form a loop.)
Elevation gain:	About 300 feet. Lowest elevation is 2,900 feet; highest elevation is 7,150 feet. (Add 4,250 feet if you're riding from Downieville to form a loop.)
Tread:	Mostly singletrack, ranging from smooth and hard-packed to loose and rocky. There are short sections of dirt and paved roads.
Aerobic level:	Easy (with shuttle).
Technical difficulty:	1–3 (mostly 3).
Highlights:	Descend from 7,150 feet (surrounded by red fir forests and alpine meadows) to 2,900 feet (to the lower part of a yellow pine forest) beside roaring streams on some of the nicest technical singletrack found anywhere.
Land status:	Tahoe National Forest.
Maps:	USGS Downieville, Sierra City. The best map is "Downieville, California, published by TerraPro

See map on Page 164

GPS Surveys Limited," available locally.

Access: Most people take a shuttle from Downieville to Packer Saddle, then ride from Packer Saddle back to Downieville. Shuttle services are available in Downieville, or you can arrange your own: Leave one vehicle in downtown Downieville and drive the other east on California Highway 49. Turn left onto Gold Lake Highway about 20 miles east of Downieville, turn left again toward Sardine Lakes after 1 mile, and follow the signs to Packer Saddle. (The road is paved but becomes very narrow toward the end, and is used by logging trucks.) It's also possible to do this ride as a loop from Downieville by riding up California Highway 49 about 6 miles to Union Flat Campground, then riding up the dirt Gold Valley Road (Road 93) for about 12 miles and turning left onto the paved road coming down from Packer Saddle. The downside to riding a loop is the 4,250-foot climb on paved and dirt roads!

Notes on the trail: The Downieville Downhill can be ridden in three ways: down the Butcher Ranch Trail, down the Pauley Creek Trail, or down the Big Boulder Trail. All three options involve riding on the Third Divide Trail to Lavezzola Road (dirt), taking Lavezzola Road to the First Divide Trail, and riding back into downtown Downieville. Each is progressively more difficult in terms of climbing and mileage. All are usually ridden point-to-point with a shuttle from Downieville to Packer Saddle, but they can also all be ridden as loops from Downieville.

The least technical and most dangerous part of each ride is from Packer Saddle to where the pavement ends. Many riders get anxious to descend, go too fast, and slide out on small patches of loose gravel. Please take it easy on this section! The Butcher Ranch Trail is fairly steep and technical. Most of it is class 3, with short sections of class 4. Intermediate riders should be able to ride most of it, advanced riders all of it; beginning riders should skip this trail to prevent damage to themselves, their bikes, and the trail. If you find that your rear tire is sliding as you brake, either get your weight far enough back so that it won't slide or dismount and walk your bike through the steep and loose sections. The trail surface is varied: bedrock, hard-packed dirt, loose rocks, mixtures of rocks and dirt. It also passes through varied terrain, including old-growth forests, meadows, streams, and wildflower gardens.

After crossing the bridge over Pauley Creek and riding up to the top of the ridge, you have two options: the Second Divide Trail or the Third

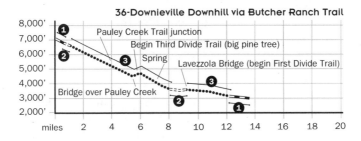

36-Downieville Downhill via Butcher Ranch Trail

Divide Trail. I suggest you take the Third Divide; the Second Divide is more technical and quite exposed in places—a sometimes damaging combination. Third Divide is less steep and less technical. Remember that hikers, equestrians, and other mountain bikers may be around the next corner. Slow down when your visibility is limited to avoid catching them by surprise. Yield the right-of-way by stopping and moving off the trail when you meet them. No matter which trail you take, you'll end up on Lavezzola Road. Take the First Divide Trail back into town.

The Ride

0.0   Ride down the paved road heading west from the parking area at Packer Saddle. Don't forget that pavement is often slippery.

0.5   After reaching a Y, turn right onto a paved road that quickly turns to dirt. The sign will direct you toward Butcher Ranch Meadow. (If you decided to ride up Gold Valley Road from Union Flat, turn left at this intersection and continue as described.)

0.8   End of the pavement. Slow down; the road can get quite rough at this point.

1.2   As you proceed through a long right turn, look for a sign that reads: BUTCHER RANCH OHV TRAIL. Take this trail left off the dirt road. It starts off steep and loose, passing through a meadow filled with mules-ears and a couple of streams.

1.9   The OHV trail heads off to the right and the Butcher Ranch Trail (singletrack) begins. This trail throws a little bit of everything at you, beginning with a steep descent into a rocky gully and a steep climb back out. Get ready for rocks of all shapes and sizes, streambeds, jagged bedrock, loose dirt, roots, sharp turns, steep cliffs overlooking a roaring stream, and steep descents. Don't let your rear tire slide, and remember to stop to enjoy the wildflowers along the streams and springs. You don't have to set a speed record getting back to Downieville. If you want to race, sign up for the Downieville Classic downhill or cross-country race!

3.8	Pauley Creek Trail junction. Continue straight, unless you want to explore a couple of miles to the end of the singletrack. It's a very challenging, scenic, and enjoyable ride, both up and back.
5.6	Bridge over Pauley Creek. Gear down for a climb.
6.0	Junction with the Second Divide and Third Divide Trails. The Second Divide Trail is technical and exposed; the Third Divide is fast and smooth for the most part. Continue straight to take the Third Divide Trail.
6.2	You're at the top of the Third Divide Trail. For the rest of the ride, refer to mile 8.5 in Ride 35, Divide Loop.
13.7	Arrive back at the center of town a much richer and dirtier person than when you left. Betcha can't ride it just once. . . .

Downieville Downhill via Pauley Creek Trail

Location:	Ride or shuttle from downtown Downieville on California Highway 49, about 2 hours either northwest of Lake Tahoe or northeast of Sacramento.	See map on Page 164
Distance:	19.1 miles point-to-point. (Add 18.0 miles if you're riding from Downieville to form a loop.)	
Time:	2.5 hours. (Add 2 hours if you're riding from Downieville to form a loop.)	
Elevation gain:	About 800 feet. Lowest elevation is 2,900 feet; highest elevation is 7,150 feet. (Add 4,250 feet if you're riding from Downieville to form a loop.)	
Tread:	Dirt road and singletrack, ranging from smooth and hard-packed to loose and rocky.	
Aerobic level:	Moderate.	
Technical difficulty:	1–3 (mostly 3).	
Highlights:	Descend from 7,150 feet (surrounded by red fir forests and alpine meadows) to 2,900 feet (to the lower part of a yellow pine forest) beside roaring streams on some of the nicest technical	

singletrack anywhere. The Pauley Creek Trail
is particularly rocky, technical, and scenic.

Land status: Tahoe National Forest.

Maps: USGS Downieville, Sierra City. The best map is
"Downieville, California, published by TerraPro
GPS Surveys Limited," available locally.

Access: See Ride 36, Downieville Downhill via Butcher
Creek Trail.

Notes on the trail: Again, see Ride 36; you'll be sharing that trail for
much of the way. To get to the beginning of the Pauley Creek singletrack,
you must travel for several miles (and do some climbing) on dirt roads, but
you'll pass a gorgeous meadow filled with wildflowers and get to
ride/wade/swim across Pauley Creek. In fact, it might not be possible to
safely cross Pauley Creek during early summer after a heavy winter. The
Pauley Creek singletrack is steep, rocky, technical, wet, lined with wildflowers, and passes beside a roaring stream. It's a long and delightful 2
miles! Intermediate riders should be able to ride most of it, advanced riders all of it; beginning riders should skip this trail in order to prevent damage to themselves, their bikes, and the trail.

The Ride

0.0 Ride down the paved road heading west from the parking area at
Packer Saddle. Don't forget that pavement is often slippery.

0.5 After reaching a Y, turn right onto a paved road that quickly turns
to dirt. The sign will direct you toward Butcher Ranch Meadow.
(If you decided to ride up Gold Valley Road from Union Flat, turn
left at this intersection and continue as described.)

0.8 End of the pavement. Slow down; the road can get quite rough at
this point.

1.2 As you proceed through a long right turn, you'll pass a sign that
reads: BUTCHER RANCH OHV TRAIL. Ignore this trail, continuing on
the dirt road (Road 99–3) by bearing to the right.

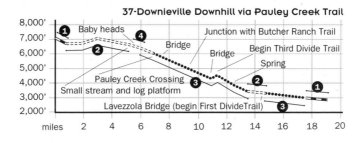

2.6 Do not take the right fork up the hill.

3.5 Follow the main road. Don't turn down 99-3-3.

4.4 Don't take the old dirt road that takes off to your left.

4.8 Cross over a small stream.

4.8+ A log platform and small dirt road take off to your left. A sign on a distant tree to your left reads: OHV TRAIL. GOLD VALLEY 1½. PAULEY CREEK 2. SMITH LAKE 2½. This is it—turn left. *Warnings:* It's very easy to miss this turnoff, because the small sign and dirt road are hard to spot. You're also approaching a steep, rough, rocky descent.

5.9 Cross a small stream.

6.1 After a jarring descent, turn left at the intersection. The sign reads: GOLD VALLEY, PAULEY CREEK TRAIL, SMITH LAKE, LEFT.

6.7 Reach a beautiful campsite on the edge of a gorgeous meadow. Cross Pauley Creek. This can be a very difficult (and dangerous) crossing when the water is high. Cross with caution—or turn back if you have any doubts. The road then climbs steeply up over loose rocks to a junction with the Smith Lake OHV Trail to the right and the Pauley Creek Trail to the left. Head left.

7.2 The dirt road ends and the singletrack begins. Remember to keep your rear wheel rolling rather than sliding.

7.5 Cross over a bridge with a roaring creek below. The singletrack now heads steeply down along the creek and becomes quite rocky and technical. It can also be wet in early summer. This is as good as it gets. Enjoy!

9.2 After more rocks, roots, and wildflowers than you can count, the trail levels out and arrives at a junction with the Butcher Ranch Trail. Turn right.

11.0 Bridge over Pauley Creek. Gear down for a climb.

11.4 Junction with the Second Divide and Third Divide Trails. The Second Divide Trail is technical and exposed; the Third Divide is fast and smooth for the most part. Continue straight to take the Third Divide Trail.

11.6 You're at the top of the Third Divide Trail. For the rest of the ride, refer to mile 8.5 in Ride 35, Divide Loop.

19.1 Arrive back at the center of town a much richer and dirtier person than when you left.

Nice rock work in the Downieville area.

38

Downieville Downhill via Big Boulder Trail

Location:	Ride or shuttle from downtown Downieville on California Highway 49, about 2 hours either northwest of Lake Tahoe or northeast of Sacramento. See map on Page 164
Distance:	20.8 miles point-to-point. (Add 18.0 miles if you're riding from Downieville to form a loop.)
Time:	3 hours. (Add 2 hours if you're riding from Downieville to form a loop.)
Elevation gain:	About 1,600 feet. Lowest elevation is 2,900 feet; highest elevation is 7,150 feet. (Add 4,250 feet if you're riding from Downieville to form a loop.)
Tread:	Dirt road and singletrack, ranging from smooth and hard-packed to loose and rocky. It can be very narrow in places!
Aerobic level:	Moderate to strenuous.
Technical difficulty:	1–3 (mostly 3).
Highlights:	Descend from 7,150 feet (surrounded by red fir forests and alpine meadows) to 2,900 feet (to the lower part of a yellow pine forest) beside roaring streams on some of the nicest technical singletrack anywhere. The Boulder Trail is little traveled and extremely narrow—definitely off the beaten path.
Land status:	Tahoe National Forest.
Maps:	USGS Downieville, Sierra City. The best map is "Downieville, California, published by TerraPro GPS Surveys Limited," available locally.
Access:	See Ride 36, Downieville Downhill via Butcher Creek Trail.

Notes on the trail: Again, see Ride 36; you'll be sharing that trail for much of the way. To get to the beginning of the Big Boulder singletrack, you must travel for several miles (and do some significant climbing) on dirt roads, but you'll pass a gorgeous meadow filled with wildflowers and will get to ride/wade/swim across Pauley Creek. In fact, it might not be possible to safely cross Pauley Creek during early summer after a heavy winter. You'll also climb to the top of a ridge with views toward the northwest and southeast. It's very easy to get lost in this region; keep track of where you've been in case you have to return the way you came.

The Big Boulder singletrack begins near an old mine. It's an old trail that has been recently resurrected, meaning that shrubs have been cut back and deadfall has been removed—but the trail surface itself has been pretty much left the way it was, narrow, loose, and rocky in places. If you love narrow singletrack, this is as good as it gets. Not many people ride this trail. Please be self-sufficient and careful. You could have a long wait for help. Intermediate riders should be able to ride most of the trail, advanced riders all of it; beginning riders should skip this trail in order to prevent damage to themselves, their bikes, and the trail.

At the end of the Big Boulder Trail, you can take either the Second Divide Trail or the Third Divide; I recommend the Third Divide, which is less steep, less technical—and fast, smooth, and fun! Either way, you'll end up dumped onto Lavezzola Road. Take the First Divide Trail back into town.

The Ride

0.0   Ride down the paved road heading west from the parking area at Packer Saddle. Don't forget that pavement is often slippery.

0.5   After reaching a Y, turn right onto a paved road that quickly turns to dirt. The sign will direct you toward Butcher Ranch Meadow. (If you decided to ride up Gold Valley Road from Union Flat, turn left at this intersection and continue as described.)

0.8   End of the pavement. Slow down; the road can get quite rough at this point.

1.2   As you proceed through a long right turn, you'll pass a sign that reads: BUTCHER RANCH OHV TRAIL. Ignore this trail, continuing on the dirt road (Road 99-3) by bearing to the right.

2.6   Do not take the right fork up the hill.

3.5   Follow the main road. Don't turn down 99-3-3.

4.4   Don't take old dirt road that takes off to your left.

4.8   Cross over a small stream.

4.8 +   A log platform and a small dirt road are on your left. A sign on a distant tree to your left reads: OHV TRAIL. GOLD VALLEY 1½. PAULEY

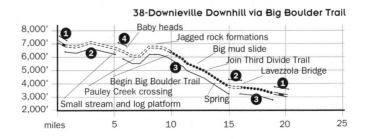

38-Downieville Downhill via Big Boulder Trail

CREEK 2. SMITH LAKE 2½. This is it—turn left. *Warnings:* It's very easy to miss this turnoff, because the small sign and dirt road are hard to spot. You're also approaching a steep, rough, rocky descent.

5.9   Cross a small stream.

6.1   After a jarring descent, turn left at the intersection. The sign reads: GOLD VALLEY, PAULEY CREEK TRAIL, SMITH LAKE, LEFT.

6.7   Reach a beautiful campsite on the edge of a gorgeous meadow. Cross Pauley Creek. This can be a very difficult (and dangerous) crossing when the water is high. Cross with caution—or turn back if you have any doubt. The road then climbs steeply up over loose rocks to a junction with the Smith Lake OHV Trail to the right and the Pauley Creek Trail to the left. Head right.

7.4   Pass by another beautiful, flower-filled meadow.

7.5   Intersection on top of a ridge. Instead of heading down to Smith Lake, turn left and ride up the ridge.

8.1   Ignore the small singletrack taking off to the right. Continue to climb the ridge. Nice views!

8.2   Tree across the trail. The road goes way around the tree, down and back up. To avoid this detour, climb over the tree and keep going.

8.5   Jagged rock formations on your left; nice views toward the northwest. Continue following the ridge on a smooth dirt road through a red fir forest.

9.3   Fork in the road. The left fork dead-ends with a view to the southeast. Turn right, swinging up and over the ridge and passing through a thick young forest. The road then becomes narrow and heavily eroded as it passes steeply down through a manzanita thicket to an old mine.

10.1 Old mine. The Big Boulder Trail starts here.

10.2 Reach a high spot after a short downhill and a short climb up. This is one narrow singletrack! It's also steep in places, and covered with large pinecones.

11.0 It looks like you're about to leap off into the canyon below. Walk your bike through the rocky section unless you're an expert: It's steep, loose, and on the side of a cliff. Do stop and enjoy the view. What's the hurry?

11.2 Large roots will try to throw you off your bike.

11.6 Carry your bike across a big mudslide.

12.0 Zigzag steeply down through the woods on a 4-inch trail along an extremely steep hillside on extremely loose stuff.

13.3 The Big Boulder Trail ends just below Third Divide Ridge, on the Third Divide Trail. Turn right to take the Third Divide Trail. For the rest of the ride, refer to mile 8.5 in Ride 35, Divide Loop.

20.8 Arrive back at the center of town a much richer and dirtier person than when you left.

Nevada City, Auburn, and Donner Pass Area

This diverse area bounded by Nevada City, Auburn, and Donner Pass extends from foothills to summits. The foothills seldom receive snow in winter and are quite hot during the summer, but the trails are ridable year-round. The high country receives a lot of snow in winter, and some of the trails don't become ridable until late summer.

All the rides that I've described are within the Tahoe National Forest or administered by the Bureau of Land Management, and most trails in this area are open to mountain bikes. I appreciate their progressive view of allowing mountain biking on most of their trails. We can show our appreciation by minimizing our impact and conflicts while riding, and by writing them to thank them or by stopping by a ranger station to thank them in person. There are many more trails in this area than I've described, but most are too technical for me (class 4). Books describing many of those trails are available locally.

In this region you can ride beside rivers, among lakes, through dense old-growth forests, and on top of scenic ridges. Not only is the area diverse, but so is its mountain biking!

South Yuba National Trail

Location:	Off California Highway 20, near Nevada City, about 1.5 hours northwest of Lake Tahoe and about 1.5 hours northeast of Sacramento.
Distance:	21.6 miles, point-to-point.
Time:	5 hours.
Elevation gain:	About 3,600 feet. Lowest elevation is 1,900 feet; highest elevation is 3,150 feet.
Tread:	Narrow and hard-packed, mostly smooth but sometimes very rocky.
Aerobic level:	Strenuous.
Technical difficulty:	2–3+ (mostly 3).

Highlights: A wonderful singletrack undulating through a shady forest on the side of a river canyon overlooking a roaring river in spring and early summer, and deep pools in late summer and fall. No motorcycles are allowed on this trail.

Land status: Tahoe National Forest, Bureau of Land Management, South Yuba River State Park.

Maps: USGS Nevada City, North Bloomfield, Washington.

Access: **Car 1:** From the corner of California Highway 20 and California Highway 49 in Nevada City, reset your odometer and drive north on California Highway 49 toward Downieville. At mile 0.3, turn right onto North Bloomfield Road. At mile 0.8, turn left onto Lake Vera Road at the sign for Purdon Crossing, then bear right onto Lake Vera/Purdon Road. At mile 3.5, go straight onto Purdon Road. At mile 4.7, the pavement turns to dirt and gravel. At mile 5.5, you may wish to park at the wide turnouts on the left side of the road. If you have a high-clearance vehicle, you can drive another mile to the bridge at Purdon Crossing, turn right onto the dirt road just prior to the bridge, and drive a short distance to the parking area at the end.

Car 2: From the corner of California Highway 20 and California Highway 49 in Nevada City, reset your odometer and drive east on California Highway 20 toward Truckee. At mile 13.2, turn left onto Washington Road toward the town of Washington. Pass through the town of Washington, drive over the bridge, and turn left at mile 19.2. (A sign will direct you to the South Yuba Trailhead.) At mile 19.5, turn left onto Relief Hill Road. (A sign will again direct you to the South Yuba Trailhead.) At mile 20.0, the pavement becomes dirt and gravel. At mile 21.3 there's a sign for South Yuba Trailhead Parking. An outhouse is available at the trailhead, but no water. (Water, drinks, and food may be purchased at the store in the town of Washington.) If you cannot arrange a shuttle, you may arrange to spend the night in Nevada City, drive your car up to the town of Washington, do the ride, take Lake Vera/Purdon Road

South Yuba National Trail

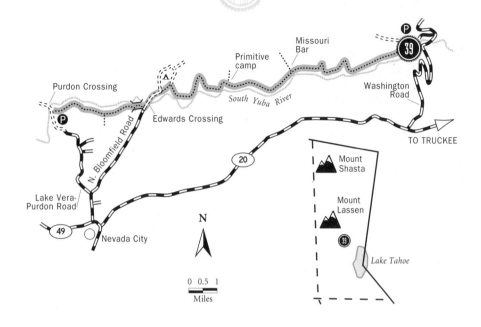

back into Nevada City, spend the night, and ride back up to your car the next day.

Notes on the trail: This is one of the longest continuous (except for 0.5 mile of dirt road) singletracks in California, and travels through an incredibly beautiful river canyon. It's not appropriate for beginning singletrackers, but is quite ridable by those with well-developed intermediate technical skills. *Warning:* This ride includes a lot of climbing even though it ends up downstream of where it started. It also involves several hours of riding. You must be a strong rider with good endurance to complete it! You won't encounter any signs of civilization for the first 17 miles. The trail is built on the side of a cliff in several locations, particularly immediately downstream from Edwards Crossing. I've classified this section as 3+, meaning that the trail alternates between class 3 and class 4. Walking your bike when you're concerned about your safety is perfectly acceptable and recommended. If you become hurt or have bike trouble, you're on your own: No one regularly patrols this trail. Know that rattlesnakes frequent the area. The trail at Primitive Camp dips below the high-water mark Do not attempt to continue past this point when water is covering the trail, because the currents can be quite dangerous. Poison oak is abundant along the trail.

This is best done as a point-to-point ride. Shuttle companies come and go in Nevada City, so it's wise to bring two cars, placing one at Purdon Crossing at the lower end of the trail, and then driving the other car and bikes up to the upper end near the town of Washington. If you cannot arrange a shuttle, you can ride out-and-back downstream from the upper end to Missouri Bar or Primitive Camp, out-and-back upstream from Edwards Crossing to Primitive Camp, or out-and-back downstream from Edwards Crossing to Purdon Crossing. If you wish to shorten the ride to only 17.1 miles and 3,200 feet of climbing, place car 1 at Edwards Crossing by driving on North Bloomfield Road from Nevada City.

The best month for swimming is July: Currents are gentle, the water isn't too cold, and the rocks haven't yet become too slippery from algae. If you plan to swim and sunbathe, add another hour or two to this ride.

The Ride

0.0 Start by riding in a digger pine forest beside shiny green serpentine rock.

0.9 A river access heads down on your left. Continue straight on the sometimes rocky, sometimes smooth, and always narrow singletrack.

1.4 Ride on a lovely bridge over McKilligan Creek and head up through a Douglas fir forest. The trail now begins to roller-coaster and becomes rockier.

1.6 Ignore the primitive trail coming down from the right.

2.3 Enjoy the beautiful views of the South Yuba River below.

2.9 Time to climb.

3.8 Cross a small creek.

4.0 An old trail heads down to your left. Ignore it and continue to climb.

4.1 Another bridge over a lovely creek. Upstream is a nice waterfall. Continue to climb. This would be a nice destination for a short out-and-back ride from the Washington end.

4.9 Head downhill on a leaf-covered trail through a forest of ponderosa pines, Douglas firs, California black oaks, and canyon live oaks.

5.1 Cross over Cecil Creek and continue to ride downhill.

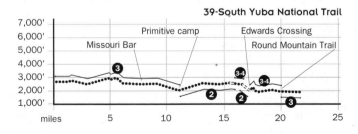

South Yuba River.

5.2	Begin to climb again.
5.5	This is the high point of the ride. Get ready for a long downhill on a smooth trail with several perfectly built switchbacks.
7.6	Arrive at the South Yuba River at Missouri Bar. This is a great place to take a swim, soak your feet, or just wash off the poison oak. It would also make a good destination for an out-and-back ride from the Washington end.
7.7	Cross the bridge over Missouri Creek.
7.8	Trail junction: Take the lower trail to continue on the South Yuba Trail. (The upper trail is the Missouri Bar Trail.)
9.3	A river access takes off to the left. Bear right to continue with this ride.
11.0	Arrive at Primitive Camp. This is another great place to take a swim, soak your feet, wash off poison oak oils, have a snack, or just take a rest. It would also make a nice destination for an out-and-back ride from either the Washington end or Edwards Crossing. Several river access trails take off to the left. Bear right at each junction to continue downstream.
11.2	Starting just before the bridge over Humbug Creek, the trail is washed out for about 100 yards. If water is covering the trail, please don't continue; you could be swept away in the current. Instead, go back the way you came. If not, carry your bike across the rocks to the junction on the South Yuba Trail and the Humbug Trail and bear left to continue on the South Yuba Trail.
12.8	A river access trail takes off to your left. Bear right. You will basically be climbing until mile 15.6. Fortunately, enough downhill sections are thrown in to make the climb quite enjoyable.
14.1	Turnoff to Overlook Picnic Site. Bear right.
15.0	Turn right onto the old dirt road and head uphill.
15.2	Turn left onto the singletrack.
15.5	Cross the bridge over Kenebec Creek. A sign alerts you that a waterfall exists upstream.
15.6	The trail forks, with a map display on your left. Take the left fork.
15.6+	The trail ends at a narrow, paved road in the middle of a campground. Turn left and ride down the paved road.
15.9	Just past campsite 12 is a sign that directs you to the trail on your left. Just prior to that is a bathroom and water. After filling up, prepare for some class 4 sections scattered among class 3 sections.
16.6	Don't take the steep trail on your left that leads down to the river. Instead, bear right and continue a short distance to the gravel road above.
16.6+	Arrive at the gravel road (North Bloomfield Road) and head carefully down to Edwards Crossing. This is the only part of the ride that's not on singletrack.
17.1	On the other side of the bridge is an outhouse and a trail sign for the South Yuba Trail. You're entering a technical and cliffy section.

You're probably also fairly tired, because you've climbed more than 3,000 feet. Please ride with extra caution!

17.5 Head downhill very carefully while keeping your speed under control.

19.7 A river access heads off to your right. Bear left.

19.9 Junction with the Round Mountain Trail. (If you have lots of energy left, you can ride up and back down this trail, a wonderfully built singletrack that zigzags up and down the mountain.) The trail becomes smoother now and very playful, with lots of blind corners. Please keep your speed under control. You'll also encounter many more trail users, mostly hikers. From now on there will be several river accesses taking off to your right. Head down any of them for a swim. Bear left in each case to remain on the South Yuba National Trail.

21.6 End of the South Yuba Trail. If you parked up above, ride down this dirt road to Purdon Crossing, and ride up the dirt road to your car. If you parked here, you're lucky! A good river access can be reached by heading upstream on the dirt road. I highly recommend scrubbing the poison oak oils off your arms, legs, and face before leaving. *Warning:* This section of river tends to be clothing-optional.

Upper Pioneer/Omega Trails

Location:	Off California Highway 20, near Nevada City, about 1.5 hours northwest of Lake Tahoe and about 1.5 hours northeast of Sacramento.
Distance:	20.4 miles, out-and-back.
Time:	3.5 hours.
Elevation gain:	About 2,230 feet. Lowest elevation is 3,700 feet; highest elevation is 5,300 feet.
Tread:	Mostly smooth and hard-packed, with some rocky and loose sections.
Aerobic level:	Moderate.
Technical difficulty:	2–3 (mostly 3).
Highlights:	Dogwoods; several miles of wonderful, narrow singletrack.

Land status:	Tahoe National Forest.
Maps:	USGS North Bloomfield, Washington.
Access:	From Truckee on Interstate 80, take the California Highway 20 exit and drive 16 miles to the White Cloud Picnic Area. From the junction of California Highway 49 and California Highway 20 in Nevada City, take California Highway 20 east for 10 miles to the White Cloud Picnic Area. Bathrooms and water are available. A campground is located across the highway.

Notes on the trail: This ride is not appropriate for beginning single-trackers, and certainly not for beginning mountain bikers. Without well-developed intermediate technical skills, you could do a lot of damage to the trail—and to other trail users. The second half of this ride is definitely class 3. Both the Lower and the Upper Pioneer Trails were built by the Gold Country Trails Council of Nevada City, an equestrian group that has been very generous in opening up its trail to mountain bikes. If you meet anyone on horseback, please thank them for building, maintaining, and sharing the trail. And don't forget to yield the right-of-way to both equestrians and hikers by stopping and moving off the trail before they feel compelled to do so.

The Pioneer Trail is marked by green arrows on carsonite posts and by white diamonds on trees. The Omega Trail is a multiuse trail for hikers, equestrians, mountain bikers, and motorcyclists, and was built by the Nevada County Woods Riders. It's marked with orange arrows on carsonite posts.

The singletrack starts about 100 yards west of the entrance to the picnic area, takes off on the south side of the highway, and parallels the highway for many miles. You'll basically be riding up for a couple of hours, but you'll encounter many downs as well (some quite steep), along with highly varied terrain (hard-packed dirt, loose dirt, sand, loose rocks, roots, narrow trails, sharp turns, and more). The trail is built in several sections. As you come to the end of one section, usually at a dirt road, look around for the start of the next section. Keep doing this until you're dumped back onto the highway. For the last few miles, two singletracks parallel each other—the Upper Pioneer Trail and the Omega Trail. I chose the Omega Trail at this point because it offered better singletrack. Then turn around and come gliding back down, watching closely for other trail users, of course. The trail stays away from the highway for the most part, but comes close enough in several sections that you can easily bail out if you wish. Please keep track of the trail junctions so that you can find your way back. I will only guide you "out." This trail is particularly nice to ride in May when the dogwoods are in bloom, or in October when they've turned.

Upper Pioneer/Omega Trails

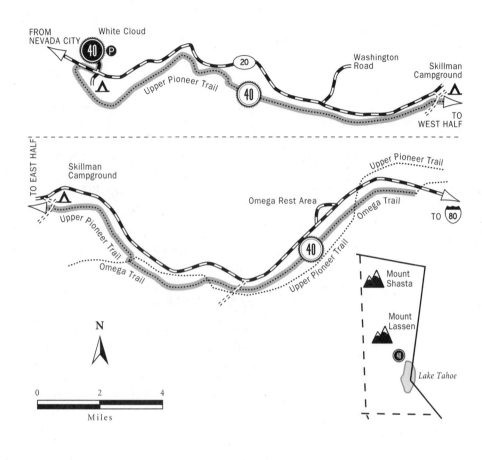

The Ride

0.0 Ride the pavement out of the picnic area and turn right (west) onto California Highway 20.

0.3 Carefully cross the highway to the beginning of the singletrack.

0.6 Cross over the dirt road and keep going.

0.9 Steep downhill. At the bottom is a trail junction. Bear left to stay on the Upper Pioneer Trail and ride along the bank of an old ditch. (Remember this junction on the way back.)

1.1 Another steep downhill. Is your weight back?

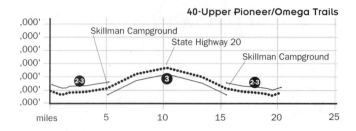

40-Upper Pioneer/Omega Trails

Skillman Campground
State Highway 20
Skillman Campground

,000'
,000'
,000'
,000'
,000'
,000'
,000'

miles   5   10   15   20   25

1.5 It looks like the trail should continue along the ditch bank, but instead, the Upper Pioneer Trail turns sharply left and begins to climb steeply. (Remember this on the way back so you don't slide your wheel down; you'll also want to make a sharp right turn at the bottom of it.) Ride through a dense forest of California black oaks, ponderosa pines, incense cedars, and Douglas firs.

2.1 Ignore the trail coming down from the left.

2.3 Steep climb.

2.9 Large gravel area (the Overlook Equestrian Trailhead). Ride across the gravel and find the singletrack on the other side.

3.3 Another steep, loose downhill.

3.5 Ride across a loose and rocky section through a manzanita grove on a south-facing slope. It can get hot here. The rocks are of volcanic origin.

3.8 Leave the rocks and manzanita and ride back into the forest. Watch for manzanita-berry-filled bear scat along the trail. Lots of dogwoods also occur along this section.

4.9 The singletrack turns into an old dirt road.

5.0 Just before you're tossed out onto a gravel road, notice the wooden sign to your left reading: PIONEER TRAIL, CONSTRUCTED BY VOLUNTEERS UNDER THE DIRECTION OF GOLD COUNTRY TRAILS COUNCIL AND THE U.S.D.A. FOREST SERVICE. At this point a small singletrack marked with a carsonite post takes off to your right. Take it.

5.0 + Turn right onto the gravel road, ride about 50 feet, and turn left onto the singletrack at the green gate.

5.1 Bear left at the trail junction and ride along an old ditch among white firs, hazelnuts, and dogwoods.

5.4 Be watching for a carsonite post that directs you to turn right at the junction. If you miss it, you'll end up in a campground.

5.6 The trail comes very close to the highway and then begins to follow an old logging road as it leaves the highway and climbs very steeply.

6.0 A sign on your left reads: NO MOTORCYCLES. Shortly thereafter you'll find yourself on a gravel road. Turn right, ride 100 feet, and turn left onto the singletrack.

6.7 You're tossed up onto an old dirt road that leads to a fork. The left fork zigzags steeply uphill. The is the Pioneer Trail. The right fork leads to a second fork. Now is the time to leave the Pioneer Trail for the more exciting Omega Trail. Head for the second fork and turn left. You're on a connector trail that will take you to the Omega Trail.

6.8 Reach a T and turn left onto the Omega Trail.

7.2 Cross an old dirt road (which is really the Pioneer Trail) and continue on the Omega Trail.

7.8 Cross the old dirt road (which is really the Upper Pioneer Trail again) and continue on the Omega Trail. It's marked by signs depicting hikers, equestrians, bicyclists, and motorcyclists.

8.0 The singletrack heads for the highway and turns right just before hitting it.

8.2 When you hit the dirt road, bear slightly right and find the indistinct singletrack taking off again. For a motorized multiuse trail, this one sure is narrow! Ignore singletracks taking off toward the highway.

10.2 You're abruptly tossed out onto the highway about 1 mile east of the Omega rest stop. The narrow Omega Trail continues for another couple of miles on the other side of the highway, but for this ride, turn around at the highway and enjoy the trail in the other direction. If on the way back you accidentally get off the playful Omega Trail and onto the Upper Pioneer Trail sooner than you'd like, don't worry; you'll end up on the Upper Pioneer Trail eventually anyway.

20.4 Back at your car.

Option: If you happen to have two cars, you can combine the Lower Pioneer Trail and Upper Pioneer/Omega Trails, plus add a couple more miles of the Omega Trail by driving 1.8 miles east of the Omega Rest Area, turning left onto Road 20–16, entering the primitive campground, and jumping onto the singletrack at the last campsite on the left. It's mostly downhill all the way down to the Harmony Store.

Shotgun "Lake"

Location:	About 2 hours east of Sacramento and 1 hour west of Truckee, off Interstate 80 and California Highway 20.
Distance:	10.9 miles, out-and-back.
Time:	3 hours.
Elevation gain:	About 1,650 feet. Lowest elevation is 6,500 feet; highest elevation is 7,000 feet.
Tread:	Mostly rocky, mostly hard-packed.
Aerobic level:	Moderate.
Technical difficulty:	3–4 (mostly 3).
Highlights:	Five beautiful lakes to visit, wildflower-filled meadows, challenging technical singletrack.
Land status:	Tahoe National Forest.
Maps:	USGS Graniteville, English Mountain.
Access:	From Sacramento, drive 75 miles east on Interstate 80. From Truckee, drive 24 miles west on Interstate 80. Take the California Highway 20 exit toward Nevada City. Drive 4.0 miles to a sign that reads: SIERRA DISCOVERY TRAIL, BOWMAN LAKE 16. Turn right onto the narrow road (National Forest 18). A bathroom and water are available at the parking area for the Sierra Discovery Trail. At the turnoff to Grouse Ridge Lookout, continue straight toward Carr and Feeley Lakes. At 8.5 miles from California Highway 20, turn right onto National Forest 17 toward Carr and Feeley Lakes. *Warning:* The road is dirt and/or gravel from here to Carr Lake. Still, I've a low-clearance two-wheel-drive car, and it made it fine. At the split in the road, take Carr and Feeley Lakes to the right onto National Forest 17–06. At the gate, turn right into the parking area. No water or bathrooms are available at the trailhead, but an outhouse is available as you ride past Carr Lake. Walk-in camping is available at Carr Lake.

Shotgun "Lake"

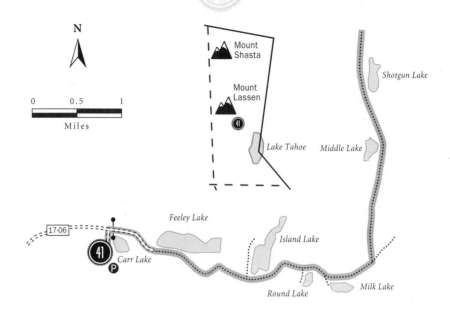

Notes on the trail: A more correct title for this ride would be "Swim, Hike, and Bike to Shotgun Lake." You'll pass by five lakes in which you can swim, you'll have to hike your bike from time to time, and you'll also find some enjoyable biking. Shotgun Lake caught me by surprise, though. It's actually a very large meadow that's very wet at one end. So if you ride to Shotgun Lake expecting to find a beautiful green meadow surrounded by lodgepole pines, you won't be disappointed.

Don't let the technical nature of the first few miles cause you to turn back; the trail grows easier in the last few miles. But in general this is a technical ride, with most of it alternating between class 3 and class 4. If you have some solid class 3 skills, this ride can be a lot of fun. I suggest that you wait until after July 15 to ride these trails, because they dry out late in the season. They're also heavily used by hikers, backpackers, and equestrians. Please ride slowly, watch carefully for others, and yield to everyone. It's good to take occasional breaks anyway, right?

The Ride

0.0 Ride through the gate and continue on the dirt road past Carr Lake.

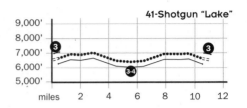

0.2 Cross the stream below the dam. This can be a very interesting crossing during high water—another good reason to wait until after July 15 to do this ride.

0.3 At the top of the dam, Feeley Lake comes into view and a wide singletrack begins.

0.6 The trail climbs up and away from Feeley Lake through a mature red fir forest.

1.0 Pass by a tiny lake becoming a meadow and cross the log and rock bridge over the outlet creek.

1.2 Another small lake is visible on your left, and you reach a trail junction. The left fork leads to Crooked Lakes. Take the right fork.

1.3 Island Lake comes into view. The trail begins to alternate between class 3 and class 4. It's particularly rough when it passes through jagged reddish metamorphic rocks.

1.6 A nice view of Island Lake.

1.9 A pond is on your left. Lots of small, blue lupines are blooming along the trail. Granite is appearing on your left, reddish metamorphic rock on your right.

2.0 Please carry your bike through any mud here.

2.0+ Trail junction. You need to go left, but if you want to visit Round Lake, ride or walk a short distance to the right and come back.

2.4 A meadow filled with corn lilies and large blue lupines.

2.5 Trail junction. You need to go left, but if you want to visit Milk Lake, ride or walk a short distance to the right and come back.

2.5+ Trail junction. Turn left onto the well-used trail.

3.3 Trail junction. Turn left onto the narrow singletrack.

3.9 Walk your bike down this steep section if you cannot ride it without sliding.

4.6 There's a sign for Middle Lake on your left. But Middle Lake isn't really a lake, it's a meadow.

4.8 The trail makes an S turn.

4.9 Cross a large seasonal creek.

5.1 Notice the large meadow on your right. This is the beginning of Shotgun "Lake."

5.4 This is the end of Shotgun "Lake." Since there were so many trail junctions, and since signs were not always present, I'll guide you back.

7.6 Bear to the right at this junction, toward Feeley Lake.

8.3 Turn right at this junction, toward Feeley Lake.

8.4 Bear right at the Milk Lake junction—unless you want to go for a swim.

8.9	Bear right at the Round Lake junction—unless you want to go for another swim.
9.3	High spot, with a good view of Island Lake.
9.6	A good place to stop for a swim in Island Lake.
9.8	At the intersection, bear left.
10.3	A great place to swim in Feeley Lake!
10.9	Back at the parking lot.

Loch Leven Lakes Loop

Location:	About 1.5 hours east of Sacramento and about 30 minutes west of Truckee on Interstate 80.
Distance:	10.5-mile loop.
Time:	3 hours.
Elevation gain:	About 1,950 feet. Lowest elevation is 5,800 feet; highest elevation is 6,550 feet.
Tread:	Mostly rocky, sometimes hard-packed and sometimes loose.
Aerobic level:	Strenuous.
Technical difficulty:	2–4 (mostly 3).
Highlights:	Deep granite-enclosed lakes perfect for swimming, green wildflower-filled meadows, challenging technical singletrack.
Land status:	Tahoe National Forest.
Maps:	USGS Cisco Grove.
Access:	From Truckee, drive 21 miles west on Interstate 80. From Sacramento, drive 74 miles east on Interstate 80. Take the Yuba Gap exit and set your odometer to 0.0. At 0.3 mile, turn right onto Lake Valley Road. At 1.5 miles, turn left onto Mears Meadow Road (dirt), National Forest 19. (A bathroom, but no water is available at the Silvertip Picnic Area.) At 5.7 miles, turn left onto National Forest 38 toward Huysink Lake. At mile 6.4, park in the wide space on your left. No bathrooms or water are available at the trailhead.

Loch Leven Lakes Loop

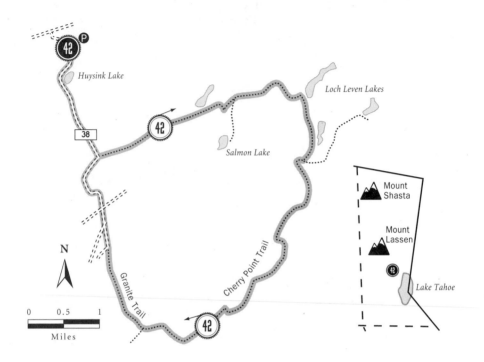

Notes on the trail: Most of this loop alternates between class 3 and class 4. Riders with intermediate technical skills and intermediate strength will be carrying or pushing their bikes for about 40 percent of the time; those with advanced technical skills and strength may be able to ride 95 percent of it. Allow an extra hour for the side trips to Salmon Lake and Upper Loch Leven Lake. This ride can be shortened considerably by riding out-and-back to any of the lakes along the way. I suggest waiting until after July 15 to do this ride to give the trails time to dry out after the deep winter snows melt. Many hikers, backpackers, and equestrians use these trails. Please ride in a nonthreatening manner and yield the right-of-way to them.

The Ride

0.0 Begin by riding down the dirt road toward Huysink Lake.

0.8 Pass Huysink Lake on your left. It's on private property, so just look, don't touch.

1.4 As you climb this dirt road, concentrate on the paintbrushes blooming along the side.

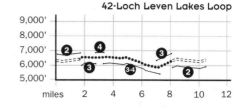

1.6 Turn left onto the singletrack at the sign for Salmon Lake and Lower Loch Leven Lake. Pass beside a very green meadow and climb through a red fir forest.

1.8 The trail levels out and begins to descend. Be sure to keep your weight far enough back that your rear wheel doesn't slide.

2.3 Smell the bark of the mature Jeffrey pine on your right. Butterscotch or vanilla?

2.5 A small and shallow lake surrounded by lodgepole pines.

2.8 Salmon Lake is at the end of the right fork, about 0.2 mile from where you're standing. It's certainly worth a visit, either on foot or on bike. After you return, take the left fork to continue this ride.

3.0 Walk or carry your bike through the meadow if it's muddy.

3.3 Ride through gorgeous meadows filled with wildflowers.

3.5 Arrive at a trail junction at Lower Loch Leven Lake. This is a great lake for swimming or sunning. Turn right and head for Middle Loch Leven Lake.

3.8 Climb steeply through a forest of western white pines, with skinny cones and plated bark.

3.9 Arrive at Middle Loch Leven Lake. Another swim? More sun?

4.1 Trail junction. Upper Loch Leven Lake is to your left. If you want to see this lake, it would probably be just as fast and easy to leave your bike here and hike up 0.3 mile. Once you get there you're faced with another granite-enclosed lake perfect for swimming. In fact, this lake is smaller and shallower than the rest, providing warmer water. After returning from your swim, you have an important decision. If you head on, you'll be riding on alternating class 3 and class 4 sections, sometimes steeply downhill on very loose surfaces. You'll then take on a long uphill climb. Do you feel up to it? If you choose to continue, turn right onto the Cherry Point Trail.

4.5 Ride through a very lush meadow and get ready to climb again.

5.3 Pass through another flower-filled meadow. Please carry your bike through the muddy section.

6.3 The narrow singletrack ends as you're dumped out onto an old logging road. Fortunately, it's recovering into a wide, class 3 singletrack.

7.1 Cross Little Granite Creek. Start looking for a singletrack heading up on your right.

7.2	This isn't an easy trail junction to spot. Look for a small pile of rocks on your right. The Granite Trail is delineated by two small logs and a series of rocks. Turn right onto this singletrack and get ready to climb steeply.
7.5	Stop climbing to enjoy the mature sugar pine that has been dropping its huge cones.
7.6	Cross a small stream and notice the large trees with reddish bark. These are incense cedars.
7.8	Ride *through* an incense cedar! (You'll see what I mean when you get there.)
7.9	A campsite with a bench. The singletrack now turns into a real doubletrack.
8.1	The doubletrack becomes a dirt road.
8.3	At a large cairn, you intersect a dirt road. Bear right onto this road.
8.3 +	Arrive at another intersection. Follow the sign to Huysink Lake by going through the intersection toward the FOREST SERVICE 38 sign.
8.8	Arrive back at the Salmon Lake Trailhead.
10.5	Tired?

Hole-in-the-Ground Trail

Location:	At the top of Donner Pass, on U.S. Highway 80, about 1.75 hours east of Sacramento and about 1.25 hours west of Reno.
Distance:	17.3-mile loop.
Time:	3.5 hours.
Elevation gain:	About 2,300 feet. Lowest elevation is 6,300 feet; highest elevation is 7,700 feet.
Tread:	Mostly singletrack, some smooth and hard-packed, some moderately technical, most narrow and well built.
Aerobic level:	Strenuous.
Technical difficulty:	1–4 (mostly 3).
Highlights:	This is some of the nicest Sierran landscape that mountain bikers are allowed access to. Enjoy views of Castle Peaks, two pristine and beautiful swimming lakes, meadows filled with

Hole-in-the-Ground Trail

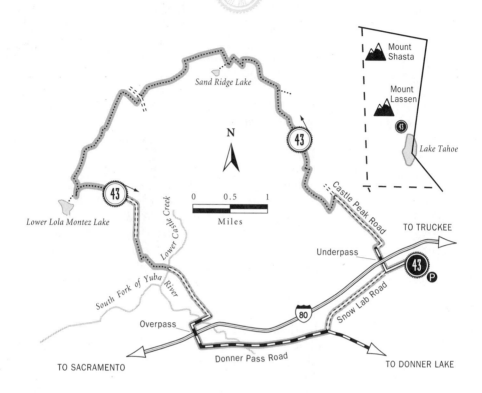

wildflowers, red fir and mountain hemlock forests, and well-built, narrow sections of lightly to moderately technical singletrack. No motorized vehicles are allowed on the single-track.

Land status: Tahoe National Forest.

Maps: USGS Norden, Independence Lake, Soda Springs, Webber Peak (the trail is not shown).

Access: Take the Castle Peak/Boreal Ridge Road exit off Interstate 80. Follow signs for Pacific Crest Trailhead and for Sno Park until the end of the road. Park in the lot for the Pacific Crest Trail. Water and bathrooms are available.

Notes on the trail: This ride passes through the kind of country that you've hiked and backpacked in, and wished you could've mountain biked in—and now you can. Thanks to the Tahoe National Forest, mountain bikes can ride this wonderful trail. Even the dirt road up to the beginning of the singletrack is scenic, with views of Castle Peaks and flower-covered meadows. The singletrack begins by climbing to the top of Andesite Ridge on a hard-packed and smooth surface at an incline that's perfect. From the top of the ridge, there are good views to the south, east, and north. A narrow trail allows you to climb to the top of Andesite Peak for even better views of the area. The singletrack then becomes more technical as it heads down through red fir and mountain hemlock forests and passes beside granite ridges and outcroppings. The singletrack climbs and descends over several ridges. Two highlights—each just 0.25 mile off the trail—are alpine lakes. Both are pristine and beautiful—perfect examples of small Sierran lakes. Wildflowers are abundant at several locations along the ride, and are as varied as are the locations. I was especially impressed with the mule's-ears, tiger lilies, and columbines. After the second lake, singletrack is interspersed with dirt road until you reach U.S. Highway 80. The trip back to the car on paved and dirt roads is relatively short and scenic. You could ride this trail as an out-and-back from either end, but it undulates so much that you'd be left with a much more strenuous ride. The return trip to the car is so short that arranging for a shuttle for a point-to-point ride probably isn't worth the effort.

The land manager is particularly concerned about this trail because sections of it are new and haven't been thoroughly cured, and because this book might attract more trail users—who might increase the wear and tear on the trail to the point of permanent damage. Please treat this trail with extra care and help educate others in low-impact riding techniques. It's usually wet or covered with snow until late July. Please let it dry out before you ride it. Waiting until August would be a good idea. Don't let your rear tire slide on steep downhill sections and before turns. Control your speed at all times so that you can stop without skidding. Walk your bike through wet or muddy sections. If you cannot ride over a water bar, carry your bike over it rather than ride around it. If you see others abusing this trail, please help educate them. I'm taking a chance by including this ride in the book. I believe that education will save trails such as this from abuse. Please prove me right!

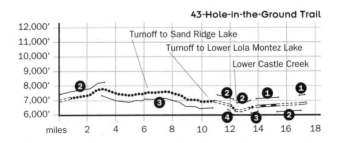

43-Hole-in-the-Ground Trail

Warning: Lower Castle Creek at the lower end of the ride sometimes becomes impassable during peak runoff in early summer. Also, snow lingers deep and late along sections of this ride. If you come off the top of Andesite Ridge and find the trail covered with snow, it's better to turn back than to risk losing the trail and becoming lost in this wild terrain. Just another reason to wait until August before riding here.

The Ride

0.0 Ride back toward the freeway off ramp.

0.5 Take the underpass to Castle Peak Road.

0.8 The pavement ends. Take the dirt road through the green gate.

0.9 Take the right fork (toward the sign depicting a cross-country skier).

1.1 Ignore the pull-outs where people camp and continue on the dirt road that climbs steeply.

1.2 Catch the views of Castle Peak and the meadow.

1.4 There's a spring on your left and a fork in the road. Bear left to continue climbing. Don't take the fork that descends into the meadow below.

1.8 Trailhead for the Hole-in-the-Ground Trail. The singletrack begins to the left of the sign.

2.3 The trail climbs steeply, but it's all ridable. Views of Squaw Valley, Heavenly Valley, and Desolation Valley appear to the south.

2.5 Ride through an old-growth red fir forest growing in deep volcanic soil.

2.6 Climb out onto the top of the ridge and enjoy the views.

2.9 Climb through young red firs with bases bent from snow moving downhill during the winter.

3.2 Ride among volcanic rocks (andesite). A small trail comes down from the top of Andesite Peak. You can wander up for a better view of the area. After returning, lower your seat and get ready to ride downhill.

3.9 Pass through a red fir forest with a granite ridge to your right while being careful to avoid sliding your rear tire. Watch for other trail users coming up.

4.4 Ride through a rocky section in a mountain hemlock forest. (Mountain hemlocks, with their droopy limbs, indicate areas of deep snow.)

4.8 Cross a small stream surrounded by red firs.

5.1 Trail junction. Take the left fork toward Sand Ridge Lake. (The right fork leads to the Pacific Crest Trail, where bicycles are not allowed.)

5.7 Cross a small stream on a granite slab.

5.8 Nice trail work across a wet meadow!

Singletrack on Andesite Ridge on the Hole-in-the-Ground Trail.

6.1 Trail junction. Take the trail marked SAND RIDGE LAKE, 1/4 MILE across granite slabs to the small, pristine lake for a snack or lunch and swim. Then return to this point. Please protect the lakeshore by not riding around the lake.

6.6 Cross a small stream.

7.2 Snow lingers late in this area.

7.6 Get ready for some fun downhill by lowering your seat and getting your weight back.

8.4 Cross a dirt road and continue downhill.

9.5 Stream crossing. Don't get your brake pads wet, because you'll need them shortly when you ride down some granite slabs.

10.0 The trail flattens out for a while and it passes through a lodgepole pine forest.

10.1 Creek crossing.

10.4 Signed intersection. First take the trail 0.25 mile west to see Lower Lola Montez Lake. This is a beautiful deep lake that deserves to be visited. (Please don't ride on the lakeshore.) Then return and take the trail east to head for the trailtail. From now on you'll probably encounter more trail users—especially hikers—than you have before, because many people hike up the trail to visit Lower Lola Montez Lake.

10.8 The singletrack ends here and the dirt road begins. This dirt road tends to be fast; don't forget about hikers. You're also riding on private property from here to mile 13.6. Be respectful.

11.4 Ignore the dirt road with a chain across it.

11.6 Ignore the private driveway.

11.9 Sign: LOLA MONTEZ TRAIL TRAILHEAD, 1 3/4. Take this singletrack. Warning: It gets very steep and loose in places.

12.4 Turn left on the dirt road at the sign that states: LOLA MONTEZ TRAIL TRAILHEAD, 1 3/4. (This mileage is not correct.)

12.7 Cross Lower Castle Creek if it appears safe to do so. (If the creek is too high to safely cross, you can turn back or spend the night and wait for lower water in the morning.)

13.2 Ignore the driveway.

13.3 Watch for a small sign to your right saying: TRAIL. You want to turn left onto a small singletrack just before this sign. (This is an easy turnoff to miss.)

13.6 Trailtail. Hit the pavement and ride downhill to the right.

13.9 Turn left onto Donner Pass Road and cross over the freeway.

14.5 Soda Springs store. Did you bring some money?

15.3 A sign on the left side of the road hiding behind a group of lodgepole pines reads: HEADQUARTERS, CENTRAL SIERRA SNOW LABORATORIES. Take the dirt road just past this sign. This dirt road is locally known as "Snow Lab Road."

15.5 The dirt road forks. Take the left fork and climb.

15.6 You're passing through private property. Please stay on the dirt road and ride quietly. At this point, the dirt road regenerates into a steep and rocky doubletrack.

16.0 A strange-looking building with a sign saying DANGER—CHLORINE appears on your right. Just ahead of you is a small sign saying FREEWAY. Continue pedaling just a little farther to . . .

16.5 Boreal Ridge parking lot. Cross the parking lot until you get to . . .

16.9 Castle Peak/Boreal Road. Pedal back to the Pacific Crest Trail parking area.

17.3 Back at the car. Wasn't that one of the best experiences you've ever had on your bike?

Stevens Trail

Location:	Near Colfax on Interstate 80, about 1 hour east of Sacramento.
Distance:	7.6 miles out-and-back.
Time:	1.75 hours.
Elevation gain:	About 1,550 feet. Lowest elevation is 1,275 feet; highest elevation is 2,400 feet.
Tread:	Mostly narrow, hard-packed, rocky, exposed singletrack.
Aerobic level:	Moderate, with one long, strenuous climb.
Technical difficulty:	2–3 (mostly 3).
Highlights:	A narrow singletrack perched on the side of a cliff overlooking the North Fork of the American River; a multitude of wildflowers in spring, especially yellow sticky monkey flowers; great swimming holes at the river. No motorcycles are allowed on the trail.
Land status:	Bureau of Land Management.
Maps:	USGS Colfax.
Access:	On Interstate 80, 14 miles east of Auburn, take the Colfax/Grass Valley/Rollins Lake exit and turn left. Drive 0.1 mile and bear right onto North Canyon Way. (Don't cross over the freeway.) Drive another 0.6 mile to the signed

Stevens Trail

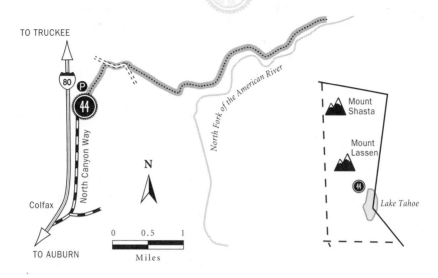

parking area for Stevens Trail. (You'll be paralleling the freeway, and will pass by a cemetery.) Please park only within the parking area or along the paved road on the side marked for overflow parking.

Notes on the trail: This trail is very narrow and exposed. You must have well-developed skills. In particular, you need to be able to instinctively move your weight toward the cliff edge whenever your bike is getting too close to it. If you try to move your weight away from the cliff edge, your bike will probably turn toward the cliff and might run right off. You also need to be able to ride over rocks without getting thrown off the trail: There is little room for error on this ride. There are a number of class 4 maneuvers that caused me to get off and walk my bike, but each was very short, allowing me to ride perhaps 90 percent of trail down and 80 percent on the way back up. I've rated the first section at 2–3, meaning that it's mostly class 2, but alternates with class 3 sections; and the second section at 3–4, meaning that it's mostly class 3, but alternates with class 4 sections. The views of the river below are constant and impressive, but I suggest you stop riding when you look at the scenery!

It's also unlikely that you'll be able to both ride safely down this trail and avoid hitting poison oak. Better to forget about the poison oak and concentrate on staying on the trail; just wash thoroughly when you reach the river, and again when you reach your car. During the summer you may wish to avoid riding in the middle of the day, because it gets quite hot on this south-facing slope. In fact, you might consider bringing a sleeping bag, riding down in the evening, spending the night beside the river, and riding out the next morning. Many hikers use this trail, especially on weekends. I suggest riding during the week and being willing to yield the right-of-way to everyone you meet. This is a great trail on which to demonstrate that mountain bikers can be good trailmates.

The Ride

0.0 Start by riding through a cool, moist valley filled with blackberry bushes on a mostly smooth, wide singletrack.

0.7 An eroded and rocky chute leads up to a dirt road with a sign that instructs you to turn right. Climb up the dirt road to the top.

1.0 While you're enjoying the shade at the top of the hill, look ahead and see the singletrack taking off to the left, about 100 feet below you. It's marked by two white arrows on a brown metal post. This singletrack is narrow, steep, and rocky.

1.4 The majority of mountain bikers will have to get off and walk their bikes down this section and across the creek bed.

1.6 Be careful of the loose rocks as the trail traverses a scree slope. A cliff is beginning to develop on the right side.

1.7 Enjoy the first good view down into the river canyon. Get ready for a scary exposed section. If you find your bike moving too close to the edge, move your weight *toward* the edge; your bike will move away from it. Do not move your weight away from the edge, or the bike will go over the cliff—with you on it.

2.3 The trail now becomes less exposed and passes through a shady forest.

2.5 Begin another scary exposed section. The good news is that the trail levels out a little.

3.2 Ignore the trail that heads off to the right. In fact, ignore all trails that head off to the right from now on. They all head down to the river.

3.8 The trail suddenly drops down into a permanent stream. Stop either just before or just after the stream. This is where the Stevens Trail meets the North Fork of the American River. There

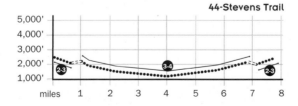

are several good places to enjoy the river, both upstream and downstream from here. If it's a hot day, I advise getting as cool as you can before heading back up!

6.3　You've just pushed your bike up a steep chute. You're faced with a choice: a gentle dirt road straight ahead, or a steep uphill singletrack to your right. Take the steep uphill singletrack, of course! (It's funny how much steeper a trail becomes when you ride it uphill.) While you're gasping for air, notice the huge grapevines growing into the manzanitas. It's unusual to find them growing together.

6.6　Hit the dirt road, turn right, and ride up for 100 feet, enjoy the shade at the top, then glide down to the awaiting singletrack.

6.8　Hang a left onto the singletrack and head for your car.

7.6　You made it.

Foresthill Divide Loop

Location:	Near Auburn on Interstate 80, about half an hour east of Sacramento.
Distance:	11.5-mile loop.
Time:	2 hours.
Elevation gain:	About 1,800 feet. Lowest elevation is 1,250 feet; highest elevation is 1,600 feet.
Tread:	Mostly smooth, hard-packed singletrack.
Aerobic level:	Moderate.
Technical difficulty:	2.
Highlights:	Just a well-built new multipurpose singletrack.
Land status:	Auburn State Recreation Area.
Maps:	USGS Auburn, Greenwood (the trails are not shown). A good topographic map of the Auburn State Recreation Area is published by SOWARWE-WERHER, and is available locally.
Access:	From Interstate 80 in Auburn, take the Auburn Ravine Road/Foresthill Road exit south toward Foresthill. At 0.4 mile, you'll enter the Auburn State Recreation Area. Pass over a huge bridge perched above the canyon of the North Fork of

Foresthill Divide Loop

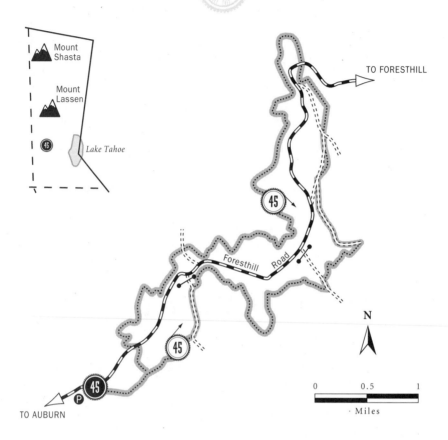

TO FORESTHILL

Mount
Shasta

Mount
Lassen

45

Lake Tahoe

45

Foresthill Road

N

45

45

P
TO AUBURN

0   0.5   1
· Miles

the American River at 0.9 mile. At 3.2 miles, pass the Old Foresthill Road turnoff to Cool and Placerville, and continue on Foresthill Road toward Foresthill. At 4.8 miles, pull into the parking area to your right. No facilities of any kind exist at the trailhead.

Notes on the trail: This singletrack loop was built by both the Auburn State Recreation Area and a local mountain biking club, FATRAC (Folsom-Auburn Trail Riders Action Coalition). I've given the whole loop a class 2 rating, because the trail surface is, with rare exceptions, smooth; the trail is of medium width; inclines and declines are mostly gradual; and there's little exposure. Riders with beginning technical skills should be able to ride this loop without damaging themselves or the trail—just remember to keep your weight back when descending so your rear wheels don't slide.

This isn't a good trail to ride during the summer, unless you get out early or squeeze the ride in before dark. It's a good trail to ride in fall, winter, and spring. All I ask is that you give it a week to dry out after a major winter storm. Weekends are also not good times to ride this trail, which can become quite crowded with other mountain bikers, hikers, and equestrians. This is a multipurpose trail: Mountain bikes must yield the right-of-way to other trail users by stopping and moving off the trail. Uphill mountain bikers also have the right-of-way over downhill mountain bikers. Ticks are common in spring. There's some poison oak, but the trail is wide enough that you'll seldom touch it.

The Ride

0.0 Grab your bike and head for the gate. Ride up to the multipurpose sign, review IMBA's rules of the trail, and turn left.

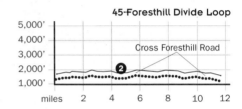

0.4 Ignore the minor trail that heads off to the right and continue to ride among grasses and chaparral on the flats, with a few ponderosa pines on the knolls.

0.6 FORESTHILL DIVIDE LOOP TRAIL, DRIVERS FLAT 5 MILES. The loop is best ridden counterclockwise, so head right. Watch your speed on the downhill sections, because many trail users enjoy this trail, and visibility is sometimes limited.

1.0 Turn left onto, and climb up, an old dirt road.

1.5 A singletrack veers off to the right. Keep left.

2.1 The trail begins to climb with a vengeance.

2.5 Enjoy the knoll under the shade of some California black oaks. You're approaching a fast, smooth downhill.

3.3 Turn left onto the old dirt road. After 100 feet, turn right onto the singletrack.

3.5 Ride over a huge wooden bridge. A small spring-fed pond is on your right. Then ride steeply downhill.

3.8 Turn left onto the old dirt road, cross over onto the east side of the ridge, and ride through a Douglas fir forest. Notice the pleasant smelling ground cover of kit-kit-dizzie, also known as mountain misery.

4.3 Take the singletrack to your right, just before the green gate.

4.4 You're ejected onto a narrow paved road. Turn right, ride for 100 feet, and take the singletrack to your right.

4.9   Pop out onto the paved road again and ride into the gravel parking area for Ruck-A-Chucky (Drivers Flat Road). The singletrack is hiding behind a live oak tree on the other side of the parking area.

5.4   The trail turns into an old gravel road and swings left. At the bottom of the hill, the singletrack swings up and to the right.

5.6   Arrive at Foresthill Road and carefully cross. (*Warning:* Cars are going 60 miles per hour and visibility is limited.) If you get to the other side intact, head south for 200 feet to the beginning of the next segment of the singletrack. An outhouse and picnic table are available. I wish I could say that it was all downhill back to the car, but it isn't. Start off the return trip by climbing through a forest of California black oaks.

6.2   Ride through chaparral.

7.6   It *is* mostly downhill from here. Have fun, but watch carefully for other trail users.

9.0   Cross a well-used dirt road.

9.9   Descend gently through a shady grove of live oaks.

10.2   The trail makes a sharp left-hand turn.

10.4   *Warning:* The trail descends to an opening in a fence. A horizontal bar guards the trail against motorcycles. If you're going too fast and the sun gets in your eyes, you may not see this bar in time. Now carefully cross the road, head south for 100 feet, and turn right onto the singletrack.

10.8   Arrive back at the sign for Foresthill Divide Trail. Bear right to return to your car.

11.5   Back at the car.

Darrington/Salmon Falls Trail

Location:	About 30 minutes south of Auburn on Interstate 80; about 1 hour west of Sacramento.
Distance:	15.6 miles, out-and-back.
Time:	2.5 hours.
Elevation gain:	About 1,400 feet. Lowest elevation is 450 feet; highest elevation is 550 feet.
Tread:	Rocks and hard-packed dirt on a mostly medium-width singletrack.
Aerobic level:	Moderate.
Technical difficulty:	3.
Highlights:	Long, semitechnical singletracks like this are hard to come by. I also enjoyed the constant views of Folsom Lake (a reservoir) and the changing environments of chaparral and oak woodlands. There are many places where you could go for a swim on a hot day. No motorcycles or horses are allowed on the trail—just mountain bikers and hikers.
Land status:	Folsom Lake State Recreation Area.
Maps:	USGS Pilot Hill, Clarksville (the trail is not shown).
Access:	From Auburn on Interstate 80, take the Grass Valley/Placerville/Highway 49 exit south toward Placerville. Lots of Highway 49 signs will lead you through Auburn. At mile 6.8, pass the turnoff to California Highway 193 in the town of Cool and continue on California Highway 49. At mile 10.6, turn right onto Salmon Falls Cutoff (this is the road just after the road to Rattlesnake Bar). After 1 block, turn left onto Salmon Falls Road. At mile 17.2, turn left into the lower parking lot, just before the bridge over the South Fork of the American River. A nominal fee is charged for parking. A clean outhouse, but no water, is available. The trailhead is located across the road, at the upper parking lot.

Darrington/Salmon Falls Trail, Sweetwater Trail

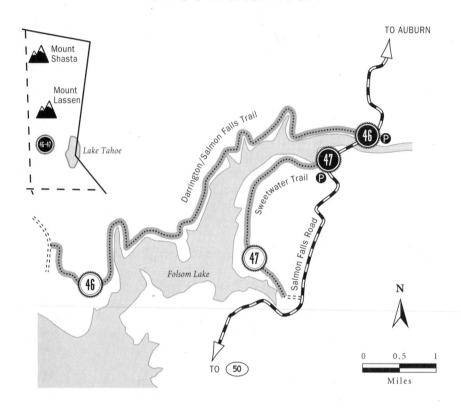

Notes on the trail: This is not a trail for beginning singletrackers. Although portions of it are smooth, most of it is rocky and requires intermediate technical skills. It can get quite hot here in summer. If you choose to ride then, get out early in the morning or wait until early evening. But summer is a busy time on the lake, and lots of boats will be cruising by. Rattlesnakes can also be abundant in this season. Fall is a perfect time to ride. Winter can also be quite nice—between storms. I researched this ride on December 24, and the weather was perfect. Bright red toyon berries can also be seen in late fall and winter. Since the trail is hard-packed sand, it needs only a few days to dry out after a storm. Spring brings high water in the reservoir, green grasses, and wildflowers, but also ticks and poison oak.

Although you don't have to worry about encountering horses or motorcycles on this trail, you do have to be concerned about meeting other mountain bikers and hikers. Please stop and get off your bike when meeting hikers, yield the right-of-way to uphill mountain bikers, and use caution when passing other mountain bikers. One more note: Despite the name, don't expect to see a waterfall on this ride.

The Ride

0.0   The trailhead isn't presently signed, but is marked with a picture of a bicycle. Ignore the heavily eroded trail coming down from above.

0.1   The real trail is the lower one.

0.1 + You then encounter a steep, loose, and rocky climb that's probably better walked than ridden. Below you is Folsom Lake, a reservoir. You're riding through chaparral, almost exclusively chamise, with small needlelike leaves and small white flowers in spring.

0.8   The trail swings inland through a shady live oak forest.

1.0   The singletrack joins an old paved road and traverses along the high-water mark. In late spring and early summer, water will be lapping at the trail. In late summer, fall, and winter, grasses will be growing on the exposed reservoir bottom.

1.5   The dirt road becomes a singletrack again.

1.8   The trees form an arch over the trail. There is some evidence of mountain bikers riding up on the side of the trail. This widens the trail; please don't do it.

2.3   There's some poison oak along the edge of the trail, but as long as you're riding in the middle, you won't hit it.

2.8   As you approach the fence, there appears to be a fork in the trail. Take the more heavily traveled left fork.

3.1   You'll find yourself on top of a knoll. The lake is spreading out more.

3.3   Take the left (lower) fork. Some people have been riding around obstacles. Please don't do this: It widens the trail. Either ride or walk over the obstacles.

3.9   Take the more traveled trail to the right. Keep your weight back on the steep downhill so your rear wheel doesn't slide. The sandy soil is easily eroded.

4.4   Pop out onto an old dirt road, turn left, cross the creek, and jump back onto the singletrack.

5.1   Ignore the trail heading up the hill to your right.

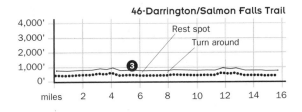

Darrington/Salmon Falls is a great trail.

5.2	You're approaching several tricky places; keep your weight back.
6.2	A small trail heads left about 100 feet to a small peninsula overlooking the reservoir. This is a perfect place for lunch or a break—under the shade of a digger pine. This is also a good end point, if you don't want to continue.
7.5	You hit a low spot and begin to climb on a singletrack that looks like it was built on an old dirt road.
7.8	The singletrack dumps you out onto a dirt road. Unfortunately, this is the end of the singletrack. For some reason, the trip back to the car seemed shorter and easier to me than the trip to this point, so turn around and enjoy it (but watch carefully for other trail users).
15.6	Back at the car.

Sweetwater Trail

Location:	About 30 minutes south of Auburn on Interstate 80; about 1 hour west of Sacramento.
Distance:	5.4 miles, out-and-back.
Time:	1 hour.
Elevation gain:	About 600 feet. Lowest elevation is 450 feet; highest elevation is 575 feet.
Tread:	Mostly smooth, hard-packed, and narrow singletrack.
Aerobic level:	Easy.
Technical difficulty:	3.
Highlights:	A wonderfully built, narrow trail that meanders through forests and chaparral with constant views of Folsom Lake.
Land status:	Auburn State Recreation Area.
Maps:	USGS Pilot Hill (the trail is not shown).
Access:	From Auburn on Interstate 80, take the Grass Valley/Placerville/Highway 49 exit south toward Placerville. Lots of Highway 49 signs will lead you through Auburn. At mile 6.8, pass the turnoff to California Highway 193 in

See map on
Page 208

the town of Cool and continue on California Highway 49. At mile 10.6, turn right onto Salmon Falls Cutoff (this is the road just after the road to Rattlesnake Bar). After 1 block, turn left onto Salmon Falls Road. At mile 17.3, cross the bridge over the South Fork of the American River, then turn right into the parking area. A nominal fee is charged for parking. A clean outhouse, but no water, is available. The trailhead is located at the far end of the parking lot.

Notes on the trail: I was surprised to find such a wonderfully built trail tucked away at the far end of a parking lot. It is narrow and hard-packed; contains dips and turns; traverses dense forests, chaparral, and grassland; and provides many good views of Folsom Lake (actually a reservoir). It's a short trail, but highly enjoyable. Please realize, though, that it's multipurpose, and therefore frequented by hikers and equestrians as well as mountain bikers. This is another of several wonderful trails built by FATRAC (Folsom-Auburn Trail Riders Action Coalition) and the state park system. Please show respect for the trail and for the trail builders by riding or carrying your bikes over obstacles rather than riding around them so you don't widen the trail, and by preventing your rear wheel from sliding by keeping your weight back so that you don't erode the trail. The trail surface is composed of fine soils that tend to retain water. Please wait at least a week after a major storm to let the trail dry out before using it. Show respect for other users by stopping and pulling off the trail whenever you meet them. I've given this trail the same technical rating as the Darrington/Salmon Falls Trail, although it's less rocky; it is much narrower.

The Ride

0.0 Start riding in a dense and shady forest, and cross a fern-lined creek.

0.7 This is the most technical part of the ride. If your technical skills aren't well developed, you may wish to walk your bike through this section.

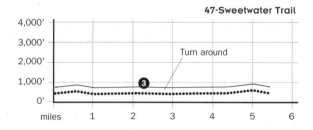

1.0 The trail traverses onto a west-facing slope and tunnels through tall chaparral.

1.1 Hang a right at the fork.

2.4 Ignore the primitive trail coming in from the left and bear right.

2.5 Notice the rare bunchgrasses growing along the trail. These were abundant in California before sheep and cattle were brought in.

2.6 This region stays wet and muddy for a long time after a major storm. Please walk your bike around the mud.

2.7 The singletrack hits a dirt road. That's all there is, folks! Turn around and enjoy the trail in the other direction.

5.4 Back at the car.

Lake Tahoe Area

Lake Tahoe is one of the most beautiful places in the Sierra Nevada, and perhaps in the world. Mountain biking through a variety of life zones with views of the lake as a backdrop is incredibly inspiring.

Many of the rides described in this book follow portions of the Tahoe Rim Trail. This trail was envisioned and built by hikers and equestrians. It's very well built and passes through some of most scenic country in the Sierra Nevada. Most of it is moderately technical (narrow and rocky) and not appropriate for beginning singletrackers. If you cannot ride down steep sections without sliding your rear wheel, or cannot descend a narrow trail without riding off the edge, don't ride these trails. If you cannot ride over water bars and aren't willing to carry your bike over them, don't ride these trails. (Riding around water bars defeats their purpose and contributes to trail erosion.) And as always, ride slowly when visibility is limited, treating other trail users with the utmost of respect. Also consider contributing to trail upkeep or participating in maintenance projects. Information about contributing and participating is available at the trailheads.

Motels and bike shops are available in Truckee, Tahoe City, and King City. Campgrounds are available along California Highway 89. You'll need reservations on weekends, and often during the week.

The rides described in this chapter start north of Lake Tahoe near Truckee and end south of Lake Tahoe near Luther Pass.

Commemorative Emigrant Trail, East from California Highway 89

Location:	On California Highway 89, north of Truckee. Truckee is located on U.S. Highway 80, about 2 hours east of Sacramento and 1 hour west of Reno.
Distance:	20.6 miles, out-and-back.
Time:	3 hours.
Elevation gain:	About 2,000 feet. Lowest elevation is 5,700 feet; highest elevation is 6,100 feet.

Commemorative Emigrant Trail, East from State Highway 89

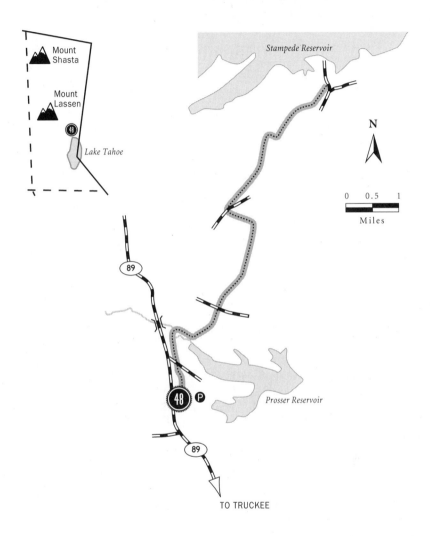

Mount Shasta

Mount Lassen

48

Lake Tahoe

Stampede Reservoir

N

0   0.5   1
Miles

89

48 P

Prosser Reservoir

89

TO TRUCKEE

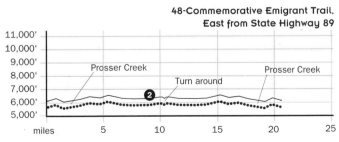

**48-Commemorative Emigrant Trail,
East from State Highway 89**

Prosser Creek

Turn around

Prosser Creek

2

11,000'
10,000'
9,000'
8,000'
7,000'
6,000'
5,000'

miles   5   10   15   20   25

Tread:	All smooth, hard-packed singletrack.
Aerobic level:	Moderate.
Technical difficulty:	2.
Highlights:	No technical skills are necessary, besides being able to ride down a narrow singletrack. You pass through a creek, through meadows, and through forests. Yellow-flowered mule's-ears are abundant in early summer. The trail melts out and dries sooner than other trails in the Lake Tahoe area. No motorized vehicles are allowed on the trail.
Land status:	Tahoe National Forest.
Maps:	USGS Truckee, Hobart Mills, Boca (the trail is not shown).
Access:	From Truckee, drive north 2.8 miles on California Highway 89 and turn right into the Donner Camp picnic area. The trailhead begins in the parking lot. A bathroom, but no water, is available.

Notes on the trail: This ride is at the boundary of high desert and montane forest. It varies from sagebrush to Jeffrey pine forest to white fir forest. The snow melts relatively early here, allowing you to ride this trail before others in the area are ready. Please allow enough time for the trail to dry out, though; it remains muddy for a while after the snow melts, and riding through or around the mud can damage it.

During the summer this ride can be quite hot. Take at least two liters of water and avoid the early afternoon. Even though the mileage is high, the climbs are gentle and limited, allowing you to easily ride the trail out-and-back. Follow the signs to Stampede Reservoir for the return trip, and signs to Prosser Reservoir/Creek on the way back. The trail is well signed in both directions. Beginning riders can choose to ride as far as they wish and head back. The top of the ridge at mile 4.5 is a good place to head back. To keep the map here simple, I didn't include all of the dirt roads.

This trail receives heavy use from a variety of users. To protect it, please don't allow your rear tire to slide on steep downhills and on turns: Keep your weight back or walk your bike when you cannot ride without damaging the trail. Please yield the right-of-way to horses and uphill travelers, and make sure you ride in a nonthreatening manner.

The Ride

0.0 The trail starts off through a meadow. Notice the extensive trail work; it was done to reduce impact on the meadow.

0.4 Cross over the dirt road.

0.8 Arrive at the top of a ridge.

1.0 Pass over the paved road.

1.3 Pass by a dirt road.

1.8 Pass over the dirt road

1.9 Ride downhill to a signed intersection: HIGHWAY 89 BRIDGE CROSSING to the left, and PROSSER CREEK FORD (NOT RECOMMENDED FOR HIKERS AND BICYCLISTS DURING HIGH WATER) to the right. Take the right fork and check out the creek. If it doesn't look safe to cross, or if you don't feel like wading, go back and take the left fork. It will take you out to California Highway 89, across a bridge, and back on the other side of the creek.

2.0 Ford. Look out for slippery rocks!

2.1 Signed intersection: The left fork is coming back from the HIGHWAY 89 BRIDGE CROSSING. Turn right to continue toward Stampede Reservoir.

2.2 The singletrack climbs up to a dirt road, joins it for a few feet, and takes off up the hill to your left.

2.3 Prosser Reservoir comes into view.

2.4 Pass over the paved road.

3.4 Ride through a dense Jeffrey pine forest and pass over the dirt road.

3.6 Notice the birdhouses along the edge of the meadow.

4.1 Pass through a forest of white fir, green-leaf manzanita, and yellow-flowered mule's-ears.

4.3 After a smooth descent, pass over the dirt road.

4.5 Pass over the dirt road and climb.

5.4 Top of a ridge. This is the halfway point, and the trail goes down a lot from here. You have a choice: Keep going or turn back. How are you feeling? (You've climbed a total of 710 feet so far.)

5.6 Pass over the dirt road. A nice downhill is coming up.

6.2 Cross the paved road. Notice how lush the forest is.

6.7 Cross the dirt road and ride down steeply.

7.2 Enjoy this section: straight downhill, with good visibility.

9.2 Cross a gravel road.

9.9 Pass over two parallel dirt roads.

10.1 Signed trail junction: The left fork goes to Captain Roberts Boat Ramp; the right fork continues to the trailtail. There's no water or food at the boat ramp.

10.2 Cross the dirt road. Stampede Reservoir can be seen in the distance.

10.3 Trailtail: Turn around and head back. The signs are easy to follow, and the trip back has more downhill, is more fun, and takes less time.

20.6 You're back at the parking lot, feeling very mellow, I imagine.

Watson Lake from Brockway Summit

Location:	At the top of Brockway Summit, about 10 miles southeast of Truckee on California Highway 267. Truckee is located on U.S. Highway 80, about 2 hours east of Sacramento and about 1 hour west of Reno.
Distance:	12.8 miles, out-and-back.
Time:	2.5 hours.
Elevation gain:	2,100 feet. Lowest elevation is 6,800 feet; highest elevation is 7,500 feet.
Tread:	Singletrack, ranging from smooth and hard-packed to rough, dusty, and rocky.
Aerobic level:	Moderate.
Technical difficulty:	2–3 (mostly 3).
Highlights:	A newly built, technical singletrack leading to a peaceful lake, fir forests and meadows, wildflowers in June and July, swimming. No motorized vehicles are allowed on the trails.
Land status:	National Forest, Lake Tahoe Basin Management Unit.
Maps:	USGS Martis Peak, Truckee, Kings Beach, Tahoe City (the trails are not shown).
Access:	From Truckee, drive southeast on California Highway 267 to Brockway Summit (about 10 miles). The trailhead is 0.5 mile south of Brockway Summit on the right (west) side of the road. No water or bathrooms are available at the trailhead.

Notes on the trail: This trail is part of the Tahoe Rim Trail system. No motorized vehicles are allowed. Bicycles are allowed, though they're not mentioned on the trail signs. Typical of trails through fir forests, it can become very muddy just after the snow melts or just after a summer thunderstorm. Please don't ride the trails when they're muddy. This particular trail is usually dry by mid-June. It can also become quite dusty between thunderstorms. It's ridable until the snow returns in October or November.

Watson Lake from Brockway Summit, Watson Lake from Midway Bridge

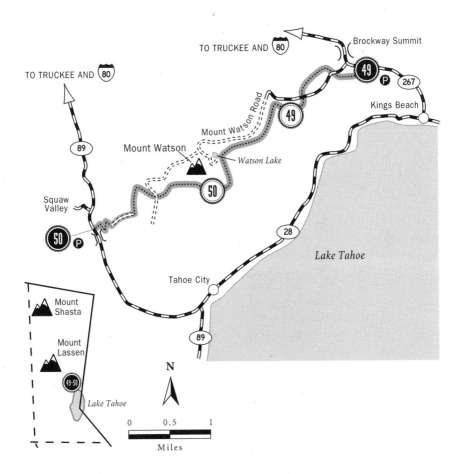

The trail is newly built and contains both smooth and hard-packed, and rocky and technical sections. Please prevent your rear wheel from sliding by keeping your weight back or by walking down steep sections. Two wild-flowers are especially abundant in late June and early July: bright red snow plants and yellow mule's-ears. Watson Lake is shallow, and therefore warms up faster than most lakes. This makes it great for swimming. (But don't forget to check for leeches—especially between your toes.) This trail is heavily used by hikers and equestrians. Please ride in such a manner that you don't catch them by surprise, and yield the right-of-way when you meet them.

The Ride

0.0 Take the single-track leaving from the turnout.

0.1 Note the small blue sign for the Tahoe Rim Trail. You'll be following similar signs throughout this ride.

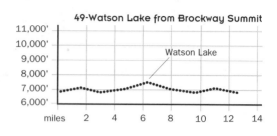

0.3 Continue on this sweet singletrack as it passes over a dirt road and becomes moderately technical.

0.4 The singletrack crosses a paved road (Mount Watson Road) and continues on other side. Prepare for hard climbing and rocky sections. The shrubs with shiny leaves, bunches of small white flowers, and sweet fragrance are ceanothus, also called deerbrush.

1.0 Cross over an unsigned dirt road. The trail becomes hard-packed at this point.

1.7 Intersect the paved road again and ride downhill on a dusty section. Keep your weight back to prevent your rear tire from sliding. Views of Lake Tahoe appear through the trees.

2.0 Continue to ride among white fir trees with bright green needles and grayish bark.

3.1 Gracefully traverse a very rocky and technical section. (Walking your bike is okay!)

3.7 Cross an unsigned dirt road. Notice the yellow-flowered mule's-ears and the bright red snow plants.

3.8 Cross another unsigned dirt road and get ready for a mean uphill climb that's steep and loose, and seems to go on forever.

4.9 Cross over yet another unsigned dirt road. (Old logging roads are abundant in this region.)

5.2 Enter a clearing decorated with a huge incense cedar and mule's-ears as far as the eye can see.

6.4 After a final steep climb, descend to Watson Lake. Don't be surprised to see cars here, because a dirt road also leads to this lake. Don't forget to check your bodies for leeches after swimming (standard procedure after swimming in shallow Sierran lakes). This is your turnaround point.

12.8 Back at the car.

Option: A point-to-point ride with a car shuttle from California Highway 267 to California Highway 89 will increase the mileage to 15.1 miles, but the elevation gain will remain the same. Also, heading for California Highway 89 will give you a lot more downhill. In order to do this, just reverse the ride description for Ride 50, "Watson Lake from Midway Bridge."

Watson Lake from Midway Bridge

Location:	About 10 miles south of Truckee on California Highway 89. Truckee is located on U.S. Highway 80, about 2 hours east of Sacramento and about 1 hour west of Reno.
Distance:	17.4 miles, out-and-back.
Time:	4 hours.
Elevation gain:	2,900 feet. Lowest elevation is 6,000 feet; highest elevation is 7,600 feet.
Tread:	Dirt road, smooth singletracks, rocky and challenging singletracks.
Aerobic level:	Strenuous.
Technical difficulty:	2–3 (mostly 3).
Highlights:	Views of Squaw Valley Ski Area and the entire Lake Tahoe Basin, red and white fir forests, wildflowers in spring (June and July), and some of the best downhill singletrack in the area on your return trip. No motorized vehicles are allowed on the trails.
Land status:	National Forest, Lake Tahoe Basin Management Unit.
Maps:	USGS Kings Beach, Truckee, Tahoe City (the trails are not shown).
Access:	From Truckee, drive south for 8.5 miles on California Highway 89 until you reach the turnoff to Squaw Valley. Continue for another 0.8 mile to Midway Bridge over the Truckee River. Cross the bridge and park on the other side (south). Locate a paved bike trail leaving the parking area on the right (west) side of the highway and heading under the bridge. No water is available at the trailhead, but bottled water can be purchased at the convenience store at the turnoff to Squaw Valley.

See map on Page 219

Notes on the trail: Before you decide not to ride this trail because it's too far or involves too much climbing, please realize that there are several places where you can turn around and enjoy a glorious downhill back to your car. (These shortcuts are marked in the ride with an *.) The first section of this ride is a well-built, hard-packed singletrack that's part of the Western States Trail system and enjoyable to ride in either direction. The turns are gentle and perfectly banked and bermed. The second section is a steep, exposed dirt road. Third comes a newly built part of the Tahoe Rim Trail that's also a pleasure to ride in either direction. Finally you'll ride the fourth section, another part of the Tahoe Rim Trail, which roller-coasters up to Watson Lake. Watson is shallow, so it warms up faster than most lakes. This makes it a good spot for swimming. (But don't forget to check for leeches—especially between your toes.) When you encounter other users on the singletracks, please yield the right-of-way to them by stopping and moving off the trail before they feel compelled to do so. When riding steeply downhill, keep your rear wheel from sliding by keeping your weight back or by walking your bike down these sections.

The Ride

0.0 Take the right fork of the paved bike trail under the bridge to the singletrack marked with a sign for Western States Trail. This singletrack is hard-packed and well built, with wooden bridges over streams and marshy areas. Locals call this trail "Twin Bridges."

0.6 A piped spring is on your right. You're riding through a cool and shady white fir forest, but since the slope faces west, the snow melts off comparatively early.

1.3 Reach the top of the Western States Trail singletrack. Turn left on the dirt road—a continuation of the Western States Trail—and continue to climb.

* If you decide to turn around now, you'll have traveled 1.3 miles and climbed 700 feet, and it's all downhill back to the car.

1.7 Take the left fork (straight ahead).

2.0 Take the right fork (bear right) and attack "The Wall"—a steep, exposed, and often hot climb. When you need a break, turn around and look at the snow-covered peaks of Squaw Valley behind you.

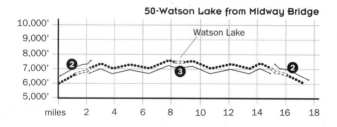

50-Watson Lake from Midway Bridge

2.3. You've climbed 1,000 feet and are resting in the shade of red firs at the top of a pass. The narrow Tahoe Rim Trail singletrack is visible on your left. Once you've caught your breath, continue by climbing up the singletrack.

3.1 You're on top of a ridge with interesting rocks and a view of Lake Tahoe. The singletrack you just rode up is especially fun on the way down. *Warning:* Even though the lake is only 100 feet above you, you'll climb another 800 feet on this trail before reaching it, and you'll have to climb another 700 feet on the way back. But if you're feeling ambitious, pedal on!

* If you decide to turn around now, you'll have traveled 3.1 miles and climbed 1,400 feet. It's downhill all the way back to your car.

3.9 Cross the unsigned dirt road and continue on the Tahoe Rim Trail.

5.2 An unsigned trail enters from the left. Go right to continue on the Tahoe Rim Trail.

6.7 An unsigned trail comes up from the right. Go left to continue on the Tahoe Rim Trail.

7.2 Stop at the rocky outcropping overlooking the entire Lake Tahoe Basin. It's quite a view.

7.9 An unsigned trail comes down from the left. Go straight on the Tahoe Rim Trail.

8.5 You're dumped out onto an unsigned dirt road. Hang a left onto this road.

8.7 Turn right onto the short continuation of the Tahoe Rim Trail singletrack to the lake. Now take a good break at the lake before climbing for another 700 feet to get back to the top of the ridge and then gliding back down to your car. If you go swimming, don't forget to check for leeches.

17.4 Back at the car. Wasn't it a great feeling drifting gracefully down the switchbacks on the Western States Trail?

51

Tahoe Rim Trail to Tahoe City Loop

Location:	In Tahoe City, about 13 miles south of Truckee. Truckee is located on U.S. Highway 80 about 2 hours east of Sacramento and about 1 hour west of Reno.
Distance:	5.5-mile loop.
Time:	1.5 hours.
Elevation gain:	About 1,100 feet. Lowest elevation is 6,150 feet; highest elevation is 7,250 feet.
Tread:	Climb on dirt roads, sometimes smooth and sometimes rocky. Descend on singletrack, mostly rough and rocky, sometimes smooth and hard-packed.
Aerobic level:	Moderate, with one long, strenuous climb.
Technical difficulty:	2–4.
Highlights:	Views of Alpine Meadows and Lake Tahoe, piles of volcanic rocks, bright green mats of pine-mat manzanita covering the forest floor, a narrow and pristine singletrack, rocky technical sections on which to test and improve your skills, green and flower-filled meadows. No motorized vehicles are allowed on the singletrack.
Land status:	National Forest, Lake Tahoe Basin Management Unit, and Burton Creek State Park.
Maps:	USGS Tahoe City (the trail is not shown).
Access:	Turn left onto Fairway Drive just after entering Tahoe City on California Highway 89 from Truckee. If you're entering Tahoe City from the south, turn left onto California Highway 89, then right onto Fairway Drive. After 0.2 mile, park at Fairway Community Center.

Notes on the trail: The first part of the ride is on dirt roads, sometimes gentle and sometimes steep. The second part is on technical singletrack—a portion of the Tahoe Rim Trail. I once tried to ride/push my bike up the

Tahoe Rim Trail to Tahoe City Loop

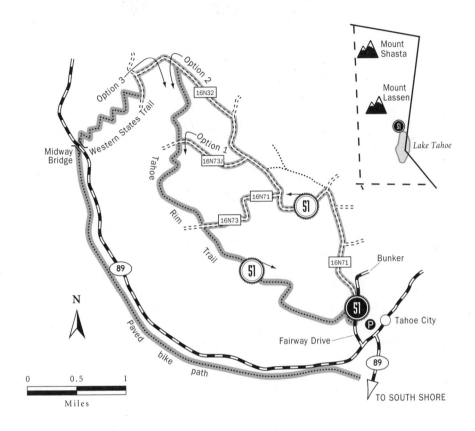

Tahoe Rim Trail from Tahoe City and found it less than enjoyable. This loop will allow you to more easily access this portion of the Tahoe Rim Trail in the downhill direction.

Warning: Sections of the singletrack are quite technical. You'll be riding over rocks of all sizes, some fixed, some loose. With intermediate technical skills, you should be able to ride most of it, and it should be a fun learning experience. With advanced technical skills, you should be able to ride all of it and feel good about your skill level. But if you have only beginning technical skills, plan to walk a lot, learn quickly, or hurt a lot! Expect other trail users on the trail, and ride accordingly. Yield the right-of-way by stopping and moving off the trail when you meet them. Prevent your rear wheel from sliding on steep downhills by keeping your weight back or by walking through these sections.

51-Tahoe Rim Trail to Tahoe City Loop

The Ride

0.0 Go up Fairway Drive.

0.1 Turn left onto Bunker.

0.3 This looks like a driveway, but it quickly turns to dirt; a sign says: FOREST PROTECTION ROAD. Take it.

0.6 This section is steep and rocky, and passes through a mixed forest of incense cedars, Jeffrey pines, sugar pines, and white firs.

0.7 Ignore the dirt road heading off to your left.

0.9 Ignore the dirt road heading off to your left.

0.9+ Major dirt-road intersection: Go straight (bear left), heading north.

1.1 You'll reach a sign for the state park boundary. This is Burton Creek State Park.

1.4 Ignore the road on your right signed: NOT A THROUGH ROAD. The upcoming section of road gets rough and rocky and steep for a while.

1.5 Major intersection. A dirt road forks to the right (east), a dirt road forks to the left (west), and a singletrack goes straight ahead (north). Take the dirt road that forks to the left.

2.1 One sign says: TRAIL, 16N73. The other says DESIGNATED TRAIL. You're on the right road; keep climbing.

2.2 Intersection: Take the dirt road to your left (west), Trail 16N71.

2.5 You've been climbing steeply. A ridge of volcanic boulders is on your right. The road has turned southwest. Keep climbing.

2.8 The forest floor is covered with bright green pine-mat manzanita. You've reached the top of the ridge. Trail 16N73K is a doubletrack and takes off to your left. Singletracks take off both right and left. Take the singletrack to your left, heading south. A sign that says TRAIL CLOSED TO MOTORIZED VEHICLES marks the beginning of this segment of the Tahoe Rim Trail. Lower your seat and get ready for some adventure.

3.2 A gentle downhill introduces you to lots of shalelike rock. Keep your weight back and let go of the brakes when in trouble. When you get a chance, look up for views of Alpine Meadows and Desolation Valley.

3.3 Extensive rock gardens. Depending on your experience and skill level, you may need to walk some of this, but it's surprisingly ridable if you keep your weight back, keep the wheels rolling, and pick good lines through the rocks. Try to look at where you want to go rather than where you don't want to go.

3.6 Enjoy this section of smooth and hard-packed trail, because more rock gardens are coming up.

3.9 More rock gardens, interspersed with smooth and hard-packed trail. Look up for views of Lake Tahoe through the trees.

4.9 Cross a severely eroded dirt road. After this point, the trail is less technical.

5.5 Trailtail. How's your adrenaline level? Want to ride it again? Go ahead!

Options: To lengthen this ride and include more of the Tahoe Rim Trail singletrack, here are three possibilities:

1. Continue on 16N73 for 0.5 mile, then take 16N73J left (west) for 0.9 mile to its junction with the Tahoe Rim Trail.

2. Continue on 16N73 for 1.2 miles and take 16N32 left (west) for 0.9 mile to its junction with the Tahoe Rim Trail.

3. Ride up the Western States Trail from Midway Bridge on California Highway 89 to the top of the saddle, and ride down 16N32 a short distance to its junction with the Tahoe Rim Trail, and return to your car on the paved bike path along the Truckee River.

The Flume Trail Loop

Location:	On the east side of Lake Tahoe, at the intersection of California Highway 28 and U.S. Highway 50.
Distance:	22.7-mile loop.
Time:	4 hours.
Elevation gain:	3,100 feet. Lowest elevation is 6,625 feet; highest elevation is 8,050 feet.
Tread:	Dirt roads and singletrack, mostly smooth and hard-packed, with some sandy sections.
Aerobic level:	Strenuous.
Technical difficulty:	2–3.

Flume Trail Loop

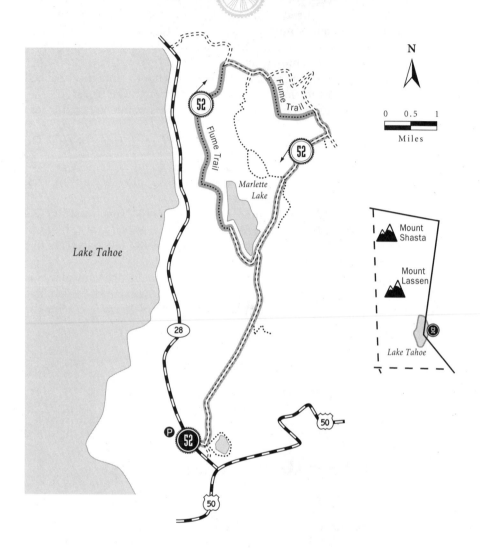

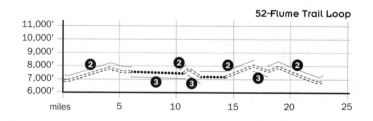

Highlights:	Views of Lake Tahoe and Marlette Lake, wildflowers and aspen groves, some nice singletrack, and a real wilderness feeling. No motorized vehicles are allowed on the singletrack.
Land status:	Spooner Lake State Park.
Maps:	USGS Marlette Lake, Glenbrook. A free and well-drawn topographic map is also available at the entrance station.
Access:	From the east shore of Lake Tahoe or from Carson City, drive to the junction of U.S. Highway 50 and California Highway 28. On California Highway 28, turn into the parking area at the sign for Spooner Lake. Pay a nominal fee for day use and enjoy the real bathroom with flush toilets and sinks. Water is available near the bathroom.

Notes on the trail: I almost didn't include this ride, because it has been written up in so many books, but it's such a classic that the book wouldn't be complete without it. In contrast to most of these rides, there's more dirt road than singletrack, but the singletrack boasts views that can be seen nowhere else, and the dirt road passes through exquisite aspen groves, hillsides and meadows filled with wildflowers, and some pretty wild country. (I came across a mother bear and her cubs on my last ride here.) Most of the Flume Trail has a smooth, sandy, hard-packed surface, but I've rated it class 3 because it's narrow and perched on the side of a cliff. Being able to steer on a narrow singletrack is an essential skill for staying alive here. You'll also need good downhill sand skills at mile 11.1. The descent beginning at mile 16.8 is rutted in places.

Everywhere, you need to be aware of other trail users, because many people use these trails and roads, especially on weekends. The speed limit is 20 miles per hour. Seldom, if ever, would you want to go this fast. (Hitting a sand trap at 20 miles per hour could definitely change your future.) The speed limit around other users or when visibility is limited is 5 miles per hour. Please slow down more than you think you should when near other trail users: Your speed may seem a lot faster and more threatening to them than it does to you. If you meet another user on the singletracks, please stop and yield the right-of-way by moving off the trail.

The Ride

0.0 Locate the sign that reads TO ALL TRAILS and follow its arrow. Shortly thereafter a sign for Marlette Lake and another for North Canyon Trail send you on your way.

0.4 Pass through an aspen forest and prepare yourself for the fact that you'll be climbing for a long time.

On the Flume Trail.

0.9   Please read the instructions that pertain to mountain bikers on the information board.

1.6   Ignore the singletrack on your right to Wild Cat Cabin and continue climbing on the dirt road.

2.9   Ignore the singletrack on the right and continue climbing on the dirt road. The outhouse, by the way, is operational, is supplied with T.P., and doesn't smell all that bad.

3.9   Ignore the singletrack on the right and continue climbing on the dirt road.

4.0   A sign at the top of the hill reminds you to control your speed, avoid locking your brakes, lower your speed around other users, and yield to other users on singletracks. Sounds like good advice.

5.1   Follow the sign for Marlette Lake Dam and Flume Trail by turning sharply left. As you head off, notice the variety of wildflowers growing in this lush area.

6.0   If the water is high, you'll have to portage your bike across the rocks and over to the dam. A sign reads: WELCOME TO THE HISTORIC MARLETTE FLUME TRAIL. You'll be riding on the base of what used to be a wooden water flume. Old boards can be seen along the way. And since it carried water, you'll be descending all the way—gradually. The one exception will be the descent off the dam.

6.1   Cross the outlet stream and climb up onto the flume base. The grand view of the Lake Tahoe Basin for which the flume trail is famous begins almost immediately. Feel free to stop at any time to enjoy the views. To enjoy them fully while riding puts you in danger of becoming part of them.

8.6	Crawl over a huge boulder.
8.7	Carry your bike over a bunch of rocks.
9.0	Crawl over a slippery boulder.
10.5	Carry your bike through the muddy section.
10.6	A singletrack on your left goes out to a view spot. This is a great place to rest or snack or just to enjoy the view.
10.7	The Marlette Flume Trail comes to an end at a dirt road. Moment of decision: If you really loved the singletrack and don't want to climb hard anymore today, turn back now and enjoy the scenery in the other direction. But if you're feeling strong and adventuresome, then turn right, toward the Red House, and pedal steeply up a short distance.
11.1	That was short but nasty!
11.3	Ignore the singletrack to your right and continue riding on the dirt road toward Red House. Now the fun begins! This section is steep and sandy. Pretend you're riding a toboggan.
11.8	At the junction, bear right toward the Red House.
12.0	Turn right onto the Red House flume. Just follow the pipe. This flume trail isn't quite as narrow as the other, but it resembles a singletrack in places. As you pass through a fir forest, watch for bright red snow plants in July.
13.7	The hillside is filled with bright yellow mule's-ears in July.
14.0	Don't turn down toward the Red House. Instead, head straight toward Marlette Lake, following the big pipe.
14.3	The Red House Flume Trail ends at a lush aspen forest with abundant wildflowers. Carry your bike down to and then carefully across the small dam, then up to the dirt road. Ride briefly down to the intersection and turn right to head for Marlette Lake. You're now on Hobart Road. I call this section from here to the top of the ridge "Sucking Air Hill," because that's what you'll be doing for the next 2.5 miles.
14.7	Turn right to continue toward Marlette Lake. You're now climbing through the largest expanse of mule's-ears I've ever seen—anywhere! In July they're particularly colorful.
15.0	A view of Hobart Lake is to your left. Pass above the mule's-ears and climb into a forest.
16.4	Ignore the singletracks coming down from your right and taking off to your left. Continue climbing on the dirt road.
16.8	You're at the top. Did you leave any air for the rest of the world?
17.3	Stop as you pass by the meadow to get a good look at the wildflowers. Watch out for loose sand and ruts as you drift down toward the lake.
18.1	This should be a familiar intersection. Turn sharply left to pump up to the top of the hill (it's all downhill on the other side).

Hopefully a cool afternoon breeze will hit you in the face as you head up.

18.8   The speed limit with good visibility and no one else on the road is 20 miles per hour. Please approach other trail users slowly. Also watch carefully for rocks and ruts. It would be a shame to bring a wonderful ride to a bloody end!

22.7   Back at the car safe and sound—and probably fairly tired, too.

53

Spooner Summit to Bench Overlook

Location:	At Spooner Summit, on U.S. Highway 50, between Lake Tahoe and Carson City.
Distance:	11.8 miles, out-and-back.
Time:	2.5 hours.
Elevation gain:	About 2,200 feet. Lowest elevation is 7,150 feet; highest elevation is 8,800 feet.
Tread:	Singletrack, mostly smooth and hard-packed, some rocky and technical.
Aerobic level:	Moderate.
Technical difficulty:	2–3.
Highlights:	Beautifully built trail, and the best view of the Lake Tahoe Basin around. No motorized vehicles are allowed on this trail.
Land status:	National Forest, Lake Tahoe Basin Management Unit.
Maps:	USGS Glenbrook (the trail is not shown).
Access:	From the east shore of Lake Tahoe, head east on U.S. Highway 50 for about 1 mile from California Highway 28 to the Spooner Summit Rest Area on the right side of the highway. From Carson City, head west on U.S. Highway 50 over Spooner Summit to the Spooner Summit Rest Area on the left side of the highway. There's a paved parking lot and a bathroom, but no water. The trail zigzags up from here.

Spooner Summit to Bench Overlook, Kingsbury Grade to Bench Overlook

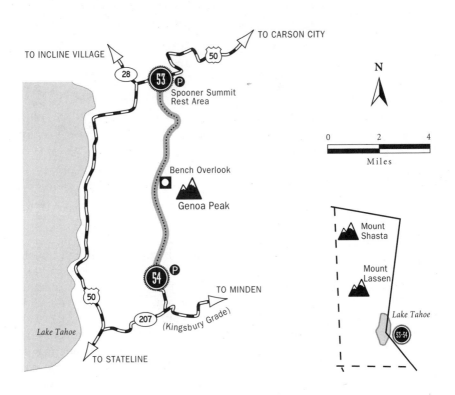

TO CARSON CITY

TO INCLINE VILLAGE

28

53 P

Spooner Summit
Rest Area

50

N

0   2   4
Miles

Bench Overlook

Genoa Peak

54 P

TO MINDEN

50

207

(Kingsbury Grade)

Lake Tahoe

TO STATELINE

Mount Shasta

Mount Lassen

Lake Tahoe

53-54

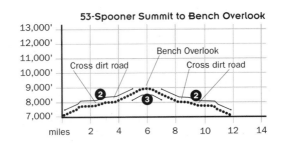

53-Spooner Summit to Bench Overlook

13,000'
12,000'
11,000'
10,000'
9,000'
8,000'
7,000'

Bench Overlook

Cross dirt road   Cross dirt road

2   3   2

miles   2   4   6   8   10   12   14

A rocky, technical section near "The Bench" on Spooner Summit to Bench Overlook.

Notes on the trail: This well-built singletrack zigzags up through forests and emerges on the side of an exposed ridge with the best view of Lake Tahoe I've ever encountered. It's basically all up to the viewpoint, and all down back to the car. On the return trip, keep your rear wheels from sliding to prevent damage to the trail, and keep your speed down when visibility is limited so you don't startle other trail users. Since hikers and equestrians built this trail, please be extra hospitable when meeting or overtaking them. Always yield the right-of-way by stopping and moving off the trail. Eye contact and a big smile contribute greatly to our acceptance on singletracks.

The Ride

0.0   Put yourself in a frame of mind for steady climbing, and begin this ride by zigzagging up through a white fir forest on hard-packed dirt. This trail is perfect a few days after a rain.

1.2   The trail flattens out a bit and is covered with pine needles.

1.8   Jeffrey pines grow on the sunny exposure and white firs grow on the shady exposure. Chinquapin shrubs grow along the trail.

2.4   Cross the dirt road and keep going. A small blue sign reading TAHOE RIM TRAIL leads the way.

2.8   You're dumped onto a doubletrack jeep trail. Head south for about 40 feet to find the continuation of the singletrack.

3.2   You're climbing steeply. The trail is exposed to the afternoon sun. This could hurt on a hot day!

3.6   Cross a well-used dirt road and keep going.

4.0   You're climbing hard.

4.8   You're still climbing hard.

5.0   Enter a thick forest of mountain hemlock. These trees grow in places where snow lingers deep and long. Expect to find snow on the trail in early summer.

5.1   Come out of the dense forest into an open area with views of everything. Continue riding to "The Bench" for the best view.

5.9   "The Bench." I hope you can stay for a while and absorb the view. The opening to Emerald Bay can be seen across Lake Tahoe; the higher peaks in Desolation Wilderness Area are visible behind Emerald Bay. You'll soon find yourself gliding gracefully and peacefully back to the trailhead.

11.9 Back at the trailhead. Don't you feel like you can fly?

Option: If you can arrange a shuttle, you can ride from U.S. Highway 50 to California Highway 207, using this ride description along with Ride 54, but you'll miss out on the wonderful downhill back to the trailhead!

Kingsbury Grade to Bench Overlook

Location:	On California Highway 207 (Kingsbury Grade) near Heavenly Valley North, between Stateline and Minden.	See map on Page 233

Distance:	13.8 miles, out-and-back.
Time:	2.5 hours.
Elevation gain:	About 1,900 feet. Lowest elevation is 7,800 feet; highest elevation is 8,800 feet.
Tread:	All singletrack, mostly smooth and hard-packed with some rocky and technical sections.
Aerobic level:	Moderate.
Technical difficulty:	2–3.

	Fantastic view of the entire Lake Tahoe Basin
Highlights:	at the end of the ride; a great combination of smooth and hard-packed sections, and rocky and technical sections. No motorized vehicles are allowed.
Land status:	National Forest, Lake Tahoe Basin Management Unit.
Maps:	USGS Glenbrook, South Lake Tahoe (the trail is not shown).
Access:	From Stateline at Lake Tahoe, travel east on California Highway 207 (Kingsbury Grade) for 2.8 miles until you reach the sign for Brautovich Park. At this point, turn left onto North Benjamin. If you arrive at the top of Daggett Pass, you've gone too far. From Minden, Nevada, travel west on California Highway 207 (Kingsbury Grade) over Daggett Pass and for another 0.5 mile to the sign for Brautovich Park. At this point, turn left onto North Benjamin. Follow North Benjamin as it turns into Andria Drive. Pass Brautovich Park and continue on Andria Drive until the pavement ends. Limited parking is available. A large sign marks the trailhead. No water or bathrooms are available at the trailhead.

Notes on the trail: I like this trail because it's narrow; it's smooth in some places, technical in others; it passes from a transition forest composed mostly of ponderosa pines, up through a transition forest composed mostly of white firs, and on through a forest composed of red firs, lodgepole pines, western white pines, and mountain hemlocks; it ends up on a high ridge with a fabulous view; and it's fun coming back down. This ride combines rocky technical sections with smooth hard-packed sand, and dense forests with open viewpoints. It ends at "The Bench," which overlooks the entire Lake Tahoe Basin with Emerald Bay and Desolation Valley Wilderness Areas in the distance. It's hard to find trails this nice.

Please don't ride this trail unless you can ride downhill without sliding your rear tire; you can ride over water bars or are willing to carry your bike over them; and you can ride in a way that doesn't frighten other trail users. Yield the right-of-way by stopping and moving off the trail. This is a quality singletrack that bikers are allowed to use. I want to keep it that way! Remember to be extra thoughtful to hikers and equestrians, because they planned and built this wonderful trail.

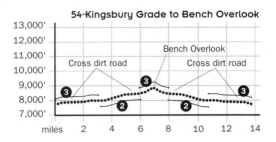

54-Kingsbury Grade to Bench Overlook

The Ride

0.0   This ride begins in granite country. Zigzag up on hard-packed granite sand between granite boulders.

0.5   After reaching a high spot, head downhill on smooth, hard-packed sand with occasional rocky spots.

1.0   Cross over a dirt road in the middle of a red fir and lodgepole pine forest.

2.0   I hope you enjoy roller coasters.

3.0   Until this point, the singletrack has been newly built. Now it follows an old dirt road and continues to wander through a red fir forest.

4.1   The trail again turns into a newly built and perfectly designed singletrack.

4.9   Ride through a dense forest with large granite boulders.

5.6   Cross a dirt road and head for the huge TAHOE RIM TRAIL sign. The rock changes from granite to metamorphic as you climb to "The Bench." The trail also becomes more rocky and technical as it ascends.

6.9   "The Bench." I hope you can stay for a while to absorb the view. The opening to Emerald Bay can be seen across Lake Tahoe; the higher peaks in Desolation Wilderness Area are visible behind Emerald Bay. You'll soon find yourself gliding gracefully and peacefully back toward the trailhead.

13.8   Back at the car.

Option: If you can arrange a shuttle, you can ride from California Highway 207 to U.S. Highway 50 by following this ride description along with Ride 53.

Star Lake from
Heavenly Valley North

Location:	On California Highway 207 (Kingsbury Grade) near Heavenly Valley North, between Stateline and Minden.
Distance:	17.6 miles, out-and-back.
Time:	5 hours.
Elevation gain:	About 2,900 feet. Lowest elevation is 7,500 feet; highest elevation is 9,000 feet.
Tread:	Singletrack, sometimes rocky and technical, sometimes hard-packed and smooth, sometimes sandy and smooth.
Aerobic level:	Strenuous.
Technical difficulty:	2-4 (mostly 3).
Highlights:	Views of Carson Valley, a pristine subalpine lake, a well-built trail, a wonderful wilderness feeling. No motorized vehicles are allowed on this trail.
Land status:	National Forest, Lake Tahoe Basin Management Unit.
Maps:	USGS South Lake Tahoe (the trail is not shown). This trail is shown on the Eldorado National Forest Service map.
Access:	From Stateline or Minden, take California Highway 207 to Daggett Pass and turn south onto Tramway at Heavenly Valley North. At the intersection with Jack Drive, head for Stagecoach Lodge, past a small grocery store and pizza parlor. Take the one-way road to Tahoe Village. The road becomes very narrow. A sign on the left reads: RIDGE TAHOE HEAVENLY STAGECOACH. Continue until you reach a parking lot next to the ski lift. The Tahoe Rim Trail starts next to the Stagecoach ski lift.

Notes on the trail: This section of the Tahoe Rim Trail passes through some of the most scenic and wild country available to mountain bikers in

Star Lake from Heavenly Valley North, Big Meadow to Freel Pass, Big Meadow to Pacific Crest Trail

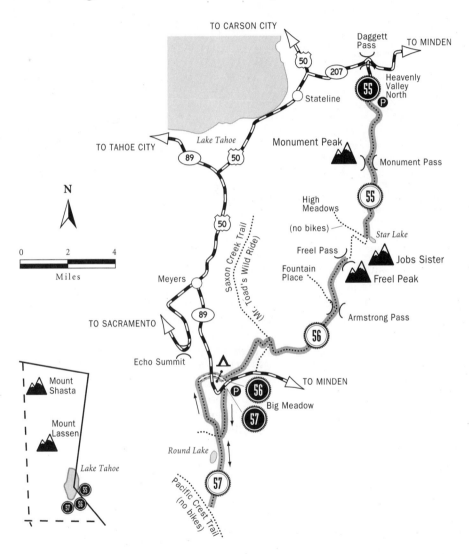

TO CARSON CITY

Daggett Pass

TO MINDEN

50

207

Heavenly Valley North

55
P

Stateline

Monument Peak

Monument Pass

TO TAHOE CITY

Lake Tahoe

89   50

55

High Meadows

(no bikes)

Star Lake

50

Freel Pass

Jobs Sister

Fountain Place

Freel Peak

N

Saxon Creek Trail

(Mr. Toad's Wild Ride)

0   2   4

Miles

Meyers

Armstrong Pass

TO SACRAMENTO

89

56

Echo Summit

TO MINDEN

56

Big Meadow

Mount Shasta

P

57

Mount Lassen

Lake Tahoe

Round Lake

57

55

Pacific Crest Trail (no bikes)

57   56

Star Lake.

California—and it's also one of the least traveled. If you feel left out because you're not allowed to ride your bike in wilderness areas or national parks, then this is the trail for you. After an initial push up a steep slope through sand, the trail takes off through a red fir forest and climbs gently on a slightly technical and hard-packed surface. Just before the top of a ridge, it turns steep and rocky with sharp switchbacks, but on the other side it returns to its easily ridable state. As it approaches Monument Pass, the trail becomes progressively more technical and exposed; most people will be carrying their bikes before the top of the pass. From the top of Monument Pass to Star Lake, the going is smooth and fairly fast. You'll undulate gently up and down while heading in a straight line through the forest to the lake. Views of Desolation Valley and Lake Tahoe are abundant. Star Lake is incredibly beautiful—a pristine, blue, deep, glacial lake at the foot of Jobs Sister. Bring a lunch. If you have the time and energy, you can ride another 2 miles and climb another 800 feet to the top of Freel Pass. And if you can arrange a shuttle, you can ride all the way to California Highway 89—but you'd miss some beautiful downhill on the way back.

This is a new and beautifully built trail. It's hard to find trails this nice! Please don't allow your rear wheel to slide, don't let your bike run off the edge of the trail, and don't ride around water bars. The first mile is frequented by hikers; the remainder of the trail is used mostly by equestrians and mountain bikers. Remember to be extra thoughtful to hikers and equestrians, because they planned and built this wonderful trail. Yield the right-of-way to them by stopping and moving off the trail.

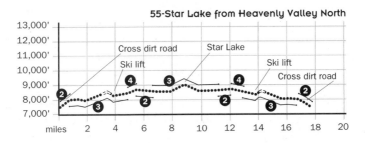

55-Star Lake from Heavenly Valley North

The Ride

0.0 Notice the small blue TAHOE RIM TRAIL sign on the fence. The trail goes up from here.

0.3 Cross the dirt road and continue on the singletrack across the meadow and into the forest.

0.8 The trail changes from class 2 to class 3.

1.3 Top of the ridge. A sign reads: AREA BOUNDARY, DON'T SKI BEYOND THIS POINT! It's okay to ride, though.

1.8 Stream crossing, followed by a steep climb through a red fir forest and large granite boulders.

2.6 Top of the ridge. Smell the bark of the large Jeffrey pines. Butterscotch, yes?

3.4 You're thrown out onto a dirt road. The small blue sign on the far side of the road would lead you to believe that the Tahoe Rim Trail singletrack continues on the other side, but it doesn't. Turn right onto the dirt road and ride downhill. *Warning:* This dirt road is steep and loose, with huge water bars.

3.7 As the dirt road makes a sharp turn to the left, the Tahoe Rim Trail singletrack takes off to the right. Take it, but be careful, because the trail becomes quite exposed in places.

3.8 Cross under the ski lift, ride through the creek, and attack the "helluva steep climb." Thousands of feet below you is Carson Valley. Don't tumble down! Above you, to the right, is Monument Pass.

4.8 The switchbacks are getting tighter and steeper. The rocks are getting larger. At some point, you'll give up and start carrying your bike.

5.0 The trail here is definitely class 4, both up and down.

5.3 The top of Monument Pass. You're surrounded by picturesque rock formations, white bark pines, and mountain mahogany. The trail down from here is sandy—quite fast when it's moist and quite slow when it's dry.

6.6 Stop to enjoy the view of the Desolation Valley Wilderness Area in the distance, with Pyramid Peak on the left. The trail becomes narrower and rockier.

7.2 This is a great little trail built on the side of a cliff with views of Lake Tahoe and Desolation Valley.

7.5 Stop to admire the huge old juniper with Jobs Sister in the background. Star Lake is in the glacial cirque below the peak.

7.8 Cross a tiny stream in a lodgepole pine forest.

8.8 Star Lake. I hope you brought a lunch and have enough time to stay here for a while, because this is one of the most beautiful places you're allowed to bike into. It's tempting to bring a sleeping bag and spend the night . . . maybe next time. You've climbed a total of 2,250 feet to this point, and will climb another 650 feet on your way back.

Options

1. You can bike another 2 miles and climb another 800 feet to the top of Freel Pass for additional views.

2. If you arrange a shuttle, you can then follow the Ride 56 description from Freel Pass to California Highway 89.

Big Meadow to Freel Pass

Location:	South of Lake Tahoe at the top of Luther Pass on California Highway 89, between U.S. Highway 50 and California Highway 88.
Distance:	25.6 miles, out-and-back.
Time:	6 hours.
Elevation gain:	About 4,800 feet. Lowest elevation is 7,200 feet; highest elevation is 9,500 feet.
Tread:	Singletrack, mostly rocky, mostly hard-packed.
Aerobic level:	Strenuous!
Technical difficulty:	3.
Highlights:	Some of the best moderately technical singletrack to be found, meadows filled with wildflowers, views of the Lake Tahoe Basin to the north and the Carson-Iceberg Wilderness to the south, riding into the alpine environment. No motorized vehicles are allowed on the trail.

See map on Page 239

Land status:	National Forest, Lake Tahoe Basin Management Unit.
Maps:	USGS South Lake Tahoe (the trail is not shown). This trail is shown on the Eldorado Forest Service map.
Access:	From the south shore of Lake Tahoe, take California Highway 89 toward Luther Pass. Just before the top of the pass, the road makes a wide left turn. At the end of this turn is a sign for Tahoe Rim Trail/Big Meadows Parking. You'll find a nice outhouse, a large posted map, and a water faucet, but no water.

Notes on the trail: Don't ignore this ride just because it's long and strenuous. It's possible to ride to an overlook about halfway to Freel Pass and turn this into a 13.6-mile moderate ride. (This shortcut is marked in the ride with an *.) Either way, this ride is for people who love moderately technical riding—and would enjoy riding through a subalpine environment with views of both the Lake Tahoe Basin to the north and the Carson-Iceberg Wilderness to the south. The trail itself was constructed by hikers and equestrians as part of the Tahoe Rim Trail system. It was beautifully built and although it will withstand a lot of use, I encourage you to keep your rear wheel from sliding when descending (or walk your bike on steep descents), to avoid riding off the edge of the trail, and to avoid riding around water bars. And since it was planned and built by hikers and equestrians, please be extra hospitable when you meet them on the trail. Yield the right-of-way by stopping and moving off the trail.

Freel Pass is located within an alpine ecosystem—it's one of the few places where you can ride into such an environment. The ride back is mostly downhill, a long technical descent that keeps your mind in the present and your emotions in the positive. It's enough to bring tears to the eyes of a naturalist mountain biker. Take lots of water—or a water filter or purification tablets—on this great out-and-back ride

The Ride

0.0 Head east out of the parking lot and continue straight on the small paved road through the open gate. At the beginning of the Tahoe Rim Trail is a sign for Grass Lake, Armstrong Pass, and Star Lake.

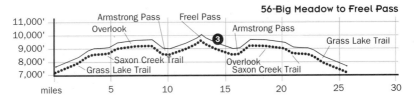

56-Big Meadow to Freel Pass

0.5 Creek crossing on a slippery log—be careful. The trail is hard-packed sand passing through open pine forests, aspen groves, and wildflower gardens—perfect.

2.1 Trail junction; bear left to continue to Freel Pass. At this point, the trail changes from class 2 to class 3. Prepare for a nasty climb.

3.7 Views of Lake Tahoe are showing up through the trees. Enjoy the roller coaster.

4.7 Trail junction. The left fork leads down the Saxon Creek Trail, otherwise known as "Mr. Toad's Wild Ride." I don't recommend that beginner or intermediate riders use this trail: It takes an expert rider to avoid damaging it. Bear right to continue toward Freel Pass.

5.6 A flower-filled and very green meadow is appearing on your left. Snow lingers late in this region.

6.0 Another beautiful meadow with wildflowers and lodgepole pine trees.

6.8 You suddenly find yourself at an overlook with an expansive view of the Lake Tahoe Basin. Freel Pass is appearing in the distance toward the east. The multitrunked trees are white-bark pines—a subalpine species.

* This is a good turn around point if you don't want to ride all the way to Freel Pass.

7.3 You're passing through a high desert meadow filled with wildflowers and with a view of the Carson-Iceberg Wilderness to the south. From here to mile 8.7, you'll roller-coaster along the top of a ridge.

8.7 It's all downhill to Armstrong Pass. Get ready for a joyful ride.

9.6 Armstrong Pass. To the left is a turnoff to Fountain Place. (It's a wonderful forest service trail, but it ends by dumping you out onto private property.)

9.7 To the right is a turnoff to Horse Meadow. (I haven't ridden this, but I understand that it's very steep.) Continue straight to Freel Pass. Gear up, because you have 1,000 feet left to climb.

11.8 The trail is getting steeper. There are juniper trees and loud, obnoxious Clark's crows. There's also water, but be sure to filter or purify it. From here, zigzag all the way to the top.

12.8 You made it to the top of Freel Pass—no small feat. If you have any energy left, and if your brain is working at this altitude, notice the pillars of granite rocks and white-bark pine shrubs. Please don't walk off the trail—some rare alpine plants grow up here. As you head back, keep an eye out for other trail users, be gentle with the trail, and enjoy one of the best downhill experiences in California.

25.6 Arrive back at your car feeling tired but emotionally refreshed.

Options

1. If you're not ready to ride back yet when you reach the top of Freel Pass, you may wish to ride for another couple of miles to Star Lake. But be warned that you'll have to climb back up about 800 feet.

2. You can also ride over Freel Pass and on to Heavenly Valley North, as described in Ride 55, provided that you've arranged for a shuttle.

Big Meadow to Pacific Crest Trail

Location:	South of Lake Tahoe at the top of Luther Pass on California Highway 89, between U.S. Highway 50 and California Highway 88.
Distance:	13.5-mile loop.
Time:	3 hours.
Elevation gain:	About 2,600 feet. Lowest elevation is 6,600 feet; highest elevation is 8,400 feet.
Tread:	From smooth pavement to rough and rocky singletrack.
Aerobic level:	Moderate, with one strenuous climb.
Technical difficulty:	1–4 (mostly 3).
Highlights:	A beautiful lake, strange volcanic rocks, wildflowers, aspen groves. No motorized vehicles are allowed on the singletrack.
Land status:	National Forest, Lake Tahoe Basin Management Unit.
Maps:	USGS South Lake Tahoe (the trail is not shown). This trail is shown on the Eldorado National Forest Service map.
Access:	From the south shore of Lake Tahoe, take California Highway 89 toward Luther Pass. Just before the top of the pass, the road makes a wide left turn. At the end of this turn is a sign for Tahoe Rim Trail/Big Meadows parking. You'll find a nice outhouse, a large posted map, and a water faucet, but no water.

See map on Page 239

Notes on the trail: This trail passes Round Lake and dead-ends at the Pacific Crest Trail. It passes mostly through forests but also through meadows and beside a lake. From the trailhead to Round Lake, the trail is heavily used and quite wide in places, but from the lake to the Pacific Crest Trail, it's more primitive. You're basically riding into a glacial lake basin with the volcanic rim of the cirque above and in front of you. Along the way you'll pass by many huge volcanic boulders. After returning to Round Lake, you ride down a class 3+ trail to the trip's low point before returning to your car via a narrow paved road. Except for the region beyond Round Lake, this trail is heavily used by hikers and equestrians. This provides a great opportunity to spread goodwill by riding in a nonthreatening and noneroding manner. Yield the right-of-way by stopping and moving off the trail. Prevent your rear wheel from sliding by keeping your weight back. Round Lake is a good place to picnic and to swim.

The Ride

0.0 From the parking area for the Tahoe Rim Trail, follow the TAHOE RIM TRAIL sign that leads you west out of the parking lot and onto a short stretch of singletrack.

0.2 Cross California Highway 89 and head for the well-used singletrack. It's rocky but ridable.

0.4 Confusing spot. The trail appears to travel left, but you should head straight up, in a southerly direction.

0.6 Gate. Just after the gate is a fork. Turn right toward Big Meadow, not left to Scott's Lake.

2.0 Pass through another gate.

2.1 A wonderful downhill through a red fir forest on a hard-packed surface.

2.4 Trail junction. Turn left (Round Lake). On the return trip you'll be taking the right fork to Christmas Valley.

2.6 Ride through an old-growth red fir forest steeply uphill among large boulders of volcanic conglomerate. One short section probably won't be ridable. Just before the lake you'll see lots of snow plants—deep red and waxy looking.

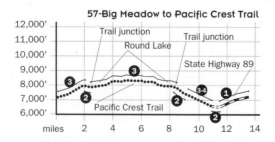

Noah at Round Lake on the Big Meadow to Pacific Crest Trail.

3.0	You're looking at Round Lake. Do you have time for a swim? When you're ready, follow the trail around the left (east) side of the lake. At first it zigzags up through some pretty rocky stuff.
3.5	Now it becomes narrow, smoother, and very enjoyable.
3.9	The top of a ridge, with big aspen trees.
4.4	A meadow with a stream: wildflower heaven.
5.3	The trail continues to roller-coaster between meadows and ridges.
5.5	Arrive at the Pacific Crest Trail. This is the end of the line for mountain bikes. Take in the views of the high country, turn around, and head back to Round Lake.
7.7	Back at Round Lake.
8.3	Trail junction. Head left, for Christmas Valley.
8.5	Don't take the trail to Dardanelles Lake.
9.2	Enter the remainder of the singletrack with alternating class 3 and class 4 sections, containing the 3 Rs: rocks, ruts, and roots.
9.8	Get ready for a very steep downhill, after which there are no more class 4 sections.
10.9	End of the singletrack. Head down the dirt road.
11.4	Turn right onto the paved road and begin to head back up.
12.4	Carefully cross California Highway 89 and head for the gated, paved, narrow road on the other side.
13.1	Pass through the gate and ride past the campground.
13.5	Back at the parking lot.

North of Yosemite

This section includes rides found along California Highways 50, 88, 12, 4, 49, 108, 120, and 140, in that order, from Lake Tahoe to Yosemite. All these highways enter or pass over the Sierra Nevada.

Even though the area is quite large, few high-quality singletracks were found that allow mountain bikes. At higher altitudes, much of this land is within wilderness areas. The rides that are open to mountain bikes receive a lot of snow in winter, and need some time to dry out after the snow melts. And many of the "trails" outside the wilderness areas that do permit mountain bikes are either dirt roads, badly eroded, or poorly maintained and therefore very difficult to ride.

Most of the maintained singletracks that allow mountain bikes are in the foothills—administered by the U.S. Army Corps of Engineers and U.S. Bureau of Reclamation. I appreciate their progressive view of allowing mountain biking on most of their singletracks. We can show our appreciation by minimizing our impact and conflicts while riding, and by writing them to thank them or by stopping by a ranger station to thank them in person. Riding here is possible year-round, but please let the trails dry out for a few days after major storms. Summers tend to be very hot, spring and fall days are usually perfect, but I've also enjoyed warm days in midwinter.

Sly Park Loop

Location:	About 60 miles and 1 hour west of Sacramento via Interstate 50 and Sly Park Road.
Distance:	8.8-mile loop.
Time:	2 hours.
Elevation gain:	About 750 feet. Lowest elevation is 3,350 feet; highest elevation is 3,400 feet.
Tread:	Hard-packed and sometimes rocky singletrack, dirt roads, and paved roads.
Aerobic level:	Moderate.
Technical difficulty:	1–3 (mostly 3).

Sly Park Loop

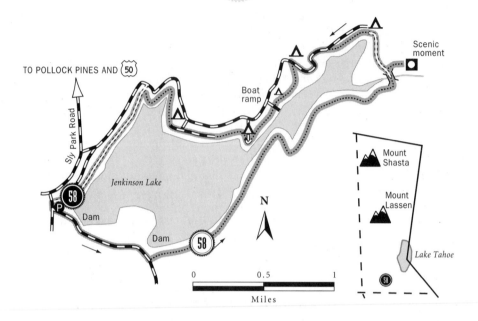

Highlights: A narrow and technical singletrack, dogwoods in bloom in spring and in color in fall, wildflowers in spring, riding alongside Jenkinson Lake, and a surprise scenic moment.

Land status: Sly Park Recreation Area, Bureau of Reclamation.

Maps: USGS Sly Park.

Access: From Interstate 50, take the Sly Park Road exit, 13.8 miles east of Placerville, and head south. Drive for another 4.3 miles, turn left into the Sly Park Recreation Area, and pay a nominal day-use fee. After entering the park, veer to the right toward the boat launch. Park near the bathroom and picnic tables next to the boat-launch parking lot. Water is also available.

Notes on the trail: After a brief interlude on a paved road, you'll enjoy several miles of narrow singletrack requiring strong intermediate technical skills. This singletrack traverses a north-facing slope through a shady forest of dogwoods, ponderosa pines, and Douglas firs just above the highwater mark. You'll then cross a bridge over the inlet creek and ride upstream for a short distance for a surprise scenic moment. The remainder of the ride is on several short lengths of dirt road, singletrack, and paved road, passing through campgrounds and picnic areas. The first part of the ride is relatively unpopulated; the second part is highly populated. Although it feels good to ride all the way around the lake, if you don't enjoy populated areas, you may wish to do this ride as an out-and-back, to the surprise scenic moment and back. If possible, I advise riding these trails during the week in summer months; weekends are quite crowded. Campgrounds are available, and can be reserved (see the appendix).

The Ride

0.0 Don't ride up the singletrack, which is reserved for equestrians. Instead, ride south across the parking lot and take the steep dirt road heading up the hill.

0.3 Reach the paved-road junction and turn onto the paved road that takes off to your left. Ride across two dams. Be careful of logging trucks.

1.0 Just past the second dam, a sign informs you that the South Shore Hiking Trail begins here. It also tells you that the trail is for advanced bikers. This is a bit of an exaggeration: Strong intermediate technical skills are needed, but not advanced skills.

1.8 Keep your weight back to avoid sliding on this downhill section. The horse trail and hiker/biker trail come close to each other. Be sure to stay on the hiker/biker trail by bearing left.

2.4 The trail becomes more technical, with more rocks and roots.

2.8 The two trails merge into one multiuse pathway.

2.9 Pass over a wooden bridge. The multiuse trail splits in two again. Bear left.

3.5 A fall could hurt here! If you're not absolutely confident, you should walk through this section.

3.6 The hiker/biker trail now splits into two separate trails. Take the biker trail to the right.

3.6 + The trails merge at the bottom of the hill.

3.7 The hiker/biker and equestrian trails come together into a multiuse trail. Pass through a small meadow filled with wildflowers in early summer.

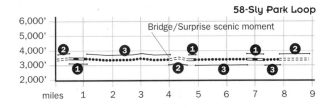

3.9 Ride on a wide bridge over the inlet creek and turn right to visit the surprise scenic event.

4.0 Wow! It's actually human-made, but quite scenic and unexpected. This is a great place for a picnic. When you're finished, return to the wide bridge over the inlet creek.

4.1 Now push your bike up the steep and rocky dirt road to your right.

4.3 Top out at 3,400 feet.

4.4 Continue on the dirt road by bearing right. Don't take any of the trails that lead down to the lake; bikes are not allowed.

4.6 A post indicates a multiuse trail for hikers, bikers, and equestrians. From now on the trail will be more populated with other users.

4.7 Walk your bike over the wooden bridge and ride on the pavement through the campground.

4.9 At the intersection, turn left onto the paved road.

5.4 Take the Chimney-Sierra Trail at outhouse 24. This is a sweet little singletrack.

5.8 Ride over a wooden plank bridge.

5.9 A boat ramp is below you. Ride up and turn left at the steps leading to the bathroom.

6.0 Cross the paved road leading to the boat ramp and jump back onto the singletrack. Ignore the paths leading down to the water.

6.5 You're guided through the campground by carsonite posts. Pass a peninsula on your left and turn onto the singletrack beside campsite 68.

6.7 Pass over a wooden bridge.

6.8 You're back on the asphalt. Turn left into Pinecone Campground.

7.3 Turn left between campsites 10 and 11 and ride through the campground to the awaiting singletrack.

7.5 A wooden bridge followed by a steep climb. Turn left onto the dirt road toward the picnic area, and turn right onto the singletrack.

7.8 Heads up for a class 4 maneuver!

7.8 + Pass over the bridge and turn left. Follow the wide dirt path through the picnic area all the way to where you began the ride.

8.8 You're back where you started.

Silver Fork Loop

Location: About 2 hours and 85 miles southeast of Sacramento via Interstate 50 and Silver Fork Road.

Distance: 9.4-mile loop.

Time: 3 hours.

Elevation gain: About 1,400 feet. Lowest elevation is 5,500 feet; highest elevation is 6,675 feet.

Tread: Hard-packed dirt, loose sand, rocks.

Aerobic level: Moderate, with one long, strenuous climb.

Technical difficulty: 3+

Highlights: Rugged high Sierra trails, two scenic streams cascading among granite boulders, meadows, old-growth forests.

Land status: El Dorado National Forest.

Maps: USGS Tragedy Spring.

Access: At Kyburtz, 30 miles east of Placerville on Interstate 50, turn right onto Silver Fork Road. This road is narrow, but paved. Drive 9.2 miles to the Silver Fork bridge. Park on either side of the bridge. Primitive campsites are available here (without bathrooms or water); a fully equipped campground is available 0.25 mile back.

Notes on the trail: This ride is on typical Sierra Nevada trails. They were probably created by deer, Native Americans, sheepherders, cattle owners, miners, and hikers—in that order. Few were planned and built, so sections of them are in erosion-prone areas. Waiting until July will ensure that the trails have dried out and the stream crossing is safe.

Expect to find a variety of rocks and sand in granite country. If you have strong intermediate skills, you'll be riding more than walking, but you'll definitely be walking some. You'll also come back a better rider than when you left. These trails are used by hikers, equestrians, motorcyclists, mountain bikers, and cows. Please be especially careful around hikers and equestrians, and yield them the right-of-way by moving off the trail and waiting until they've passed. Since some of the horses haven't encountered mountain bikes before, speak to them as they approach so they realize you're human. Please also walk your bike down anything that you

Silver Fork Loop

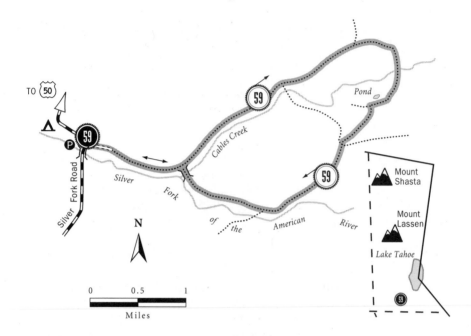

cannot ride without sliding to minimize erosion. And finally, if you're looking for fast trails, this is not the ride for you. Instead it's an opportunity for you to ride and push slowly, enjoying the scenery, the sound of the streams, and the wilderness.

The Ride

0.0 Begin at the sign for Cables Creek Trail. The first section is a narrow, rocky dirt road.

0.2 Bear left at the unsigned junction.

0.4 The trail narrows to a singletrack and becomes quite rocky.

0.7 Pass by a large granite slab.

0.9 Ride along the Silver Fork (of the American River).

1.0 Pass through the cattle gate and close it behind you. The creeks have now split; you're riding along Cables Creek.

1.3 A wooden post announces that you're heading to Government Meadow, 2 miles ahead. You're now riding in a clockwise loop, and will return to this spot later via the trail to the right. But for

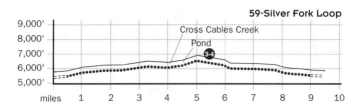

now, continue to head for Government Meadow. Ride through a dense forest of incense cedars and white firs.

2.0 Enjoy the very narrow singletrack through a very green meadow. And another meadow. And another.

2.4 Continue straight at the trail junction, toward Jake Schneider Meadow.

2.8 Climb steeply!

3.3 Trail junction. Turn right, toward Government Meadow.

3.7 Arrive at the lush Government Meadow.

3.8 Watch for bright red snow plants in this dense white fir forest.

4.0 Cross Cables Creek after making sure it's safe. This next section of trail involves a lot of climbing, but it's pleasantly narrow and untraveled. Unfortunately, the trees have not been removed from it for many years.

4.1 Head around to the left of the large fallen tree and bear right to find the trail. Ignore the small trail that heads off to the left.

4.4 Stop to enjoy a shallow pond filled with rushes and surrounded by hundreds of large blue dragonflies.

4.4+ It's tempting to take the right fork down, but don't do it: It descends steeply to a dead end. Instead, head left and up on the more traveled trail. Motorcycle use is evident.

4.7 The switchbacks are getting really steep.

4.8 An indistinct trail heads down to the right. Bear left and keep climbing toward the southwest.

5.0 Major intersection. According to the sign, the left fork leads 2 miles to California Highway 88. Take the right fork toward Silver Fork. This is the high point of the ride; it's time to head down.

5.4 The trail becomes smoother and more ridable . . .

5.8 . . . until it gets rocky again.

6.1 Arrive at Silver Fork. This is a perfect place to take a break.

6.5 At the signed intersection, bear right toward Cables Creek.

7.2 Get ready to head steeply down some switchbacks.

7.9 Cross Cables Creek on a large, modern bridge. Below is a great place to take a swim.

8.0 You've completed the loop and are back where you were at mile 1.3. Turn left and head back down to your car.

9.4 Arrive back at the Silver Fork bridge.

The Hogan Trail

Location:	About 45 minutes east of Stockton, along the north shore of New Hogan Lake (a reservoir), near the town of Valley Springs.
Distance:	10.5 miles, out-and-back.
Time:	2.5 hours.
Elevation gain:	About 1,800 feet. Lowest elevation is 650 feet; highest elevation is 850 feet.
Tread:	Rocky and hard-packed singletrack.
Aerobic level:	Moderate.
Technical difficulty:	Mostly 3 +.
Highlights:	It's rare to find a narrow, moderate to highly technical singletrack built by mountain bikers. No horses or motorcycles are allowed.
Land status:	U.S. Army Corps of Engineers.
Maps:	USGS Valley Springs (the trails are not shown).
Access:	From the north on California Highway 99, take the California Highway 12 East exit in Lodi. From the south on California Highway 99, take the California Highway 26 East exit in Stockton. In both cases, follow signs for San Andreas until you reach the community of Valley Springs. Again, head for San Andreas as you leave Valley Springs. Just outside the city limits of Valley Springs, turn right onto Lime Creek Road/St. Petersburg Road. After 0.8 miles, turn right onto South St. Petersburg Road. Follow the signs to Acorn East Campground and park in the day-use lot. Water and a bathroom are available. (You can also park in Oak Knoll Campground during the recreation season, May through September.)

Notes on the trail: If you're looking to ride the shortest, easiest route between two points, don't ride this trail. It purposefully meanders to maximize the mileage, climbs, and descents. Likewise, if you have only beginning technical skills, this isn't the trail for you. I've rated the technical level as 3 +, meaning the ride is composed of alternating class 3 and class

The Hogan Trail

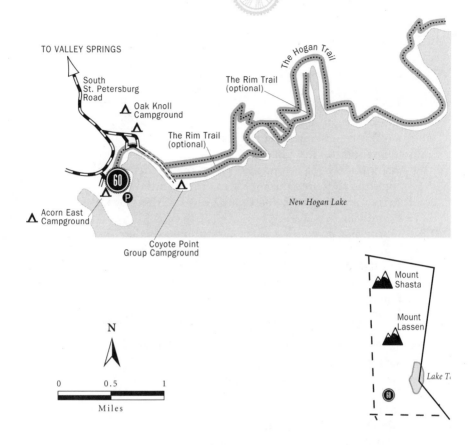

4 sections. With strong intermediate skills you should be able to ride the majority of it. Without such skills you'll be walking a lot, running the risk of getting hurt, and risking damage to the trail. Many thanks to the members of SCAAB (Stockton Cyclists Are Always Bleeding) for building (and continuing to build) this trail. The challenging Hogan Trail meanders above the easy Rim Trail, sometimes following it for short distances. Both trails are part of the Coyote Point Mountain Bike Trail system.

It's very hot here during the summer, and the lake is filled with boats. If you must ride in summer, avoid afternoons. But the crowds leave in October and don't return until May. I suggest riding in late fall, winter, and early spring.

The Ride

0.0 The trailhead is at the north end of the day-use parking lot and marked with a picture of a bike. It begins as a gravel road.

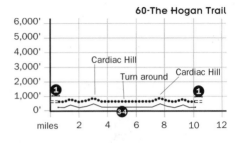
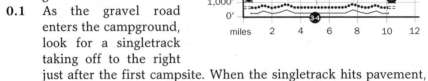

0.1 As the gravel road enters the campground, look for a singletrack taking off to the right just after the first campsite. When the singletrack hits pavement, continue to follow the bike signs through the campground.

0.4 Arrive at the gravel road and head for the Coyote Point Group Camp.

0.5 Notice the sign with a black diamond on the left side of the gravel road. This is the beginning of the Hogan Trail. Head uphill through a "forest" of chamise.

0.5 + Bear right onto the more traveled singletrack, toward the digger pine.

0.6 If you ride over a small wooden bridge and then pass a large digger pine, you're on the right trail.

0.8 Take the left fork and climb steeply. It's presently marked with a sign that reads: SINGLETRACK and SCAAB.

0.8 + Keep your weight back on the steep descent.

1.0 Ride over a small wooden bridge, through a grassy area, and climb to the top of the ridge.

1.4 Get ready to ride down.

1.4 + Stop for a good view of the reservoir.

1.6 Bear left at the fork.

2.0 Meet the Rim Trail for just a moment, then veer left to continue on the Hogan Trail.

2.2 Join the Rim Trail for about 50 feet and head up to the left again.

2.5 Rejoin the Rim Trail about 50 feet from where you left it at mile 2.2, then head up to the left again in about 50 feet.

2.9 Either fork will take you to the top of the knoll, but the left one is more gradual.

3.0 You've made it to the top of Cardiac Hill. The best part of the ride is just ahead—the switchbacks down from the top of this hill. They're built to maximize the trip down.

3.6 A sharp right turn would take you to the end of the Rim Trail, so continue straight ahead.

4.7 Take the switchbacks down to the right. They're very tight, but very sweet.

4.9	You've left the chaparral behind and are now riding through oak trees and grassland. There's also poison oak along the trail in this section.
5.3	The trail currently stops here, but is being continually extended. Come back again soon! Have a snack, go for a swim, if you wish, and head back as soon as you're rested.
7.0	Now you need to make a choice. You can bail out by taking the left fork to the Rim Trail and heading back the easy way, or you can go back the way you came by bearing right and heading up the switchbacks to the top of Cardiac Hill. It might be tempting to take the easy way out, but the Hogan Trail is a lot of fun on the way back, and the climbs aren't that long.
7.6	See, the climb wasn't that bad. Again, there are two or three ways down off the top, but they all end up in the same place.
7.8	You're back on the Rim Trail.
8.0	You see three plastic posts, about 50 feet apart. Again, it's tempting to pass them up by staying on the Rim Trail, but turning right at the first one, riding the loop, and rejoining the Rim Trail at the second one is much more fun.
8.4	You're at the second plastic post, after riding the loop. Less than 50 feet ahead of you is another post and another continuation of the Hogan Trail.
8.9	Ignore the trail swinging in from the left and continue to climb to the top of the ridge. Enjoy the switchbacks down from the top.
9.5	Cross over the little wooden bridge in the grassy area.
10.0	Hit the gravel road and head for the parking lot.
10.5	Back at the car.

Option: If you'd rather ride a trail that's easy, both aerobically and technically, then try the Rim Trail. At mile 0.7, a small sign with a bike on it will direct you to turn left onto the medium-width singletrack. A number of narrow singletracks will take off to the left along this trail. In every case, bear right to remain on the wider and smoother singletrack.

Lake Alpine Loop

Location:	About 1 hour west of Markleeville and about 2 hours east of Stockton on California Highway 4.
Distance:	5.4-mile loop.
Time:	1.5 hours.
Elevation gain:	About 1,000 feet. Lowest elevation is 7,075 feet; highest elevation is 7,600 feet.
Tread:	Mostly loose and rocky.
Aerobic level:	Moderate.
Technical difficulty:	1–4 (mostly 3).
Highlights:	Views of Lake Alpine, technically challenging singletrack.
Land status:	Stanislaus National Forest.
Maps:	USGS Tamarack, Spicer Meadow Reservoir. A free topographic map of this ride is also available from the Stanislaus National Forest, Calaveras Ranger District.
Access:	From Markleeville or from Stockton, take the Lake Alpine East Shore exit off California Highway 4. Drive 100 yards and park at the first bathroom. Flush toilets and water are available.

Notes on the trail: Even though this is listed as an easy ride aerobically, it demands solid technical skills to avoid injuring yourself, your bike, others, or the trail. You must be willing to walk your bike through sections that you cannot ride without sliding. This is not for beginning singletrackers, and certainly not for beginning mountain bikers! Many people use these trails: other mountain bikers of varying abilities, hikers, equestrians, runners. You must ride slowly, be very observant, and be willing to yield the right-of-way to all other users. I suggest avoiding weekends. I also suggest waiting until after July 15 to ride these trails, to give them time to dry out. A forest service map has been published showing an additional, small loop around the campgrounds, across California Highway 4, and back to the Bee Gulch trailhead. I haven't been able to locate all of this trail and don't recommend it.

Lake Alpine Loop

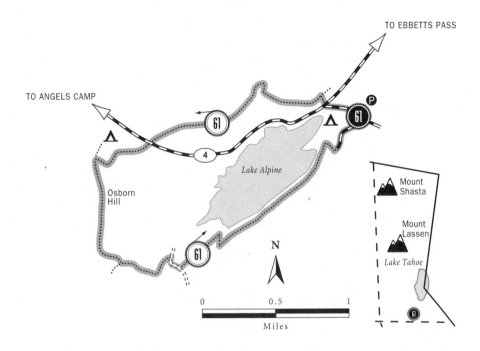

TO EBBETTS PASS

TO ANGELS CAMP

61

61

P

4

Lake Alpine

Osborn
Hill

61

N

Mount
Shasta

Mount
Lassen

Lake Tahoe

61

0   0.5   1

Miles

The Ride

0.0 Go back out to California Highway 4 and carefully cross the road to the Bee Gulch Trailhead. Expect to do some climbing.

0.3 If you can't ride through the rocky sections or over the water bars, please get off your bike and walk it over them rather than riding around them.

0.6 Creek crossing and steep climb up to a water tank. At the trail junction, turn left onto the Alpine Bypass Trail (no sign currently).

0.7 Head down through a forest of very old lodgepole pines

1.2 Please walk your bike through the spring-fed muddy section.

1.3 Cross a doubletrack and keep going. You're paralleling the highway, but just far enough away that all you can hear is the sound of the wind in the trees.

1.5 Pass some cabins on the left. The trail is smooth and it's tempting to ride fast, but the visibility is poor and many hikers and equestrians use this trail. Just drift down gently.

1.7 Abruptly hit California Highway 4. Please cross very carefully. A sign on the other side tells you that you'll be riding on the Osborne Ridge Trail.

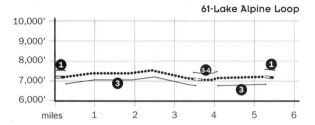

61-Lake Alpine Loop

1.9 Cross a small paved road and keep pedaling up the singletrack. After 100 feet, turn left onto a narrower singletrack. (The wider singletrack goes to Silvertip Campground.) Climb through a red fir (silvertip) forest.

2.1 At a junction, bear left to continue on the Osborne Ridge Trail. *Warning:* Don't continue to climb onto this exposed ridge if thunderstorms are building. The bright yellow clumps of flowers are sulfur plant, a member of the buckwheat family. The light lavender clumps are pennyroyal. If you squeeze a leaf, you can appreciate the fact that it's a member of the mint family. (If you're pregnant, do not taste the leaves. Native American women used these leaves as an abortifacient.)

2.4 Look closely at the bedrock and you'll realize that it's a volcanic conglomerate with larger rocks glued together with finer volcanic material. The next descent is steep, rocky, and loose.

3.1 A fence marks the bottom. If the gate was open, leave it open. If it was closed, please close it. In mid- to late summer, this small meadow is filled with small white flower heads floating above the grasses: yampah. Turn left onto the Emigrant Trail and be prepared for some challenging rocky sections.

3.5 Turn right onto the dirt (rock) road. A sign for the Lakeshore Trail will direct you.

3.6 Turn left onto the singletrack (the Lakeshore Trail). Begin a class 3+ section that may require you to carry or push your bike about half the time. Be sure to stop and get off the trail if you meet someone.

3.9 Cross the stream. The fragrant bunches of pink flowers are spirea, in the rose family.

4.0 Bear right to continue on the larger singletrack.

4.2 A good view of the lake to your left.

4.3 Back to class 3 with a hard-packed and fairly smooth trail that undulates up and down through the forest.

4.9 A trail takes off to the right toward Inspiration Point. Why do I suspect that this trail is steep? Continue straight ahead.

5.0 Take the right fork.

5.2 Pass around a gate and hit the pavement.

5.4 Turn left at the stop sign.

5.5 Back at the bathroom.

Glory Hole Upper

Location:	About 1 hour east of Stockton on California Highway 49.
Distance:	5.5 miles, out-and-back.
Time:	1 hour.
Elevation gain:	About 650 feet. Lowest elevation is 1,050 feet; highest elevation is 1,450 feet.
Tread:	Narrow to wide singletrack, hard-packed and smooth.
Aerobic level:	Easy, with one strenuous climb.
Technical difficulty:	2–3.
Highlights:	Wonderful switchbacks; constant and impressive views of the reservoir. No motorcycles or horses are allowed on the trails—only hikers and mountain bikers.
Land status:	U.S. Bureau of Reclamation.
Maps:	USGS New Malones Dam (the trails are not shown).
Access:	From the north on California Highway 49, turn right at the sign for the Glory Hole Recreation Area, 1.8 miles south of Angels Camp. From the south on California Highway 49, turn left at the sign for the Glory Hole Recreation Area, 5 miles north of the visitor center and 15 miles north of Sonora. After passing through the entrance station, drive another 0.3 mile and park in the upper trailhead parking area to your left. A sign for the Carson Creek Trail will send you on your way. An outhouse is available, but no water.

Notes on the trail: I've split the trails at the Glory Hole Recreation Area into two rides because the section from the upper trailhead parking area requires intermediate technical skills, whereas the section from the lower trailhead parking needs only beginning technical skills. This ride from the upper parking area involves riding down some wonderfully sharp switchbacks, along a cliff overlooking the reservoir, around a peninsula, and back. I've rated the switchbacks class 3, because without intermediate

Glory Hole Upper,
Glory Hole Lower

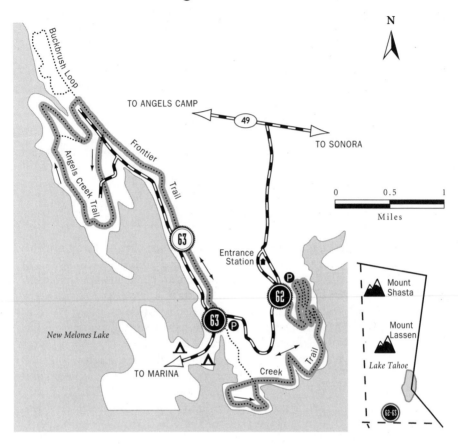

N

Buckbrush Loop

TO ANGELS CAMP

49

TO SONORA

Frontier Trail

Angels Creek Trail

63

0   0.5   1
Miles

Entrance Station

P

62

63

P

New Melones Lake

TO MARINA

Creek

Trail

Mount Shasta

Mount Lassen

Lake Tahoe

62-63

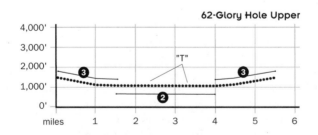

62-Glory Hole Upper

4,000'
3,000'
2,000'
1,000'
0'

"T"

3

2

3

miles   1   2   3   4   5   6

Trail near New Melones Reservoir on the Glory Hole Upper.

technical skills you'll tear up the trail; the cliff is also class 3 because the trail is narrow and a mistake would hurt a lot! Although you seem to descend a lot, the climb back up isn't that bad—and even delightful. It's a challenge to ride all the way up without stopping, but the switchbacks are built in a way that makes the ride seem easy and fun. This ride also passes through an area that has a wild feeling, even though you're beside a reservoir rather than a lake. Views of the reservoir are constant and impressive.

It gets very hot here in summer. If you must ride then, get an early start or ride late in the day. Fall, winter, and spring are the best times of year to ride, but ticks are abundant in spring, and you should let the trail dry out for at least a week after a major winter storm. This area also becomes very busy with boaters from April 1 to November 1; if you enjoy peace and quiet, choose another time. Poison oak is abundant, but the trail is wide enough that you probably won't encounter it.

The Ride

0.0   Start off riding through gentle, rolling grasslands and oak forest. Please yield the right-of-way to hikers by stopping and pulling off the trail so that they may easily pass.

1.1   Encounter a trail coming down from the right. This leads up to a helipad and picnic area, then dead-ends. Continue straight and enjoy the beautiful views of the water.

1.5	This is a gentle place where you can easily walk down to the water for a break, a picnic, or a swim. The trail now becomes class 2.
2.3	Arrive at an **X** intersection. The two trails to your left circumnavigate the peninsula. I chose to ride counterclockwise so that the water would be on my right, for a change.
2.6	A small trail zaps across to an "island" accessible by bike only when the water is low enough. Not only is this trail inaccessible at high water, but it's also not an official trail. I suggest you keep riding around the peninsula.
3.0	Another great spot to rest, picnic, or go for a swim.
3.2	Arrive back at the **X** intersection. If you're ready to head back to your car, turn right. If not, refer to the option.
5.5	Arrive back at the car. It was sort of fun riding back up the switchbacks, wasn't it?

Option: If you wish to combine the two rides, take the remaining leg of the **X** north, ride 0.7 mile to the lower trailhead parking area, follow the directions for Ride 63, return to this point, ride around the peninsula the other direction, and return to your car. The total mileage will be 15.8 miles, and the total climbing will be 1,350 feet. If you also throw in the Buckbrush Loop, add another 1.4 miles to the total for a grand total of 17.2 miles. Was that enough for you?

63

Glory Hole Lower

Location:	About 1 hour east of Stockton on California Highway 49.	See map on Page 264
Distance:	7-mile loop.	
Time:	1 hour.	
Elevation gain:	700 feet. Lowest elevation is 1,050 feet; highest elevation is 1,200 feet.	
Tread:	Medium to wide, smooth, and hard-packed singletrack.	
Aerobic level:	Easy.	
Technical difficulty:	2.	
Highlights:	Wide, smooth, and gradual singletrack; the Angels Creek Trail dips and swoops through an area that appears and feels quite wild and	

offers views of the reservoir. No motorcycles or horses are allowed on the trails—only hikers and mountain bikers.

Land status: U.S. Bureau of Reclamation.

Maps: USGS New Malones Dam (the trails are not shown).

Access: From the north on California Highway 49, turn right at the sign for the Glory Hole Recreation Area, 1.8 miles south of Angels Camp. From the south on California Highway 49, turn left at the sign for the Glory Hole Recreation Area 5 miles north of the visitor center and 15 miles north of Sonora. After passing through the entrance station, drive another 1.3 miles and park in the lower trailhead parking area to your left. You'll see a sign for the Carson Creek Trail. An outhouse is available, but no water.

Notes on the trail: I've split the trails at Glory Hole Recreation Area into two rides because the section from the upper trailhead parking area requires intermediate technical skills, whereas the section from the lower trailhead parking area needs only beginning technical skills. This ride from the lower parking area involves riding to the Angels Creek Trail, around that loop, and back. If you have intermediate technical skills, you can throw in the Buckbrush Loop (1.4 miles) as well, but without such skills you run the risk of damaging the trail.

It gets very hot here in summer. If you must ride then, get an early start or ride late in the day. Fall, winter, and spring are the best times of year to ride, but ticks are abundant in spring, and you should let the trail dry out for at least a week after a major winter storm. This area also becomes very busy with boaters from April 1 to November 1; if you enjoy peace and quiet, choose another time.

The Ride

0.0 From the lower trailhead parking area, ride back up the pavement for about 200 feet, cross the road just past the large sign, and notice the singletrack taking off toward the north.

0.1 A sign for the Frontier Trail will come into view.

1.2 A picnic table is off to your right.

1.3 Ignore the trail junction on your left and stay on the high trail.

1.8 The trail comes up to meet the road. Cross the road and ride down about 30 feet to the beginning of another singletrack. This is the beginning of the Angels Creek Trail.

2.1 Cross over a small paved road and keep going.

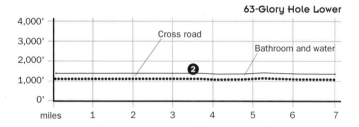

63-Glory Hole Lower

3.1 The trail narrows nicely and begins to dip and swoop through a forest of live oaks. It feels wonderfully wild at this point.

3.5 Arrive at the top of a knoll.

3.6 Ignore the trail coming in from the right and keep going straight.

4.3 Descend through manzanita shrubs and arrive at a Y. Take the left fork.

4.3 + Turn left onto the more traveled trail.

4.6 One trail heads down to the left. This leads to the Buckbrush Loop. If you have intermediate or advanced technical skills, you can ride this loop and return to this point. If not, take the other trail, which heads up. You're now back on the Frontier Trail.

4.7 Pass by a parking area with a bathroom and water.

5.1 + Remember this spot? This is where you crossed the road to begin the Angels Creek Trail. Now ride back to your car the way you came.

5.5 The trail passes right over an Indian grinding rock.

5.6 Ignore the trail coming up from the parking area.

6.9 Back to the road, just 200 feet from the lower trailhead parking area.

7.0 Back at the car.

Option: If you arrive back at the car and wish to ride more, you can take the Carson Creek Trail for 0.7 mile to an X intersection, turn right, ride around the peninsula for 0.9 mile, and return to the X; it's 0.7 mile back to your car. These trails are all class 2.

Southern Sierra Nevada

The southern half of the Sierra Nevada is higher and less civilized than the northern half. Many peaks reach more than 14,000 feet. No roads traverse the range between California Highway 120 in Yosemite National Park, and California Highway 178 south of Sequoia National Park. Therefore trails that allow mountain bikes tend to be found on either the east side or the west side, but not along the summit.

South of Yosemite

The west side is serviced by California Highway 41 and can be approached from Fresno. The rides vary from the foothills where summers can be quite hot and winters mild but wet, to the ponderosa pine forests where summers can be mild and winters cold and snowy.

The east side is serviced by California Highway 395. There aren't many high-quality, bike-legal singletracks on public lands in this area, but the ride that's here is phenomenal! The forest service is considering opening up more singletracks to mountain bikers during the fall months only, after the crowds leave and before the snow falls. The rides that I've described are within a sagebrush, piñon pine, and juniper desert. This is a high desert. Summers can become quite hot, and winters may be very cold, with occasional dustings of snow. Fall and spring are definitely the best times to ride. A large and convenient campground is located in Mammoth Lakes, along with a ranger station, bike shops, supermarkets, restaurants, and more.

Goat Mountain Trail

Location:	About 1.5 hours northeast of Fresno, and about 30 minutes south of Yosemite, off California Highway 41.
Distance:	5.8 miles, out-and-back.
Time:	1.5 hours.
Elevation gain:	About 1,230 feet. Lowest elevation is 3,775 feet; highest elevation is 5,000 feet.
Tread:	Mostly smooth and hard-packed, sometimes rocky.
Aerobic level:	Easy, with one strenuous climb.
Technical difficulty:	3–4 (mostly 3).
Highlights:	A great little leaf-covered singletrack passing through the forest. No motorcycles may use this trail.
Land status:	Sierra National Forest Recreation Area.
Maps:	USGS Bass Lake.
Access:	From the junction of California Highway 41 and U.S. Highway 99 in Fresno, set your odometer to 0.0 and drive northeast toward Yosemite National Park. At 28 miles from Fresno, turn right at the sign for O'Neals/Northfork onto County Road 200. Keep following the signs for Northfork and Bass Lake. At 42 miles from Fresno, just after a Shell station and just before entering the town of Northfork, turn left onto County Road 221. At 44 miles from Fresno, go straight through the intersection—onto Road 222—toward Bass Lake. Don't turn left to head for Goat Mountain Lookout. At 53 miles from Fresno, the trail begins at the Forks Campground. There's no trailhead parking in the campground; instead, you can park at a nearby day-use area and ride to the campground. Both water and bathrooms are available at the campground. My description begins at the campground gate.

Goat MountainTrail

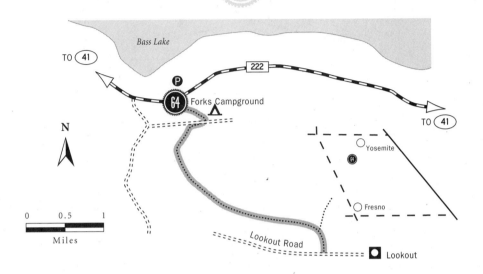

Notes on the trail: This ride may be easy in terms of total effort, but it requires strong intermediate technical skills. It's not an appropriate trail for beginning singletrackers, and certainly not for beginning mountain bikers. Although it's mostly class 3, there are several short sections of class 4.

This trail is beautifully built. It meanders up through a dense forest of ponderosa pines and incense cedars while maintaining its narrow and pristine character. In general, it becomes more technical as it ascends. Please don't ride it unless you can descend on a narrow singletrack without riding off the trail and without sliding your rear wheels, or unless you're willing to get off and walk through sections that you cannot ride cleanly. It would be easy to tear this trail up; please preserve it in its current pristine condition! There are a couple of sections that you'll probably want to walk in order to preserve your body as well, unless you have advanced technical skills.

The bottom of the trail is right at the snow line. It should melt out by April, but allow enough time for the trail to thoroughly dry out so that you don't cause any erosion. Likewise, allow the trail to dry out for a few days following any major rainstorm. Since this trail begins at a campground and leads to a lookout, many hikers and equestrians, as well as other mountain bikers, use it. Please control your speed and be able to stop at any time. When you meet other trail users or uphill mountain bikers, stop and pull off the trail before they feel compelled to do so.

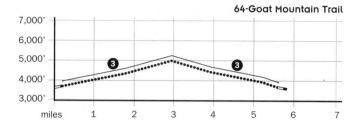

64-Goat Mountain Trail

The Ride

0.0 Begin riding at the gate to the campground. Follow the one-way paved road through the campground.

0.2 Across from site 25 look for the sign for the Goat Mountain Trail. (22E04). Then ride up through a grove of young incense cedars and older ponderosa pines.

0.4 The trail forks. Take the right fork up to the dirt road. Look to the right and you'll see the singletrack continuing on the other side of the dirt road.

1.4 The trail levels out a little and becomes more technical.

1.7 Begin to climb more steeply on a rockier trail.

2.1 Junction with the Spring Cove Trail; bear right to continue on the Goat Mountain Trail. This next 1-mile section is mostly class 3, but contains a few class 4 maneuvers and becomes very narrow and cliffy.

2.9 The trail ends at a dirt road. If you didn't notice the large manzanitas with deep red-purple bark and the bright green ground cover of mountain misery on the way up, look for them on the way down.

5.8 You're back at the gate to the campground.

Squaw Leap Loop

Location:	About 1 hour east of Fresno, off California Highway 168.
Distance:	7.8-mile loop.
Time:	2 hours.
Elevation gain:	About 1,770 feet. Lowest elevation is 900 feet; highest elevation is 2,035 feet.
Tread:	Hard-packed sand and rock.
Aerobic level:	Moderate, with one very long, strenuous climb.
Technical difficulty:	3–4 (mostly 3).
Highlights:	Views of the San Joaquin River canyon, wildflowers in spring, technical and narrow singletrack. No motorized vehicles are allowed on the trails.
Land status:	Bureau of Land Management, Squaw Leap Management Area.
Maps:	USGS Millerton Lake East.
Access:	From Fresno, drive 37 miles east on California Highway 168 and turn left onto Auberry Road toward the town of Auberry. On the far side of town, just after the school, turn left onto Powerhouse Road. After 1.9 miles, turn left onto Smalley Road at the sign for Bureau of Land Management, Squaw Leap Management Area. Follow the signs for the campground and loop trail. Pull into the parking area for campground and trailhead. The trailhead is marked obviously with a huge (maybe 6 feet by 8 feet) map display. An outhouse is available, but no water.

Notes on the trail: First, a word about water bars. Water bars are essential to trail maintenance. They direct the flow of water off the trail so it doesn't run down the middle and cause severe erosion. But water bars only work if you ride or walk *over* them. By riding or walking around them, you create a path for water around the water bars, thereby decreasing their effectiveness. The majority of water bars on this ride consist of a rubber strip attached to a wooden base. Although these strips look kind of scary, they yield to your tires easily. Simply pulling up slightly when you

Squaw Leap Loop

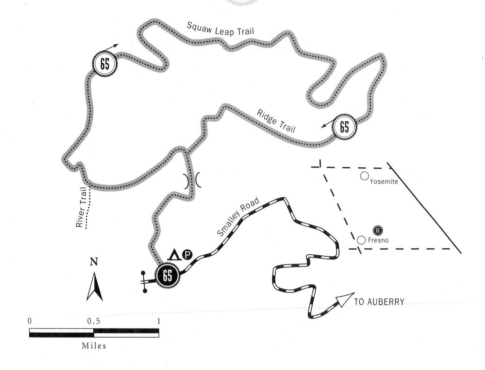

hit one will ensure that you and your bike pass over without being deflected.

There are three parts to this ride. The first part leads you down to the bridge over the San Joaquin River and up to a junction. This part is very heavily used by hikers and equestrians and requires a lot of care on your part to avoid surprising them. The second part is mostly an old dirt road that is trying to revert to a wide singletrack, but is having trouble doing so because of erosion problems. Third, you'll ride a narrow, class 3+ singletrack that sees little use. If you ride the loop clockwise, you can take the narrow, technical singletrack downhill. *Warning:* This singletrack minimally requires very well-developed intermediate technical skills. It's not a ride for beginning singletrackers! Another concern is rattlesnakes. Please look far ahead and ride in control, both for your own sake and that of the resident wildlife. In spring ticks will be out and about, as will wildflowers. This is perfect wildflower country, starting in March and extending into early May. Summers are hot here—especially on the south-facing slope on which you'll be riding. If you find yourself riding in the middle of the hot summer afternoon, take it easy on the climb, drink lots of water,

Ride over the San Joaquin River on the Squaw Leap Loop.

and rest a lot in shady places. Fall is a perfect time to ride: The weather is cool, and the trails have been well groomed since the rains of last winter. This is also granite country. The river canyon is carved from granite, and you'll be passing several outcroppings of granite.

The Ride

0.0   Remember to ride *over* the water bars.

0.5   This is the first view you get of the San Joaquin River canyon. In fall you'll see a series of deep pools; in spring and early summer, a series of whitewater cascades. The trail becomes steeper now. Move your weight back to avoid sliding your rear tire.

0.9   Cross one of the most beautiful foot/bike bridges you'll ever see and enjoy the views of the canyon both upstream and down.

1.1   Junction: The River Trail heads left, the Ridge Trail heads right. Go left and ride through grasslands with digger pines, blue oaks, and occasional chaparral plants on a old, eroded dirt road that is resisting being reduced to a singletrack.

1.9   Intersection: Bear right onto the Ridge Trail.

2.5   A spring surrounded by brilliant scarlet monkey flowers.

2.7   Begin riding on a sweet, new singletrack.

3.1   Mileage marker 3. This is probably the best view of the river canyon below, and a good place to take a break.

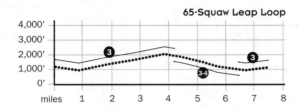

65-Squaw Leap Loop

3.4   Bear right and continue to climb on an old dirt road.

3.9   This is the high spot of the ride. It's all downhill from here!

4.1   Mileage marker 4.

4.2   Now the newly built, narrow, technical singletrack begins.

4.4   A sign reminds you that you're on the trail. A nice view of the river canyon makes itself known at this point.

5.1   Mileage marker 5.

5.6   A very narrow and steep section. Be careful!

5.8   Notice the typical table mountain in the distance in front of you, resulting from a flow of volcanic magma down what use to be the San Joaquin River. After solidifying, it was more resistant to erosion than the surrounding material, and therefore was left behind as a marker for where the *bottom* of the canyon used to be (way up there?).

6.2   Mileage marker 6.

6.7   You're back at the junction above the bridge. Turn left.

7.9   Back at the car.

Tour de Granite Adventure

Location:	About 1.5 hours east of Fresno, off California Highway 168.
Distance:	7.7-mile loop.
Time:	1.75 hours.
Elevation gain:	About 1,500 feet. Lowest elevation is 5,950 feet; highest elevation is 6,350 feet.
Tread:	Indistinct, narrow singletracks; old dirt roads; granite slabs with no visible trail; well-developed singletracks.
Aerobic level:	Moderate, with one strenuous hike-and-bike stretch.
Technical difficulty:	2–5 (mostly 3).
Highlights:	Meadows filled with wildflowers, beautiful scenery composed of granite slabs and domes, and an adventurous hike-and-bike section allowing you to test your orienteering skills and the traction provided by your shoes.
Land status:	Sierra National Forest.
Maps:	USGS Dinkey Creek.
Access:	From U.S. Highway 99 in Fresno, take the turnoff for California Highway 168 east toward Shaver Lake. When you reach Shaver Lake (51 miles from Fresno), turn right onto Dinkey Creek Road. Drive for another 5.4 miles and turn left onto a dirt road with an open green gate. (A small sign to the right of the gate will read: 9s05.) Drive for 100 yards, turn left onto a small dirt road, and park under the pines. Please don't park on the edge of the meadow. Grab your bike, your map, and your compass, and head back toward the green gate. Just before the granite slab, you'll see a small singletrack taking off to the right. Take it.

Notes on the trail: Every book has to have at least one adventure ride, and this is it. The ride follows the course of the annual Tour de Granite race. Singletracks built on old logging roads lead you to a cliff of granite.

Tour de Granite Adventure

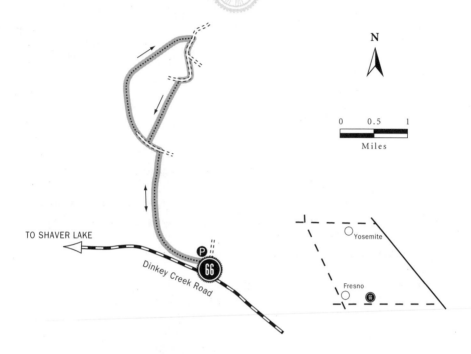

And then you get to push your bike up a cliff to another singletrack waiting at the top. The push up the cliff is very steep: Wear shoes that will grip the rock. There are no signs on this course, and only sporadic piles of rocks (ducks) to mark the path up the cliff. Only those riders with experience at following indistinct trails who have a good sense of direction should attempt this ride. *Note:* I once rode this trail on the first day of deer-hunting season. It was a bit disconcerting to find so many people wandering around in camouflage and carrying large guns. You may wish to choose another time to ride.

The Ride

0.0 Ride the singletrack as it zigzags between the trees.
0.2 Bear left onto the dirt road, ride about 100 feet, and take the singletrack that heads off to the left, between the large rocks, just before the fence.
0.4 Bear right onto the dirt road. This old road will regenerate into a singletrack just before the fence. Ride along the fence to the gate

66-Tour de Granite Adventure

and pass through it, closing it behind you. Ride west along the fence until you see the singletrack taking off toward the northwest. Skirt the edge of a meadow filled with wildflowers and bracken ferns. The trail varies from singletrack to old dirt road.

1.5 Low point. Climb through sugar pines, white firs, and incense cedars.

2.0 Arrive at a dirt-road fork. Take the left fork downhill and across the bridge.

2.3 Arrive at another dirt-road fork. Take the dirt road to the left. (You'll be returning to this point later via the dirt road on the right.)

2.7 The dirt road becomes a singletrack.

2.8 Climb very steeply up a granite rock beside manzanita bushes. The intervening bushes with spikes on them are buckbrush (ceanothus). They feel particularly nice on legs that are covered with mosquito bites.

2.9 Arrive at the top of a small granite slab with a view of a large and steep granite slab leading up to a dome. You'll soon be pushing your bike up this—but first you have to head down to the stream. Ride or walk your bike northwest along the crest of the slab until you find an indistinct trail leading down to the creek. Then carry your bike down to the creek. Use caution: The rocks here have been polished by moving water and are very slippery. During periods of high water (late spring and early summer) you may not be able to safely cross this creek. In low water you may want to cool off in the pools before carrying your bike up the steep slab in front of you. This is a wonderful destination in case you want to head back from here. But if you want to continue, you need to contour up the slab, basically upstream, heading for the small Jeffrey pine with a dead top, with two Jeffrey pines above it. Go between the two pines, along a slab, more or less paralleling the stream about 200 feet north of it. The slab turns into a crack. Walk up the crack. Continue straight as the crack makes a left-hand turn. Look for ducks (piles of rocks) to guide you. A dike in the granite provides enough traction for you to traverse a steep section. Remain about

Granite slab showing the approximate route of the Tour de Granite Adventure.

200 feet from the creek, just below the trees. Pull away from the creek as you level off. Pass by a small dead snag and a manzanita bush, then by a larger dead snag, then hang a right and head for a third dead snag near a large boulder. The route passes between two boulders, the size of small cars, and straight up the slab toward two Jeffrey pines, a single-trunked tree leaning against a double-trunked tree. Pass just to the right of these trees. Notice that the granite is lighter than the surrounding granite where people have been walking. Now head for a double snag to the right of the dome. Pass about 100 feet to the right of the double snag and an indistinct singletrack will come into view. Among a bunch of dead and down snags, veer down to the left toward the dome.

3.3   The trail now becomes visible as it passes through sand, and invisible as it passes over granite.

3.4   The trail just disappears! Push to the top of the small dome. A little forest will appear on your left. Pass by two dead, standing snags on your right.

3.5   As you get to the top of the little dome, the singletrack will become visible in the soil; it's heading a bit north of east. At a standing dead snag, you hit the granite again. Keep looking for where people have worn away the lichens. The singletrack then heads to the right toward a triplet of trees and back onto the granite. Hang a left at the next tree, down into a tiny canyon, and back up the other side.

3.6   Hang a right and follow the ducks up the granite. Head for a dou-ble-trunked Jeffrey pine, beside a rock that looks like a big finger on its side. Follow the ducks around to the right. Cross over the crack and head uphill. You're now heading east, away from the "finger rock."

3.7   Ride by a tiny dome and through a narrow pass. The route again alternates between dirt and granite. Arrive at two Jeffrey pines, facing southeast, with a view of a distant dome with a fire look-out on top (Bald Mountain Lookout). Hang a left to stay up on the slab.

3.9   You made it! Leave the granite behind and head into the woods on the well-established singletrack.

3.9 +   Turn right onto the dirt road. (This road is used by motor vehicles.)

4.1   Bear right onto the more heavily used dirt road.

4.6   Turn left onto the singletrack. This is an easy trail to miss. If you find yourself in a primitive campground with a green outhouse and several large barrels, ride back 200 feet to the beginning of the singletrack.

4.7   Watch for a sandpit followed by a creek crossing. (Keep your weight back or you'll end up on your head.)

4.9   Get ready for a steep downhill ride on a sandy, rocky, and loose singletrack. Enjoy it, but don't tear it up.

5.4   Arrive back at the dirt road you were riding at mile 2.3. Bear left and head back toward your car.

5.7   Turn right at the dirt-road junction and follow it as it turns into a singletrack and returns you to the gate in the fence. Pass through the gate, retrace your steps to the singletrack that passes between the two big boulders, turn right onto the dirt road, ride 100 feet, and turn right onto the singletrack.

7.7   And arrive back at the trailhead.

Lower Rock Creek Trail

Location:	Near Mammoth Lakes on California Highway 395, about 3 hours south of Reno and about 4 hours north of Los Angeles.
Distance:	7.8 miles, point-to-point.
Time:	1.5 hours.
Elevation gain:	0 feet. Lowest elevation is 4,975 feet; highest elevation is 6,750 feet.
Tread:	The upper section is mostly hard-packed sand, sometimes loose sand, and sometimes rocks. The lower section is mostly loose and rocky, sometimes smooth and hard-packed.
Aerobic level:	Moderate.
Technical difficulty:	1–3 (mostly 3).
Highlights:	A technical singletrack running alongside a lush stream environment in the bottom of an impressive and wild canyon. No motorcycles are allowed on this singletrack.
Land status:	Bureau of Land Management and Inyo National Forest.
Maps:	USGS Toms Place, Mount Morgan.
Access:	From the Mammoth Lakes exit (California Highway 203), drive 16 miles south and take the Lower Rock Creek Road exit from California Highway 395. Park one car in the space provided about 100 yards from the beginning of the road, right beside the sign that announces: INYO NATIONAL FOREST DAY USE RECREATION AREA LOWER ROCK CREEK. The singletrack begins across the road. No water or bathrooms are available. Drive the other car down Lower Rock Creek Road to the town of Paradise. Park across the street from the A-frame store. (They have cold drinks!)

Notes on the trail: Riders with well-developed intermediate technical skills will be able to ride most of this trail, but you'll likely find yourself carrying your bikes over several sections. It's especially important that you

Lower Rock Creek Trail

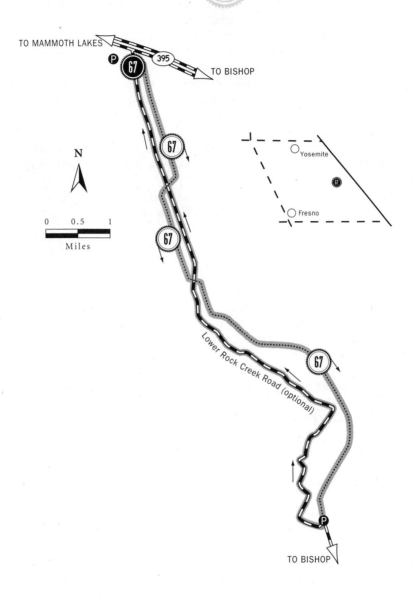

be able to ride down steep and loose sections without sliding your rear tire. Beginning singletrackers should not attempt this ride. Beginning mountain bikers shouldn't even consider it!

You're basically riding alongside a stream in a beautiful desert canyon. The trail runs beside the creek, usually in the shade of trees. Lots of trees and other water-loving plants grow along the stream, but the sides of the canyon are rocky and barren. Wild roses are especially abundant along the trail, with pink flowers in spring and bright red hips in late summer and fall. Lots of hikers use this trail—especially anglers. Please control your speed so that you can stop unexpectedly without sliding; slow down considerably when approaching blind spots; and yield the right-of-way to hikers by stopping and moving off the trail. This is a desert. It can get very hot on a summer afternoon—something to keep in mind when you're planning this ride, especially if you decide to ride back to the trailhead on the asphalt road. You must climb 2,000 feet in open desert without shade. Some people prefer to leave their car at the bottom of the trail and then ride up the road to the beginning of the singletrack. Whatever floats your boat!

The Ride

0.0 Cross the road and read the welcome sign: LOWER ROCK CREEK MOUNTAIN BIKE TRAIL, BUREAU OF LAND MANAGEMENT AND INYO NATIONAL FOREST. Thanks, people! Start off on a class 2 trail, narrow but smooth.

1.0 The trail becomes class 3, with some rocks. If you watch closely, you may be able to spot the beaver-tail cactus, to remind you that you're in a desert.

1.8 Challenging maneuver.

2.2 This stuff is looser than it looks! Slow down before you hit it, keep your weight back, and be sure you can come to a stop before you hit the road—or prepare to get creamed by a 60-mile-per-hour car. Then carefully cross the bridge and catch the singletrack on the other side of the road. This next section is cool and shady, reminiscent of a roller coaster, and more frequented by hikers.

3.2 A large rock is approaching; you'll have to carry your bike over it. If you're going too fast, you won't be able to stop in time—and you'll ride straight into the creek.

3.2 + Cross the paved road and continue on the singletrack on the other side. Ride down to and along the creek among Jeffrey pines.

3.5 Keep your weight back to preserve the trail on this steep descent.

3.7 Cross the bridge across the creek.

3.9 Some small rocks are making their appearance.

4.1 Pass through a very dense forest.

4.2 Bigger rocks are making their appearance.

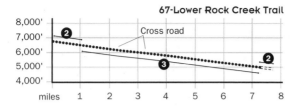

67-Lower Rock Creek Trail

4.8   A nice forest of Jeffrey pines. Stick your nose in a crack in the bark: Butterscotch or vanilla? This is a great place to enjoy the creek. Look at the columns of volcanic rock to your left—much as you would find in Devil's Postpile. Just beyond, pass through a bunch of pink volcanic boulders.

5.1   Pick up your bike and carry it through the rocks (short class 4 section)—unless you have advanced technical abilities.

5.5   Bridge.

5.7   The trail is being crowded out by plants and rocks.

5.8   Another short class 4 section.

6.3   The last short class 4 section.

6.5   A spring is coming out from under a rock.

6.6   Notice the horsetails growing in this moist and lush area.

6.8   Ride over two consecutive bridges.

6.9   Another bridge.

7.1   And another bridge.

7.2   And still another. The trail becomes smooth—and therefore fast—but you're approaching an area that's well used by anglers and hikers. Please ride slowly and just enjoy the smoothness of the trail.

7.4   End of the singletrack. Follow the dirt road.

7.6   When you reach the creek, take the singletrack to the right and ride over the small bridge. If you're riding back up to your car and it's a hot day, I suggest you wet your hair and perhaps your shirt in the creek before heading up.

7.8   If you parked across the street and began your ride here, please buy something from the store. If you're riding back up the asphalt, buy yourself a cold drink or a snack.

Appendix: For More Information

Monterey Bay Area

Ride 1: Fort Ord Public Lands, Bureau of Land Management, 20 Hamilton Court, Hollister, CA 95023; (831) 394–8314; www.monterey.edu/students/Students_D-H/farleyaaronm/world/blm/.

Ride 2: Wilder Ranch State Park, 600 Ocean Street, Santa Cruz, CA 95060; (831) 423–9703; http://cal-parks.ca.gov/districts/santacruz/wrsp456.htm.

Ride 3: Soquel Demonstration State Forest, 4750 Soquel–San Jose Road, Soquel, CA 95073; (831) 475–8643.

Western South San Francisco Bay Area

Rides 4–7: Midpeninsula Regional Open Space District, 330 Distel Circle, Los Altos, CA 94022-1404; (605) 691–2100; mrosd@openspace.org; www.openspace.org.

Eastern South San Francisco Bay Area

Rides 8–12: Henry W. Coe State Park, P.O. Box 846, Morgan Hill, CA 95038; (408) 779–2728; http://cal-parks.ca.gov/DISTRICTS/fourivers/hwcsp432.htm; www.coepark.parks.ca.gov.

North San Francisco Bay Area

Ride 13: China Camp State Park, California State Parks–Marin District, 7665 Redwood Boulevard, Suite 150, Novato, CA 94945-1405; (415) 893–1580; http://cal-parks.ca.gov/DISTRICTS/marin/ccsp202.htm.

Ride 14: Skyline Wilderness Park, 2201 Imola Avenue, Napa, CA 94559.

Ride 15: Rockville Hills Community Park, Solano Farmlands and Open Space Foundation, P.O. Box 115, Fairfield, CA 94533; (707) 421–1351.

Santa Rosa/Clear Lake Area

Rides 16–17: Annadel State Park, 6201 Channel Drive, Santa Rosa, CA 95409; (707) 539–3911; http://cal-parks.ca.gov/DISTRICTS/silverado/asp246.htm.

Ride 18: Boggs Mountain Demonstration State Forest, Department of Forestry and Fire Protection, P.O. Box 839, Cobb, CA 95426; (707) 928-4378.

North Coast Redwood Park

Ride 19: Prairie Creek Redwoods State Park, Orick, CA 95555; (707) 488-2171; http://cal-parks.ca.gov/DISTRICTS/ncrd/pcrsp.htm.

Mount Shasta Area

Ride 20: Scott/Salmon Ranger Districts, 11263 North Highway 3, Fort Jones, CA 96032; (916) 468-5351.

Rides 21-23: Shasta Lake National Recreation Area, 14225 Holiday Road, Redding, CA 96003; (530) 275-1589; www.r5.fs.fed.us/shastatrinity/.

Rides 24-26: Whiskeytown-Shasta-Trinity National Recreation Area, P.O. Box 188, Whiskeytown, CA 96095; www.nps.gov/whis/.

Mount Lassen Area

Rides 27-28: Lassen National Forest, Almanor Ranger District, P.O. Box 767, Chester, CA 96020; (530) 258-2141; www.nps.gov/.

Rides 29-30: Plumas National Forest, P.O. Box 11500, Quincy, CA 95971; (530) 283-2050; www.r5.pswfs.gov/plumas.

Downieville Area

Rides 31-38: Tahoe National Forest, Downieville Ranger District, North Yuba Ranger Station, 15924 Highway 49, Camptonville, CA 95922-9707; (530) 288-3231.

Nevada City/Auburn/Donner Pass Area

Ride 39: South Yuba River State Park, 17660 Pleasant Valley Road, Penn Valley, CA 95946; (530) 432-2546; http://cal-parks.ca.gov/DISTRICTS/ goldrush/syrp.htm. Tahoe National Forest, Nevada City Ranger District, 631 Coyote Street, Nevada City, CA 95959; (530) 265-4531. South Yuba River Recreation Lands, Bureau of Land Management, Folsom Field Office, 63 Natoma Street, Folsom, CA 95630; (530) 985-4474; www.ca. blm.gov/folsom.

Rides 40–42: Tahoe National Forest, Nevada City Ranger District, 631 Coyote Street, Nevada City, CA 95959; (530) 265-4531.

Ride 43: Tahoe National Forest, Truckee Ranger District, Truckee, CA 95734; (530) 587-3558; www.r5.fs.fed.us/tahoe/ and www.r5.pswfs.gov/ tahoe.

Ride 44: Bureau of Land Management, Folsom Field Office, 63 Natoma Street, Folsom, CA 95630; (530) 985-4474; www.ca.blm.gov/folsom.

Ride 45: Auburn State Recreation Area, P.O. Box 3266, Auburn, CA 95604-3266; (530) 885-4527; http://american.parks.ca.gov/auburn /asrabasic.htm.

Rides 46–47: Folsom Lake State Recreation Area, 7806 Folsom-Auburn Road, Folsom, CA 95630-1797; (916) 988-0205; http://american.parks. ca.gov/folsomsra/flsrabasic.htm.

Lake Tahoe Area

Ride 48: Truckee Ranger District, Tahoe National Forest, Truckee, CA 95734; (530) 587-3558; www.r5.fs.fed.us/tahoe/ and www.r5.pswfs. gov/tahoe.

Rides 49–51, 53–57: Lake Tahoe Basin Management Unit, P.O. Box 8465-870, Emerald Bay, South Lake Tahoe, CA 95731; (916) 573-2600.

Ride 52: Lake Tahoe Nevada State Park, P.O. Box 8867, Incline Village, NV 89452; (775) 831-0494.

North Of Yosemite

Ride 58: Sly Park Recreation Area, Bureau of Reclamation, P.O. Box 577, Pollock Pines, CA 95727; (530) 644-2545; camping reservations: (530) 644-2792.

Ride 59: Eldorado National Forest, 100 Forni Road, Placerville, CA 95667; (530) 644-6048.

Ride 60: U.S. Army Corps of Engineers, New Hogan Lake, 2713 Hogan Dam Road, Valley Springs, CA 95252; (209) 772-1343.

Ride 61: Stanislaus National Forest, Calaveras Ranger District, P.O. Box 500, Hathaway Pines, CA 95233; www.r5.pswfs.gov/stanislaus/calaveras/ index.htm.

Ride 62–63: U.S. Bureau of Reclamation, New Melones Lake, 16805 Peoria Flat Road, Jamestown, CA 95327; (209) 984-5248.

South of Yosemite

Rides 64, 66: Sierra National Forest, 1600 Tollhouse Road, Clovis, CA 93612; (559) 297–0706; www.r5.pswfs.gov/sierra.

Ride 65: Bureau of Land Management, Bakersfield Field Office, 3801 Pegasus Drive, Bakersfield, CA 93308-6837; (661) 391–6000; www.ca.blm.gov/bakersfield/recreation.html.

Rides 67: Inyo National Forest, 873 North Main, Bishop, CA 93514; (619) 873–2400. Mammoth Ranger District, Box 148, Mammoth Lakes, CA 93546; (619) 924–5500.

About the Author

I am an intermediate rider—in terms of strength, endurance, and technical abilities—who has a passion for riding in natural areas, especially on singletrack. I love the intimate feeling of riding on narrow and pristine trails, and enjoy light to intermediate technical challenges. There's something spiritual about gliding silently through a redwood forest or along the top of a ridge overlooking lakes and distant peaks. Mountain biking allows me to get close to nature while being aware of the changing environment. Some rides have brought tears of joy to my eyes—riding among meadows of wildflowers or cresting a ridge to find a glacial lake in the cirque of a perfectly formed peak. Others have caused me to laugh so hard I couldn't stop. Some rides made me feel good to have survived! All made me feel alive and well. When I finish a ride, it takes several hours to get the smile off my face. All the rides I've selected for this book have this spiritual quality; many are challenging in some way; and all are fun!